Second Edition

PROJECTS IN
LINGUISTICS

A PRACTICAL GUIDE TO RESEARCHING LANGUAGE

Alison Wray
Cardiff University

Aileen Bloomer
York St John University College

HODDER
EDUCATION
AN HACHETTE UK COMPANY

First published in Great Britain in 1998 by Arnold. This edition published
in 2006 by Hodder Education, part of Hachette Livre UK
338 Euston Road, London NW1 3BH

www.hoddereducation.co.uk

British Library Cataloguing in Publication Data
A catalogue record for this book is available from the British Library

Library of Congress Cataloging-in-Publication Data
A catalog record for this book is available from the Library of Congress

ISBN 978 0 340 90578 4

6 7 8 9 10

Typeset by Phoenix Photosetting, Chatham, Kent
Printed and bound in the UK by MPG Books Ltd., Bodmin, Cornwall

What do you think about this book? Or any other
Hodder Education title? Please send your comments to
the feedback section on www.hoddereducation.co.uk

PROJECTS IN
LINGUISTICS

CONTENTS

PART II TECHNIQUES FOR COLLECTING DATA

PART III TOOLS FOR DATA ANALYSIS AND PROJECT WRITING

PREFACE TO SECOND EDITION

Why we wrote this book

We wrote this book because you can't learn how to write good essays and research projects just by reading the subject textbooks. There is a lot of knowledge that a student is expected to somehow 'pick up': what good research looks like; how researchers express themselves; where to start. The alert student will gather some of this information piecemeal from tutorials, feedback on written work, talking to other students and so on, but there is usually no way of being sure that you have done all the right things until the work comes back marked.

From the marker's point of view, there are certain features that a piece of work can contain that will make it look credible. Many of the things that make the difference between a high mark and a low one are to do with having the knack of how to plan and present research effectively.

Who the book is for

The book is intended, primarily, for undergraduates taking linguistics or language studies as part or all of their degree programme, and who are expected to engage in research-type project work. However, those embarking on postgraduate research, particularly if they have not previously done data analysis in linguistics, will find the book a useful source of basic procedural information and references to key texts. Secondary- and high-school students engaged in project work should also find it approachable, even if it sometimes assumes more technical knowledge than they yet have.

What the book does

The book is arranged in three parts. Part I is divided into chapters covering some of the major sub-disciplines most commonly chosen by students for their projects. They do not always map onto a single undergraduate module or conventional sub-area of linguistics, because, in our experience, projects don't do this either. But it should not be too difficult to make the connections back to introductory textbooks or class notes. Within each of these chapters there is a brief review of introductory texts, a list of major journals and a brief account of the major research areas. **Key terms** in **bold font** can be used to find information in printed book indexes or via electronic search engines. There are also over 300 practical suggestions for projects. These are specifically aimed at the needs of the student who is required to engage with data of some kind, but who is not expecting to make an original contribution to the field (though some of the projects undoubtedly could lead to this if handled well).

Part II contains chapters on methodology, which provide techniques and guidance on how to set up and run research. The final part contains tools: guidance in practical procedures, and specific information that is often needed but not always easy to find.

But, before all that, there is an introductory chapter intended to set the scene and help the reader orientate him-/herself. We strongly recommend that this chapter is read before anything else.

What the book doesn't do

Although each of the project chapters contains an overview of the research that has been done in the area, this book is not intended to provide a full introduction to those areas. Rather than giving a great deal of primary information, already available in dedicated textbooks, we refer the reader to such books. In this way, we not only keep this book focused on its primary function but also provide the reader with the beginnings of a bibliography. Because the book is about practical projects, there are several areas of linguistics that are not covered at all. Furthermore, many of the projects that are proposed would not be suitable for a more rigorous (i.e. postgraduate or professional) research context. Rather, we have directed our attention unashamedly towards generating ideas that students will find inspiring and encouraging, and we have exploited the freedom from narrower research constraints that can still be enjoyed at this exploratory level.

The second edition

In this second edition, we have reorganized some of the chapters, added additional project ideas, and, in response to users' requests and suggestions, increased our coverage of some specific topics. Most notably, we have introduced a chapter on ethical considerations, to replace the previous narrower coverage of the British Data Protection Act, and have considerably expanded the chapters on statistics and plagiarism. Throughout, we have updated not only the references but also aspects of the content, particularly to reflect new technologies that were barely worth a mention when we were preparing the first edition nine years ago. Thus, we offer guidance on the use of the Internet as a resource, including how to reference electronic material, and we include website addresses as appropriate in the topic chapters. Our aim in making changes has been to enhance the usefulness of the book to its student and staff users, without risking the integrity of the underlying concept, which the user feedback has indicated to be unique and valuable as it stands.

ACKNOWLEDGMENTS

The key influence on us in creating this new edition was the feedback that we received in response to a users' questionnaire issued by our commissioning editor, Eva Martinez. We are very grateful to those who provided the uniformly helpful observations and suggestions, and we thank them also for their overwhelmingly positive comments on the first edition. In reworking the text, we relied heavily on the material written by Kate Trott, Shirley Reay and Chris Butler for the first edition, and we should like to thank them for giving us permission to re-use and rework it as required.

For feedback on drafts, specific observations, and providing vital information, we wish to thank: Pauline Aldous, Margaret Atherden, Chris Butler, Louise Cooper, Tom Dawkes, and Gordon Tucker.

Last but not least, we should like to thank our students at York St John University College and Cardiff University. They inspired the original concept of the book, and they continue to show us, in their writing and questioning, just how much creativity and insight a good project can unleash.

Alison Wray
Cardiff University, Cardiff

Aileen Bloomer
York St John University College, York

February 2006

INTERNATIONAL PHONETIC ALPHABET

THE INTERNATIONAL PHONETIC ALPHABET (revised to 1993, corrected 1996)

CONSONANTS (PULMONIC)

	Bilabial	Labiodental	Dental	Alveolar	Postalveolar	Retroflex	Palatal	Velar	Uvular	Pharyngeal	Glottal
Plosive	p b			t d		ʈ ɖ	c ɟ	k g	q ɢ		ʔ
Nasal	m	ɱ		n		ɳ	ɲ	ŋ	N		
Trill	B			r					R		
Tap or Flap				ɾ		ɽ					
Fricative	ɸ β	f v	θ ð	s z	ʃ ʒ	ʂ ʐ	ç ʝ	x ɣ	χ ʁ	ħ ʕ	h ɦ
Lateral fricative				ɬ ɮ							
Approximant		ʋ		ɹ		ɻ	j	ɰ			
Lateral approximant				l		ɭ	ʎ	L			

Where symbols appear in pairs, the one to the right represents a voiced consonant. Shaded areas denote articulations judged impossible.

CONSONANTS (NON-PULMONIC)

Clicks		Voiced implosives		Ejectives	
ʘ	Bilabial	ɓ	Bilabial	ʼ	Examples:
ǀ	Dental	ɗ	Dental/alveolar	pʼ	Bilabial
ǃ	(Post)alveolar	ʄ	Palatal	tʼ	Dental/alveolar
ǂ	Palatoalveolar	ɠ	Velar	kʼ	Velar
ǁ	Alveolar lateral	ʛ	Uvular	sʼ	Alveolar fricative

OTHER SYMBOLS

ʍ	Voiceless labial-velar fricative	ɕ ʑ	Alveolo-palatal fricatives
w	Voiced labial-velar approximant	ɺ	Alveolar lateral flap
ɥ	Voiced labial-palatal approximant	ɧ	Simultaneous ʃ and x
H	Voiceless epiglottal fricative		
ʕ	Voiced epiglottal fricative		Affricates and double articulations can be represented by two symbols joined by a tie bar if necessary.
ʡ	Epiglottal plosive		

k͡p   t͡s

VOWELS

Where symbols appear in pairs, the one to the right represents a rounded vowel.

SUPRASEGMENTALS

ˈ	Primary stress	
ˌ	Secondary stress	ˌfoʊnəˈtɪʃən
ː	Long	eː
ˑ	Half-long	eˑ
˘	Extra-short	ĕ
|	Minor (foot) group	
‖	Major (intonation) group	
.	Syllable break	ɹi.ækt
‿	Linking (absence of a break)	

DIACRITICS   Diacritics may be placed above a symbol with a descender, e.g. ŋ̊

̥	Voiceless	n̥ d̥	̤	Breathy voiced	b̤ a̤	̪	Dental	t̪ d̪
̬	Voiced	s̬ t̬	̰	Creaky voiced	b̰ a̰	̺	Apical	t̺ d̺
ʰ	Aspirated	tʰ dʰ	̼	Linguolabial	t̼ d̼	̻	Laminal	t̻ d̻
̹	More rounded	ɔ̹	ʷ	Labialized	tʷ dʷ	̃	Nasalized	ẽ
̜	Less rounded	ɔ̜	ʲ	Palatalized	tʲ dʲ	ⁿ	Nasal release	dⁿ
̟	Advanced	u̟	ˠ	Velarized	tˠ dˠ	ˡ	Lateral release	dˡ
̠	Retracted	e̠	ˤ	Pharyngealized	tˤ dˤ	̚	No audible release	d̚
̈	Centralized	ë	̴	Velarized or pharyngealized	ɫ			
̽	Mid-centralized	e̽	̝	Raised	e̝	(ɹ̝ = voiced alveolar fricative)		
̩	Syllabic	n̩	̞	Lowered	e̞	(β̞ = voiced bilabial approximant)		
̯	Non-syllabic	e̯	̘	Advanced Tongue Root	e̘			
˞	Rhoticity	ɚ ɑ˞	̙	Retracted Tongue Root	e̙			

TONES AND WORD ACCENTS

LEVEL			CONTOUR		
e̋ or ˥	Extra high		ě or ˩˥	Rising	
é ˦	High		ê ˥˩	Falling	
ē ˧	Mid		e᷄ ˦˥	High rising	
è ˨	Low		e᷅ ˩˨	Low rising	
ȅ ˩	Extra low		e᷈ ˧˦˧	Rising-falling	
↓	Downstep		↗	Global rise	
↑	Upstep		↘	Global fall	

1

Introduction: starting on the right foot

Choosing an area

In this book we are assuming that you are about to embark upon a data-based dissertation-length project in an area of your choice. However, even if you are preparing an essay for a specific module, there is plenty here to help you. The secret of good research is to know what it is practical to do and what it is wise to do, so here are some questions you can usefully ask yourself.

What can be researched?

There are many questions that we can ask about language, but not all of them are suitable for a research project. Some questions cannot be answered for practical reasons, such as *How many words are there in all the languages in all the world?* Even if you could settle on an adequate definition of 'word' and 'language', you could never discover that information. A good research question is one that you can envisage finding an answer to. So, never just ask the question. Always imagine the possible answers and how you would find them out.

A good project is something that is doable within the bounds of the available facilities. To ensure that it is, plan through the stages very carefully, listing what you will need. For many students, it is a problem even getting access to a quiet room, let alone to a patient during brain surgery!

What area should I choose?

Remember you will have to eat, sleep and breathe this project, perhaps for several months, so do yourself the favour of choosing something that you can live with, enjoy and know that you are doing well. It makes sense to work on aspects of language that you have already found rewarding and gained good marks in. If you cannot think of a subject, this book has hundreds of project ideas. Alternatively, take half an hour with a cup of coffee and your old files and textbooks, and simply remind yourself of the aspects of language that you have found most interesting. Try to remember what it was about language that fired your enthusiasm in the first place. Maybe your studies so far have not given you an opportunity to pursue some of the interests that you brought with you, and now might be your chance to follow them up.

If you have other projects coming up over the next year or two, prepare the ground now. As you read, think, chat and write other pieces of work, jot down any thoughts, references, etc., in a book or file marked 'Project Ideas'. Then, when it comes to it, you will have plenty of ideas to choose from.

In looking for ideas, try to use sources that are as up to date as possible, because ideas and techniques change as more is learned about the field of investigation. It is a good idea to base your work on something that someone else has done, either replicating the original study or changing one **variable** (see Chapter 19), such as the age or gender of the subjects.

Who will supervise me?

Supervising student projects can be one of the most rewarding things that a university teacher has to do. You will get most out of a supervisor who shares your interest in the subject, especially if they are personally research-active in it. Don't just base your judgement on what someone has taught you in modules, as staff don't always get to teach their favourite subjects, especially in relatively small departments. Find out from the department's list of staff research interests who works in areas that interest you, and then arrange to see them. Most people love talking about their own research and will be delighted to have you take an interest.

What am I expected to do?

There are in-house rules for project writing and presentation: they may be uniform across the whole institution or department-specific. Check any instructions you have been issued with, or your module handbook, for guidelines. In-house rules include things such as:

❑ What the **word limit** is and how you calculate it. Do quotes, appendices, and summary tables count? Are you allowed to go over or under the limit and, if so, by how much? What happens if you don't stick to the limit? What happens if you submit your work late?

❑ What the required **presentation** format is. Is it compulsory to word-process? Do you need to leave a right-hand as well as a left-hand margin? Should you write/print on one side of the paper or both, and in single, 1.5 or double spacing? How many copies are you to submit? Does the work have to be bound, or in a certain type of folder? Should your name be on every page, or is your work marked anonymously? Even if there are no specific rules, put yourself in the place of the person marking not just your project but numerous others like it (possibly at 2 o'clock in the morning), and think about the following points. If comments are to be made *on* your work, it is not helpful to put each sheet in a separate plastic envelope. In some kinds of presentation files, the words at the right-hand edge of the reverse side of the paper cannot be read because of the file-grip mechanism, so you need to leave a margin. As a general rule, the smaller the package your work comes in the better – walking home with 40 ring binders is actually a physical impossibility. See also 'Presenting symbols and numbers' near the end of this chapter.

❑ What the preferred **referencing system** is. A full description of the two most common ones (the **Harvard** and the **Humane**) can be found in Chapter 20.

Getting organized

How do I organize my time?

You have only limited time to achieve your goal. You want your work to be as good as possible, which means not rushing it, but also not wearing yourself out. You need to use your time well and know when to stop. You will have other things to do at the same time as the project, including, quite possibly, other deadlines to accommodate. Only by planning can you really identify what needs doing, in what order, and how long it will take. If you don't have some idea of this, you are leaving a great deal to chance. One way to schedule things is to work backwards (Table 1.1).

Table 1.1 Working backwards from the deadline

Date	Task
16th	DEADLINE
15th	Print final version (NB: *never* leave printing to the last day. You *know* why!!). Add any handwritten bits (symbols, diagrams, etc.); photocopy; take to the binder. (Note that while some types of binding can be done while you wait, others take longer. Check in advance, so that you can make allowances in your schedule.)
13th	Draft-print 'final version' and read it *slowly* for typing errors, style, expression, accuracy in referencing and general sense; make any alterations
12th	Write conclusion and final version of introduction
11th	Finish chapter/section X
6th	Finish chapter/section Y

It is important to honour your timetable. When you have achieved your goal, stop and rest. Getting ahead of your own schedule can be a good psychological step, but only if you don't slow down so much that you waste the time you gained. If you get wildly outside your timetable, rewrite it, taking into account any factors you overlooked last time, and making any necessary adjustments in what you hope to cover.

Making a plan

From the start, have a clear idea of what you intend to cover and what you don't. Write a list of chapter and/or section headings, and list what will go in each (see below). Whenever you come across a useful idea or reference, note it in the appropriate place on your plan, so that you can find it when you need it. You can always change your plan later, but it's better to have one. It saves you doing all sorts of unnecessary work for chapters or sections that you haven't realized you won't need to write. Also, read the 'Before you start to write' section of Chapter 22.

Structuring your work

In linguistics, and especially in 'scientific' linguistics, it is a good idea to write under headings: this helps to keep everything in its place, saves words, and makes the work much easier to read. There are various possible structures and no single way is correct (but do check what you are required to do). Typically, however, the following components will need to be included (see also 'What research looks like', below):

❐ *Title*: Make it informative about what you are finding out.

❐ *Abstract*: A short description (often only one paragraph) that summarizes your study, including what you found out. It is *not* the same as an introduction. Write the abstract last, when you have the full picture of what you have achieved.

❐ *Introduction*: A short contextualization of your topic, introducing your **topic**, and indicating why it is important to address it. A brief outline of how the rest of your write-up is structured.

❐ *Literature review*: Brief, succinct, critical evaluations of how existing research contributes to answering your focal question. See below for more on how to write such a literature review. Conclude the review by identifying one or more **research questions** that the existing research leaves unanswered, and that you aim to answer in your own study. Where possible, include predictions or hypotheses about what you will find.

❐ *Methodology*: A description of your data: your informants, how you have designed and administered your research tools (questionnaire, experiment, etc.). You may want to include a brief rationale for your chosen approach, based on the literature.

❐ *Data or Results*: A straight description of the data you have gathered.

❐ *Analysis*: Organized according to the research questions that you identified as needing answers or predictions/hypotheses that needed testing. Compare, contrast and/or evaluate patterns in your data, using graphs and statistical analyses if possible and appropriate.

❐ *Discussion*: Take your analyses back to the literature, comparing what you have found with what you discussed in the literature review, and commenting on what it means. As appropriate, consider how your findings may have been affected by limitations in the design of your work or problems with how you carried it out. But leave your reader with a sense that you have nevertheless achieved something worthwhile: project your work in a positive light where you can.

❐ *Conclusion*: Explain how the outcomes of your Discussion section help to locate your findings within the topic field. Identify any remaining questions and suggest what could be done in the future, and how, to find answers to them.

You can choose different headings for your chapters or sections from those given above, but always keep a clear sense of the purpose of each component of your account.

Using the word limit imposed for your work, calculate how many words you have for each of the above components. If you find you need more words in a section, take them from another, in order to stay inside the word limit. By identifying subsections, you can subdivide the word counts further, until you never have more than a few hundred words to write under a given heading. This will help you maintain discipline and focus, and give you clear warning when you have too much or too little to say (so that you can restructure the plan to accommodate it). It will also encourage you, since you will always know exactly how much of your project you have written up and how much you still have to do.

Using resources

Books and journals

Although **textbooks** are a good place to start, in research it is poor practice to rely heavily on them. Rather, use them as a gateway to the original literature that you need to track down and read for yourself. **Readers** can be an excellent way to access classic papers in an area of enquiry: scan the editors' introduction for a justification of why a paper was selected. **Edited collections** feature chapters by many different writers on the same theme. Some collections are more principled than others, however: some are simply papers presented at a certain conference and may not be ground-breaking. **Monographs** are complete books written by one author (or by co-authors, with no indication of who wrote what). They can be difficult to differentiate from textbooks, but normally will focus on a narrow theme and argue a particular point of view. Reading entire books is time-consuming, so use the blurb on the back, the Introduction and the Conclusion to find out what the author is claiming. Then use the index and/or the table of contents to identify the most relevant topics for your interests. **Journal articles** can be technical, but tend to be succinct and in a format not dissimilar to your own project. If you find a journal article difficult to understand, whether because of its style or because of the previous knowledge that it assumes, start by reading the abstract, the Introduction and the Conclusion, to get the main points and orientate yourself. Then go back and read the rest of the article if you judge that it is relevant enough to your needs. Use the reference lists in journal articles as a quick way of finding other relevant material. Specialist **encyclopedias** (especially Brown 2006, Crystal 1997, 2003b) and **handbooks** (e.g. Aronoff and Rees-Miller 2001; Kaplan 2002) are an excellent resource, because the top people have been asked to summarize the issues in their specialist field. You can also use **abstracting databases** (see later), **bibliographies** (these tell you who has written what in a given subject area), unpublished **MA dissertations** and **PhD theses**, and archives of past undergraduate **projects** (though remember that work by students is not usually of the same quality as published research!).

Where to look in libraries

Most libraries keep the latest issues of journals in one place, and then bind several issues together and put them on the stacks (shelves). For books, remember to check other sections than just linguistics (e.g. education, sociology, philosophy, psychology) that may have relevant books. Besides your own and any other local university or college libraries, remember to consider hospital and other institutional libraries and local archives. The local city or county library may also have useful books and, if you need inter-library loans (see below), you may be charged less there than in your own institution. Major university libraries and public libraries in large cities may not let you borrow books, but you can arrange in advance to gain read-only access. National libraries, such as the British Library in London, normally require a special ticket, and you may need a letter of introduction from your institution confirming that you are engaged in research.

Libraries in most countries operate a system of **inter-library loans**, whereby a book or journal article not available locally can be obtained from elsewhere. There is normally a charge for this service, but it may be subsidized by your department or, at a civic library, by the local government.

Electronic resources

Libraries now carry a great deal of information in electronic form: on CD, in networked databases, or through institutional subscriptions to Internet services. You may be able to access your university's materials remotely (via the Internet from your home computer) using a password. Enquire with a librarian about what is available and, if there are training sessions on how to use the resources, take advantage. Many printed journals are now also available electronically, and you can search for what you want, and then download and print out (via PDF) a copy identical to the printed edition. A great many journal papers and other resources that are otherwise not available can be obtained through the ERIC clearing house of language and linguistics (www.cal.org/ericcll/).

There are several ways of saving time by knowing how to use search tools, particularly those that look for journal articles and books on a particular topic. Particularly useful are Linguistics and Language Behavior Abstracts and the Web of Knowledge, available via institutional subscription, and Google Scholar (http://scholar.google.com), free on the Internet. All of these include an abstracts database. Abstracts databases are important because few people have the time to check every journal as it comes out, and there is therefore a danger of missing things relevant to their work. The database carries abstracts of all the papers in the various publications that it covers, updated on a regular basis. Where electronic, the entries are searchable by author, keyword, and text. The idea is that you can find many entries that may be relevant to your needs and, on the basis of the abstract, decide whether or not to obtain and read the full paper. Remember: reading the abstract is *not* a substitute for reading the article itself if you are intending to refer to the research. A brief summary cannot give you sufficient detail for your purposes, so you must read the full account in context. Some abstracts databases are also available on paper, where searching is done using multiple indexes.

The Internet

A huge amount of information is available via the Internet. There is no quality control, however, so it can be inaccurate or even positively (and deliberately) misleading. For this reason, it is a good idea to operate with caution: use what you find as a stepping stone to your goal, rather than as a goal in itself. That is, if you find on a website a claim that something is the case, don't simply accept it and quote it. Rather, look for references that back the claim up, and then track them down for yourself. Don't be satisfied until you have found evidence that is reliable (see 'Reviewing the literature' below). Where you do want to use information from websites, prefer those belonging to official organizations or to people whose credentials you can check. Students often ask specifically about the status of Wikipedia (http://en.wikipedia.org/wiki/Main_Page), a free encyclopedia that is written by, and constantly updated by, its users (that is, anyone). Although Wikipedia is vulnerable to the obvious limitations of being compiled in this way, the aim of the project is to create a reliable database by allowing its readers directly to edit existing pages, so that they, in effect, review the quality of the account, and remove any inaccuracies. Inevitably, the issue comes down to how 'accurate' and 'inaccurate' are defined, particularly when it comes to topics that are not subject to hard scientific facts. Our advice is to treat Wikipedia like any other Internet source: possibly accurate but not necessarily, and therefore a great place to orientate yourself and get ideas, but not the end of the line. Take what you discover, and check it in other sources. If you cannot find any supporting evidence for a claim, then maybe that claim is unreliable and should not be used. Having said that, the changing text in Wikipedia, along with the *talk* page for each article, have the potential to underpin a fascinating research project about the way that meaning is negotiated (see Project 163). For guidance on how to reference material from the Internet, see Chapter 20.

People

There are lots of people in the world who know things that you don't, so ask them. The golden rule is to ask sensible questions, so that you don't annoy people or waste their time. If you do your homework first, most people will be pleased to give you time and information.

Databases

Databases are resources that offer you linguistic material for research that you could not possibly gather for yourself. They include general corpora of English and other languages (see Chapter 18), and specific corpora such as the CHILDES database of child language (see Chapter 3). Not all databases are electronic. For example, you can find out the frequency with which different words occur in texts not only from web sources such as www.comp.lancs.ac.uk/ucrel/bncfreq/flists.html, but also from printed word-frequency lists such as Johansson and Hofland (1989), Nation (1986), Hindmarsh (1980), Carroll *et al.* (1971), Kucera and Francis (1967) and West (1953).

Dictionaries and glossaries

If you are unsure what a word or a technical term means, then look it up. Apart from general English-language dictionaries, there are a number of specialist linguistics dictionaries, including Crystal (2002), Trask (1993, 1995, 1999) and Richards and Schmidt (2002). In addition, many linguistics textbooks have glossaries at the back.

Being a researcher

There are certain hallmarks of being a researcher, certain assumptions that are made, and ways in which the work is approached. Here are a few pointers.

What research looks like

Most research engages with one or more **research questions** – that is, questions that you will answer through an investigation, rather than just by reading. However, the research questions are derived from what you have read, and existing **theory** creates the best foundation for asking something new, or for applying an old question to your particular data. Some kinds of theory make it possible to make a prediction about what you will find, often framed as a **hypothesis**. An experimental hypothesis makes predictions about the outcome of specific controlled events, and the outcomes actually achieved enable you to confirm or fail to confirm the hypothesis (see Chapter 12). Hypotheses and predictions can also be used in non-experimental research. They enable you to identify in advance what contrasts or features you are likely to find (and therefore should look for) in your data. For example, in an observation study, your hypothesis might be that a child will interact differently with adults from the way it does with other children. This gives you a focused goal, and reminds you to avoid introducing other differences between the two situations, such as what activities the child is engaged in. If your research is not built upon a hypothesis, there is a serious danger that you will not be able to explain what you have found out.

Much legitimate research involves rerunning experiments and analyses done by others, challenging established theories with new data and so on. Because linguistics spans the sciences and the humanities, it deals with strikingly different kinds of intellectual material:

☐   quantitative data, on which statistical tests can be done: experimental results, word counts, etc.;

☐   qualitative data: judgments, perceptions, insights, etc.;

☐   pure theory: models of internal processes which, though testable in terms of what language is like, are in essence non-experimental.

Reviewing the literature

In an essay, project or dissertation, you will normally be expected to have a literature review. It is easy for this requirement to seem overwhelming and/or to get out of hand. Simply, there is too much out there for you to read it all and it can be unclear how you should decide what to read, how carefully to read it, and how much detail to report. The following guidelines may help:

☐   Draw up a skeleton plan (e.g. contents page) of your entire project (see earlier), and work out how many words you can afford to give to your literature review. Once you have decided what issues to cover (see below), further subdivide by theme until you establish that you have an average of, say, just 350 words to cover each topic within the review. By knowing the word limits from early on, you can easily see when it will be pointless to read any more.

☐   Don't conceive of the literature review as being a description of as many different ideas in the general area of your project as you can find. If you do, you won't know what to choose or be able to say anything interesting about it.

❐ Drive your literature review by *topic*, not publication. Specifically, begin with the precise focus of your project, and from that derive interesting questions that you can ask of the literature. By asking questions you will find it easy to *harvest* books and journal articles for what they say that is *relevant*, rather than simply reporting everything they contain. You will also find it easier to compare and contrast different claims. In a project examining the differences between the language of a 4-year-old twin brother and sister, obvious questions to ask of the literature might include: How would the language of a 4-year-old non-twin girl normally compare to that of a boy of the same age? Is development of language in twins usually different from non-twins? What sorts of features are likely to be most interesting (e.g. phonology, grammar, vocabulary, social interaction)?

❐ Some of your literature review might be about methodology, focused around a question like: What methods have been successfully used by others to study the language of young children? You may choose to introduce such a topic when you reach the methodology part of your account. In fact, don't conceive of the literature review as a single lump of text (e.g. a chapter) if it makes more sense for your story to introduce it in parts, according to the questions you are asking at different stages of your account.

❐ View the literature review as a boxing ring, not a display cabinet – that is, use what you read to identify disagreements and paradoxes. You can then act as referee, commenting on who you think has the stronger argument and why. Disagreements are difficult to see if you simply describe first one author's work and then another's, but if you are using the resources to answer *your* questions, then you will naturally want to report similar (or contrasting) claims together, giving you the opportunity to comment on how they relate. See Chapter 21 for more guidance on how to achieve this.

❐ Expect to evaluate what you read, not just report it. Not every claim in print is reliable or well justified by evidence. For more guidance on how to evaluate the literature and write a critical literature review, see Wallace and Wray (2006).

How to read and how to make notes

Avoid just reading things that might be relevant in some general way. Always know why you are reading something and what you hope to find out, and don't make notes that are not specific to your work. Rather than ending up with separate pages of notes for each book or article you read, make the notes under the headings for which they are appropriate, so any page of your notes will contain references to several different works. This means that you are more likely to notice when two authors disagree. It also means that writing up can be done without wading through all the notes again. Always label a note or quote with the author's name, date of publication, and page number, so you know where to find it again. If what you have written down is a quote, put it in inverted commas, otherwise you may later think that it is in your own words. To present someone else's words as your own is plagiarism (see Chapter 21). Copy accurately, especially spelling and punctuation.

Theory-only projects

In some circumstances, it may be possible to focus entirely on the critical evaluation or the development of a theory or model without collecting any data of your own. There are two basic reasons why you might embark on a theory-only project. First, you may want to write about an aspect of language that either is not amenable to testing or cannot usefully be investigated via data collection (though, either way, it should still be possible to illustrate your points with linguistic examples). Areas of linguistic study where these criteria might apply in some circumstances include the evolution or origin of language, philosophy of language, or syntactic theory. Second, it may not be feasible to collect the sort of data that you require. In this case, you will be referring to data-based research, but it will be the published material of other researchers. Into this category might fall projects focusing on clinical linguistics, exotic languages, historical linguistics and so on. Do not see theory-only projects as an escape route from empirical research – they are difficult to do well. In addition, check that a non-empirical project is acceptable for your assessment.

If you are writing a theory-only project, begin with a clear overview of the literature. You should read around the area that interests you as extensively as is practical, because otherwise your arguments will be unsubstantiated. Identify a theory that interests you and which you feel is open for debate and then try to find an angle on it that will create an interesting discussion. One way is to apply it to a new issue. For example, an existing model of lexical retrieval for monolinguals could be discussed in the light of the needs and practices of multilinguals. Can the model cope with additional languages easily or does it need reorganizing? A model that represents the transition from thought to utterance could be explored from the viewpoint of human evolution: does it lend itself to there being a survival advantage at every stage of man's evolution? Or, if someone has proposed a model that accounts for the production of speech, how easily can it be applied to writing? Can it simply be reversed to account for comprehension? If it is a model of adult language, does it apply equally to children?

Draw diagrams to demonstrate how your model works. Diagrams should be explicit and should adequately illustrate the sequence of events that will produce the envisaged outcome. It should be possible to explain the predicted results if the structures are subject to breakdown or malfunction at any stage. Explain the ways in which your model differs in construction, process and outcome from others.

Setting up data-based research

Chapters 2–10 in this book explore the types of projects that you may be able to undertake. Different areas of research require different techniques, and these are described in Chapters 11–15. But, before you start, there are many general considerations, which we will look at now. It is very important that you read the next few pages, and that you remember to reread them as you plan and carry out your project. What is said below is, of course, subject to modification in the light of what your own course requirements are, so don't forget to check with your own supervisor or tutor what you are expected to achieve, what methods or approaches are preferred, and what equipment is available.

Making sure you know enough

Although it is best to choose a project that uses skills that you already have, this may not be entirely possible. If you need additional skills, check whether there are tutors who can help, either directly or through recommending self-study texts or other sources of assistance. Ask a tutor to give you an honest answer to the question 'Am I up to it?' See if there are modules you can opt for or specific lectures you can attend that could help. If you know well in advance what your project will be on, plan your modules to prepare you for it. Lecturers often remark that students could help themselves more during project work by looking back carefully at modules that they have previously taken, perhaps digging out old lecture notes and reading lists and generally making use of established resources.

Getting subjects and informants

Studying human language normally requires access to people. You may want to work with one person in some detail or you may need to get a number of people to perform some task, either individually or as a group. Either way, you must be sure that appropriate people will be available. How will you persuade your subjects to give up their time? What will you tell them about the purpose of your study? If you want to compare males with females, say, are you easily going to recruit the same number of each? If you are collecting your data in the vacation, whom will you use? If you recruit willing members of your family, what will be the effect of their differences in age, education, and so on?

Remember that your subjects are doing you a favour by participating. It is in your interests to keep them sweet, so be as efficient as you can in making arrangements, keeping to appointments, and clearly explaining what you want them to do. Remember to thank them afterwards. Subjects may be interested to know, at a later date, how the study turned out.

Accessing and using equipment

Establish what you need and whether it is available. Do ask for help and advice from the technicians or others (e.g. postgraduates) who know about the equipment you use. If your own department does not have what you need, another one may. If you have a clear idea of what a piece of equipment does, then you may be able to think of an alternative (cheaper, simpler, low-tech) way of achieving the same result. If you need special computer software, is there a fellow-student who can help you write it?

Safety and ethics

If you are at all unsure about the safety aspect of your data collection, get advice. You will not be very popular if you kill one subject in three, and you should really aim to avoid even sending them away with a headache. (The headaches that you get are, however, par for the course.) As for ethical matters, check if there are guidelines in your department that you need to follow (see Chapter 15 for more information).

Reducing the risk of it going wrong

Research that involves other people is sure to present all sorts of problems you haven't foreseen. If your questionnaire is ambiguous, your experimental stimuli are inappropriate, or your tape recorder doesn't work, you can end up with data that is useless or no data at all. Beware of the **observer's paradox**: your subjects' awareness that you are studying them may have an effect on their linguistic behaviour, so that the data are not representative of what would happen if no observation were taking place. There are techniques for minimizing the problem (see Chapters 11–15), but often it is sufficient simply to acknowledge that there may have been such an effect, and not worry too much about it.

By running a **pilot study** (experiments and questionnaires) or a **rehearsal** (recordings and interviews), you can identify many problems and fix them before you start. A pilot study is a trial run using a small number of people similar to those you will use as subjects. Even if you are doing an observational study, a case study, or a text analysis, you can have a dummy run by taking a small piece of suitable data and working through it to check that you will be able to achieve your objectives. Try to make the pilot as representative as possible by taking it seriously. Gather the results and practise processing them, whether through the tables and statistics (invent additional figures if that helps the number crunching) or through some process of interpretation. Ask the people who took part in the pilot or rehearsal to help you modify the procedures so that they will work better (Would two short sessions be better than one long one? Were the instructions clear?). If it is an interview study, ask your pilot subjects to help you frame the questions or procedures better. Because of their advance knowledge of the procedures and stimuli or questions, it is usually inappropriate to use pilot subjects again in the main study.

Ending up with manageable results

The biggest single error made by inexperienced researchers is not thinking about what the results will look like until they have them. It may seem as if the difficult part of the work is getting the data, but it isn't. There is nothing worse than sitting down with 40 hours of video data or 300 pieces of paper and thinking, 'What do I do with this lot?' Here are some tips:

❐ If you won't have time to listen to an hour's recorded data from each subject, don't collect so much.

❐ If you are designing a questionnaire, make sure you know how to collate the full range of answers you may get (see Chapter 13).

❐ Decide in advance what to do with a rogue result or an unhelpful respondent – can you identify in advance clear grounds for excluding such a case and no others? Do you need a couple of extra subjects as back-ups, in case you can't use someone's results?

❐ Check whether you are expected, as part of your assessment, to perform statistical tests on your results. If you are, or if you feel that it is appropriate to do so, work out in advance which test(s) you will use, and have a clear idea of how you will generate the values that go into them. Chapter 19 will help you.

Handling data and knowing how to interpret your results

Summarizing data (especially scores) into formats that are easy to digest and compare is essential if both you and your assessors are to make sense of them (see Chapter 19). Clearly thought-out and labelled tables can save space. You needn't restate in prose what is in them but you must to refer to them and interpret them. Give worked examples of some of your results, plus detailed general discussion, before drawing broader conclusions.

Numerical data may appear straightforward, but you can easily end up not knowing what the numbers actually mean. Before you start, make sure you are able to state clearly what it will mean if result A is bigger than B, B is bigger than A, A and B are the same, and so on. Know where every figure will go in a table and which ones you will want to compare with which. Use Chapter 19 on statistics before you design your study, to ensure that you will have results you can process.

Non-numerical data is often much messier and much more difficult to draw firm conclusions from. You may know that a speaker tends to put up more resistance to an interruption by person A than by person B, but how can you back that claim up adequately? Look for clear examples and ask yourself often 'Does the data really demonstrate what I think it does?' If you cannot find examples, then maybe it does not.

If you did not find the patterns you expected in your data, you still have a result. Consider why it has happened. Could the reason lie in your experimental design? Be prepared to evaluate your work critically and state how it could have been improved. This needn't be done in a self-deprecatory manner. Remember that one major purpose of research is to identify what to investigate next and how.

Discussion and drawing conclusions

Aim to draw some conclusion about an aspect of how language works or how people use or process language. At the very least, you should be able to provide some speculations, on the basis of your data, about what the phenomena that you have observed are and how they can be explained. There is nothing wrong with reasoning through various possible arguments and visibly discarding one model in favour of another: it gives the assessor a much clearer idea of how you have reached your final conclusion. Make sure that any questions you have asked in your account have been answered and that you bring the reader back to your starting point: how your study fits into the broader frame of the topic area.

Presenting symbols and numbers

❑   If you want to present phonetic symbols in your work, you can download fonts: see Chapter 16.

❑   Spell the numbers one to ten as words (except in dates). Larger numbers can be written as figures (e.g. 24). However, avoid starting a sentence with a number, so write: *Twenty-four informants took part in the study.*

Avoiding plagiarism

The threat of plagiarism is a source of great anxiety to lots of students who never have and never will plagiarize. On the other hand, unless care is taken with the way you write, you may inadvertently plagiarize. A definition of plagiarism and guidance on practical ways to avoid it, with a worked example, can be found in Chapter 21.

Being streetwise: keeping on the right side of your assessor

It pays to understand the psychology of your assessor. It is in your interests to maximize the chance that there is a smile on his/her face from the moment your project reaches the top of the pile to the moment that the grade is put onto the mark sheet. The best way to achieve this is by writing outstanding work, but there are a few other tactics as well, that will make an assessor feel that you have taken care to make your work easy to read.

❐   Obey the house rules for presentation, word counting and deadlines.

❐   Express yourself with care (see Chapter 22).

❐   Label your work clearly and, if there is any danger of pages coming loose, label every page. Use page numbers.

❐   With audio, video, or other supplementary data, make sure it is clear what it is, and how to navigate it (see Chapter 11).

❐   Indicate clearly the structure of your work, so that the assessor knows at every point what you are doing and why.

❐   Word-process. If you have to write things in by hand (e.g. phonetic symbols), then remember to do it, and make them neat and legible. If your writing is terrible, get a friend to write them in for you.

❐   When you think your work is ready to hand in, pretend to be the assessor picking it up and opening it. Will it give the impression you want? If not, fix the problems.

There is a lot to think about – perhaps more than you had realized when you decided to do a project – but much of what we have identified in this chapter can be applied quite naturally as you proceed. The key thing is to enjoy the opportunity of researching your chosen linguistic topic in depth. It will be a lot of work but there is a very good chance that your project will be the piece of work that you are ultimately most proud of.

PART I

AREAS OF STUDY AND PROJECT IDEAS

2
Psycholinguistics

Psycholinguists ask questions such as the following:

- [ ] How does our brain organize the words that it stores?
- [ ] How does it access them so quickly and efficiently?
- [ ] What causes the '*tip of the tongue*' phenomenon, when a word just won't come to mind?
- [ ] Why are we more likely to mishear something that is out of context?
- [ ] How do we know how to finish off a sentence that someone else starts?
- [ ] How similar are the processes of listening and reading?
- [ ] When the brain encounters a sentence it has never seen or heard before, does it have to look everything up in some vast dictionary and grammar store, or are there short-cuts that it can take to work out what it means?
- [ ] Does the brain process the words as soon as it hears or sees them, or does it store up strings of words and then process them all at once?
- [ ] Why don't we take idioms like *He's one sandwich short of a picnic* literally?
- [ ] How do we know when someone has made a mistake in what they have said?
- [ ] What mechanisms operate during speech production to ensure that all the words come out in the right order and with the right intonation?
- [ ] What can the language of brain-damaged people tell us about how language-processing occurs?

Just imagine trying to teach a computer to speak and understand a language exactly like a human, and it becomes clear why we shouldn't take the answers to questions like these for granted.

Textbooks and major journals

Psycholinguistics is a sub-discipline of both psychology and linguistics, and the slant within textbooks varies accordingly, so you are likely to encounter some rather different viewpoints and approaches. Aim for recent publications when you are trying to get an overview of what the current issues are. Useful introductory texts include Field (2003), Steinberg (2005), and the more detailed Steinberg, Nagata, and Aline (2001). Also check handbooks (e.g. Kroll and De Groot 2005, on psycholinguistic approaches to bilingualism) and various entries in linguistics encyclopedias (especially Brown 2006). Psychology textbooks that focus on language include Harley (2001) and there are chapters on language in Eysenck and Keane (2005) and Pinel (2003). For project ideas, Field (2005) and Prideaux (1990) are good sources, and Clark and Clark (1977) remains a classic.

Journals in the field of psycholinguistics can be rather daunting, because many of them build on complex theory and methodology. You may not be able to fully replicate anything published in a journal, but you may get some ideas about what questions are interesting and why. Useful journals for projects in psycholinguistics include the following:

Journals

Applied Psycholinguistics
Brain and Language
Cognition
International Journal of Language and Communication Disorders
Journal of Experimental Psychology: Learning, Memory, and Cognition
Journal of Memory and Language
Journal of Psycholinguistic Research
Language and Cognitive Processes
Language and Communication
Memory and Cognition
Mind and Language
Quarterly Journal of Experimental Psychology
Reading and Writing

Central themes and project ideas

There are two levels at which a project in psycholinguistics can operate:

❏ If you have some experience of experimental research and have access to specialist equipment and supervision, you can plan to replicate or adapt a published experiment. Find references to such experiments by reading overviews, and go from there back to the original account, normally in a journal. Only the original paper will give you sufficient detail of the procedures and analyses to plan your own work. Get advice at an early stage from your supervisor, and ensure that you leave plenty of time. General guidance on experimental work can be found in Chapter 12.

❏ If you are not experienced, if you have little call on equipment, and/or if your supervisor has insufficient time or specialist knowledge to support you, you are not in a position to conduct research that is compatible with the complex procedures of published work. However, there are plenty of projects that require less technical skill but which can still be used to shed light on the psychological processes of language. It is mostly projects of this sort that are suggested in the following sections.

How psycholinguists conceptualize language

Following Fodor (1983), most psychologists believe that human cognition is modular. This means that it consists of a number of independent processors. If processors operate independently, then it should be possible to find people who have impairment of one, while the others function normally. As far as language is concerned, interest lies in establishing whether the processes responsible for the production and comprehension of speech and writing are four independent ones or not. For example, clinical psycholinguists want to know whether losing the ability to process *spoken* input will affect the processing of *written* input as well: does what we see on the page have to be turned into 'speech' before it can be decoded?

Projects

1   Investigate the hypothesis that some types of extraneous sound are more distracting to linguistic processing than others. Give a difficult linguistic task to three groups of subjects, one group with speech played in the background, one with non-vocal music and one (control) group with no sound. Use the literature to make a prediction about which condition will prove most distracting.
2   Compare memory for objects with memory for words. Give one group of subjects a set of household objects to memorize. Give a second group just a list of the names of the same objects to memorize. Use the literature to decide on your hypothesis, e.g. it is easier to remember the names of objects than it is to remember the objects themselves. Consider how your experiment might help establish whether the process of memorizing an object involves naming it. What sort of processing model is most consistent with your results?
3   In order to find out if training on one linguistic task is transferable to another task, give one group of subjects training in strategies for memorizing random lists of words, give a second group no training, and then ask both groups to memorize long lists of words and recall them. In a second test, give them long lists of numbers to recall. Use the literature to decide on the most robust hypotheses to test, e.g. the trained group will perform better in the words list than the untrained group; the memorization of words and of numbers requires different skills, so training in one task will not be an advantage in another. Consider the significance of an outcome where the untrained group performed better on: the word test; the number test; both.

How we understand language

Speech comprehension

Research into the comprehension of spoken language has focused on research questions like the following: How do we deduce meaning so efficiently when the quality of the acoustic input is so variable? How do we work out so quickly what a word is – often after only the first two phonemes? One theory that offers an answer is the Cohort model (Marslen-Wilson and Tyler 1980): as soon as we hear a word begin, we 'flag up' all the words we know which have that sound at the beginning, creating a **word-initial cohort**. We then disqualify those that no longer fit when the next sound is heard, or which are unlikely because of the context. The cohort model is described in most introductory books on psycholinguistics.

Project

4   Ask as many friends and relatives as you can to jot down examples of *slips of the ear* (e.g. *Hormone treatment should be available for postmen or pausal women*: post-menopausal women), that is, when they mishear something (collect your own examples too). Give them as much time as possible – at least several weeks – and make sure they remember to make a note of things at the time. A taxonomy can be found in Garman (1990: 162–4). Use the examples to assess models of lexical processing. What characteristics do misheard items share with the items they are mistaken for? Are there any examples of mishearings that do not begin with the same sounds? If so, how can the standard models of processing account for them?

Reading

Reading is a secondary linguistic skill. Whereas a child develops naturally the facility to speak and to understand speech, reading and writing are learned. They are an extremely recent innovation in mankind's development and still have little or no role in many parts of the world. Therefore, we should expect that the processes of reading and writing are overlaid on the much older processes of understanding and producing speech. However, evidence from some kinds of brain-damaged patients suggests that, when we read, we do not always simply translate the words on the page into a phonological representation and access the meaning that way: rather, there appear to be shortcuts that do not involve the mediation of speech processes.

For models of reading, see Coltheart (2005) and Hillis (2002). Eysenck and Keane (2005: Ch. 10) review the advantages and disadvantages of five different approaches to research on reading. Questions of particular interest include: Is the recognition of a word aided by the preceding context? Do we identify words by recognizing the component letters or by overall word shape? For further information, see Eysenck and Keane (2005: 347–52). Models that aim to account for reading processes include the *logogen model*. Each word has a threshold of activation, which, when reached, triggers its recognition. Activation towards the trigger is caused by seeing the letters of the word, by context, by the general frequency of the word, and by its recent use. The logogen model is described in most introductory textbooks.

Projects

5   Investigate whether reading is mediated by phonological processing. Present on a computer screen sentences that are (a) acceptable (e.g. *Chess appeals to clever boys*); (b) nonsense (e.g. *Trees blossom during knives*); and (c) nonsense, but sound identical to acceptable ones (e.g. *Wardrobes and dressers differ in sighs*). Time subjects pressing one or other of two keys, according to whether the sentence makes sense or not. Hypothesis: sentences in set (c) will take longer to judge as nonsense than those in set (b) because the phonological form will compete with the visual one. Alternative hypothesis: there is no phonological involvement in silent reading, so (b) and (c) will take the same amount of time to decode and respond to. To counter the problem of some sentences simply being intrinsically harder than others, use two groups of subjects, each of which has homophones where the other has the correct spelling (so the second group would have *Wardrobes and dressers differ in size* in set (a) and *Chess appeals to clever buoys* in (c)). In constructing the stimuli, remember that the position in the sentence of the homophone may make a difference to the speed of processing because, if the first three words are already nonsense, you don't have to look any further. Compare your results with those of Baron (1973).

6   Base an experiment around that of Van Orden (1987): measure reaction times to questions such as: *is BREAD a FOOD?*; *is MELT a FOOD?*; *is MEET a FOOD?* Van Orden's hypothesis was that the decision for 'meet' would be affected by the fact that it sounds identical to 'meat'.

Psycholinguistics and grammatical theory

Research in both syntax and psycholinguistics has offered models of how sentence parsing (decoding) is achieved. Clifton and Ferreira (1989: 79) provide a useful list of sentence types predicted to take longer to parse according to *their* model. Parsing models by Bever, Kimball, and Frazier and Fodor are described in Garnham (1985: 77–87). For a comprehensive description of model types, see Garman (1990, Ch. 6).

   The idea that language is managed using large strings and templates is fundamental to the notion of **formulaic language**. A number of researchers, including Pawley and Syder (1983), Sinclair (1991) and Wray (2002), have suggested that language comprehension and production can be at least partially achieved using 'a large number of semi-preconstructed phrases that constitute single choices, even though they appear to be analysable into sections' (Sinclair 1991: 110). Among those noted by Pawley and Syder is: *NP be-TENSE sorry to keep-TENSE you waiting*, which generates many sentences all to the same pattern, including: *I'm sorry to keep you waiting; I'm so sorry to have kept you waiting; Mr X is sorry to keep you waiting all this time* (Pawley and Syder 1983: 210). These constructions, and others that are more fixed, such as *What in the world* and *The thing is*, are variously called **sentence frames, (routine) formulae, chunks, schemata, templates, sentence builders** and **lexical phrases**. They may be advantageous as regards processing resources (Wray 2002) and/or language learning (Nattinger and DeCarrico 1992). If quite lengthy phrases or clauses can be stored and accessed like single lexical items, there are important implications for models of how we process sentences, and certain predictions can be made about patterns in speech errors.

Project

7   Record someone recounting the same experience several times to different people (and maybe several weeks apart) to see if the same structures and expressions are used to describe the same events on separate occasions. Consider the implications of 'preferred' ways of saying things, for a standard model of language processing.

Lexical and structural ambiguity

There are potential lexical ambiguities in much of what we hear. Why do we not normally notice that, for example, *Have you got enough time for this?* could equally well be *Have you got enough thyme for this?* Researchers have wanted to establish whether all the possible interpretations of a phonetic string are available at first, and then eliminated, or whether one interpretation is assumed (possibly the most frequent) and the others remain unretrieved unless there is a problem making the chosen one fit the context. There are accounts of research into lexical ambiguity in Garnham (1985: 62–7), Aitchison (2003: Ch. 19) and Harley (2001: 168–75).

Ambiguity also occurs at the syntactic level. It entails two or more possible interpretations of the structure of a clause, as in *Hubert saw his grandmother with a telescope*. Syntactic ambiguity is of interest because it can tell us how our grammatical and semantic processing interact. If we decode a whole clause grammatically before we try to interpret it, then we should not expect to find any evidence of the semantic context having resolved the disambiguation before the clause has ended. Evidence from experiments such as those of Tyler and Marslen-Wilson (1977) suggests that we do use semantic information to help us resolve syntactic ambiguity. For further information, see Harley (2001: 254–8).

Garden-path sentences

Garden-path sentences (GPSs) are so called because they *lead us up the garden path* by misleading us about their construction. A popular type of example uses the coincidence of the simple past tense and the past participle forms of certain English verbs, e.g. *The ball bounced past the window burst*, in which the verb is read as simple past but is only comprehensible as a past participle (*The ball that was bounced past the window burst*). GPSs are significant because our problems in interpreting them as grammatical appear to depend on our decoding strategy: we seem to decide on the form of the verb before we get to the end of the sentence. For a fuller description and references to experiments, see Kess (1992: 129 ff.). A useful account of much other research into the processing of sentences is given in Eysenck and Keane (2005, Ch. 11) and Harley (2001: Ch. 9).

Projects

8   In many cases, one reading of a lexically or structurally ambiguous sentence makes more sense in the context than the other reading, but there are also cases where context does not disambiguate them. Do informants still tend to think of one of the two available readings first, even when both are equally plausible? If so, do they all think of the same one? One theory suggests that the more frequent meaning will be accessed first (see Garman 1990: 255–7, Harley 2001: 146ff., 254ff.). Construct sentences that contain ambiguity, but where the two readings seem equally likely (e.g. lexical: *Everyone enjoyed the port*; structural: *Marmaduke had a conversation with a postman riding on a horse*). Randomize the order of the sentences and audio-record them, ensuring that the way they are read does not favour one interpretation over the other. Interview informants individually. Tell them that the stimuli are ambiguous, then play them one sentence at a time, and ask them which interpretation they registered first. Use the literature to decide whether your hypothesis should be that all your informants will tend to think of the same reading first, or that either reading is as likely to be recognized first, if there is no context to aid the interpretation.

9   Do 'complex' sentences take longer to process than 'simple' ones? Time two groups of subjects responding to 'true–false' comprehension questions about a story. Group A gets half of the questions in the active voice (e.g. *What hit him?*) and half in the passive (e.g. *Who was he helped by?*). Group B gets the reverse (*What was he hit by? Who helped him?*). Hypothesis: passive questions will take longer to respond to than their corresponding active. Because any given question is framed in the passive to one group and the active to the other, you are controlling for some questions being inherently more difficult than others. Remember that some passive sentences are easier to identify than others, because pragmatics precludes the possibility of seeing the grammatical subject as the actor (e.g. *The walls were painted by the handyman*). Use a computer for the presentation and timing. Alternatively, provide the story on paper, then audio-record the entire question–answer session so that you can later accurately measure the time taken for each response.

10   Sachs (1967) asked subjects whether or not they had heard certain sentences in a passage: some sentences had been there and, of those that had not, some were paraphrases of what had been there (e.g. passive where the original was active), while others were different in meaning. Her results indicated that we discard the information about form after decoding it but remember the meaning. Replicate her experiment, perhaps with some modifications, and see if your results agree with hers. There are brief reports of the experiment in Slobin (1979: 55–6) and Garnham (1985: 139).

How we produce spoken language

In order to speak a word, we have to access a store of words, find and retrieve a match for the idea, activate the instructions about how to pronounce it, and pass those instructions to the articulators (tongue, larynx, and so on). To produce a whole utterance, there must be forward planning to ensure the words are articulated in the right order, with the correct intonation, and so on. Sometimes things go wrong.

Speech errors and 'tip of the tongue'

Inadvertent errors in the speech of normal people can provide indications of how we access individual words and how we plan the larger units of our utterances. Garrett (e.g. 1976) studied speech errors in some depth (see Caplan 1987: 273–4), and found:

☐ More errors with content words than other words, including semantic substitutions, words swapping places (e.g. *he is planting the garden in the flowers*), and the transposition of sounds between words (e.g. *shinking sips* for *sinking ships*). Where an affix gets separated from its root (e.g. *He is schooling to go* for *He is going to school*), it is the affix that stays in place and the content word that moves.

☐ Prepositions occasionally undergo semantic substitution.

☐ There is always a phrase boundary between the two words in a word swap.

☐ There is rarely a phrase boundary between the two words in a sound swap.

For an examination of a whole range of speech errors, see Garman (1990: 151–62). Fromkin (1973) provides an easy introduction to slips of the tongue and Cutler (1982) investigates them in more depth. A short assessment of the processes involved is given in Eysenck and Keane (2005: 402ff.). For some examples, see Crystal (1997: 265).

General accounts of the 'tip of the tongue' phenomenon can be found in Aitchison (2003: Ch. 12) and Garman (1990: 170–1). For discussion contextualized in other theories, see Eysenck and Keane (2005: 403ff.). An experiment designed to elicit the 'tip of the tongue' phenomenon in experimental conditions is reported in Brown and McNeill (1966). The experiment is briefly described in Harley (2001: 362–63), Garman (1990: 170) and other introductory texts.

Aphasia

Many descriptions exist of speech errors and word-finding difficulties in people with aphasia (language disturbance after brain damage) and, clearly, models of normal processing need to be able to account for the phenomenon. Among the word-level symptoms that manifest themselves in various forms of aphasia are:

☐ an inability to access content words: this is like an extreme form of the 'tip of the tongue' phenomenon;

☐ making up non-existent words (**neologisms**);

☐ semantic errors: substitution of a word with a similar or associated meaning;

☐ phonological errors: problems with sequencing the sounds, or the persistent use of a wrong sound over several attempts;

☐ more problems with verbs than nouns;

☐ memorized texts (prayers, poems, etc.) are produced more easily than novel sentences.

Broca's aphasia features agrammatism: problems with assembling words into sentences and with the elements that carry the grammatical structure, such as function words (e.g. prepositions) and word endings. People with Wernicke's aphasia produce long strings that are incomprehensible, displaying better access to the grammatical words than to content words. For brief information about the major symptoms of aphasia, see Eysenck and Keane (2005: 411ff.) and Harley (2001: 376ff.). A general consideration of how aphasia contributes to research into normal processing, and many examples of aphasic speech, can be found in Aitchison (2003). For a detailed introduction to aphasia, see Pratt and Whitaker (2006).

Projects

11   The Brown and McNeill (1966) 'tip of the tongue' experiment is reasonably easy to replicate. You may want to modify it in various ways. Reading their account may give you ideas for an experiment of a different design that elicits the same phenomenon.

12   Write a case history of a person with aphasia, include examples of spontaneous speech, recitations of well-known rhymes or lists (e.g. days of the week), specific naming tasks and so on. If you have the opportunity to conduct a longitudinal study, log the person's improvement or deterioration. What strategies does he/she have for coping with the problems? How do carers and others approach communication? Do teaching or therapy have any long-term effect?

13   Challenge one or more models of language processing (in general) or lexical retrieval (in particular) to adequately explain the patterns of word-loss described in the aphasia literature. Use a resource like Eysenck and Keane (2005) or Harley (2001) to find a suitable model.

14   Find a person with word-finding difficulties and catalogue: words consistently accessible; words occasionally accessible; words never accessible, and words said in error for other words. Look for semantic and syntactic patterns to these sets and use this to test hypotheses such as: concrete nouns are more easily accessed than abstract ones; function words (and, by, of, yet, etc.) are very difficult to access; word substitutions are always in the same word class (noun for noun, verb for verb, etc.); personal names are more difficult to access than generic nouns (e.g. John is harder to access than boy). Are whole sets of semantically linked words lost? Each case is different and the patterns you find will depend on the precise symptoms of the individual, so don't prejudge. Use the information to examine one or more models of lexical storage and access.

15   Elicit speech errors by recording subjects when tired or drunk, or when reading a technical passage aloud. Sort the errors into types and use them to evaluate a model of reading and/or speech production.

16   Collect speech errors over a long period of time or use commercially available audio- or videotaped compilations of outtakes from TV or radio. Rather than just listing your examples, use them to challenge or support models of speech

production. In categorizing and analysing your data, consider questions such as: What was said? What was intended? How soon did the speaker spot the problem? Why at that particular point? Did the listener spot the problem? Why/how? What did the speaker do? What did the listener do? Was there an actual, or potential, breakdown in communication? What is the phonetic/articulatory relationship between what was said and what was intended, and what happened in the phonological environment, e.g. did any assimilation match the intended or the actual output?

How we produce writing

In order to write a word, we need to first select it from the mental lexicon and then access information about how it is spelled. Interesting questions arise about whether speakers of different languages have different processing systems, because in languages with a good grapheme-phoneme correspondence, such as Spanish, it is possible to move between pronunciation and spelling via simple 'rules', whereas English has many words that are not pronounced as they are spelled (e.g. *knight*; *Leicester*).

Slips of the pen

As we might expect if our model of writing parallels that for reading, there is evidence that errors in writing can occur at letter-part, whole-letter, and word level. Garman (1990: 165–7) describes slips at all these levels. For many more examples, and a fuller examination of what they can tell us, see Hotopf (1983). There has been little research on errors in the writing of longer units, perhaps because we are more likely to spot them as they are happening and to repair them at an early stage. However, Hotopf examines a sizable collection of data.

Projects

17   Adapt the Sachs experiment (see Project 10) for written input. Use one of the current models of processing (such as those reviewed in Eysenck and Keane 2005) to predict in what ways changing the medium may change the outcome of the experiment. Are your predictions borne out?

18   Replicate the experiment reported by Kaufer *et al.* (1986), in which writers were asked to think aloud as they composed text and the location of their pauses was noted. It was found that experienced writers operated in larger units than inexperienced ones.

19   Get subjects to type a passage as fast as possible onto a computer without being able to see the screen (it is best if they are fairly fast typists). As they can't see what they've put in, they will be unable to go back and correct. Analyse the errors, first separating out those that are to do with adjacent keys. Are there transpositions across words, across phrase boundaries, etc.? Relate your findings to those from research into slips of the pen and dysgraphia (see below).

20   As for project 19, but use keyboard tracking software such as ScriptLog
     (www.scriptlog.net/about.asp) to reconstruct the errors that subjects make when
     typing a passage.
21   Replicate or adapt Griffiths's (1986) experiment where subjects copied a written
     passage while observers noted where they paused to look back to the original. He
     found that pausing was not random, but tended to happen at syntactic (constituent)
     boundaries. The methodology could be adapted for copying onto a computer.

Dyslexia and dysgraphia

'Dyslexia', in common parlance, actually refers to **developmental dyslexia** and
developmental dysgraphia: difficulties that some children of normal intelligence have in
learning to read and write, and which can persist into adulthood if not remedied. There
are several reasons why developmental dyslexia and dysgraphia are still not understood:

❐   Until recently, children with severe dyslexia were misdiagnosed as stupid or lazy.

❐   Bright, resourceful, and/or highly motivated dyslexics often find ways of compensating
    for their difficulties, and indeed may not always realize that they are dyslexic.

❐   The terms 'dyslexia' and 'dysgraphia' do not describe single phenomena. They are
    used of an array of symptoms and a given individual may have only some of them.
    These symptoms may indicate different levels of severity in a single brain
    dysfunction, or may be caused by different things.

To find out more about developmental dyslexia and dysgraphia, see Reid and Wearmouth
(2002) and Molfese *et al.* (2006).

  Acquired dyslexia and **dysgraphia** also exist. These conditions affect individuals
previously able to read and write but who have lost some or all of that ability after a brain
injury. Acquired dyslexia can take different forms, suggesting breakdowns at different
stages of the reading process. See Luzzatti and Whitaker (2006) for an overview that
includes theoretical models.

Project

22   Analyse data from a dyslexic child (or adult) before, during and after remedial
     help. Gauge the extent to which the problem has been solved, poor skills have
     been directly improved and/or alternative strategies have been developed to
     compensate for an immutable deficit. Incorporate your assessment into a model of
     reading, to explain what differences in the processing procedures appear to have
     been achieved in order to improve the outcome.

Language and thought

Since the work of Sapir and Whorf, there has been much interest in the question of
whether we 'simply' express thoughts through our language, or whether the way our

language operates has an effect upon the way we think. Out of this have come two hypotheses, the stronger **linguistic determinism** – the way we think is determined by our language so that we are, as Sapir put it, 'at the mercy of our language' – and the weaker **linguistic relativity**: we are more likely to interpret the world in a certain way because of our 'language habits'. The theme was taken up by George Orwell who, in an essay at the back of his novel *Nineteen Eighty-Four*, explains how a new version of English, 'Newspeak', will prevent subversive thought by containing no words capable of expressing it. For direct access to Whorf's ideas, see Carroll (1956). Slobin (1979: 174–85) explores in some detail the implications and predictions of the Sapir–Whorf hypotheses. For a critical appraisal of the debate, see Pinker (1994, Ch. 3); Pinker concludes that the Sapir–Whorf position is unsustainable, and that thought is independent of language.

Projects

23   A counsellor was recently heard to say in a radio interview, 'Before we talked about problems we didn't think about them.' This might imply that if there were no counselling culture, many of the problems it deals with would not exist. Survey the views of counsellors, clients, and people who have never used a counsellor to explore the hypotheses that talking about something (a) changes the way you perceive it; (b) can create a problem in your mind that didn't exist before; and/or (c) gives you words to express thoughts and feelings you already have. Link this to the Sapir–Whorf hypotheses of linguistic determinism and linguistic relativity.

24   Someone who does not eat meat is called a *vegetarian*, someone who eats no animal products at all is called a *vegan*, and someone allergic to gluten is referred to as a *coeliac*, but there is no commonly used term for a person who avoids just red meat or just dairy products and no clear way to differentiate between vegetarians who do and do not eat fish. Compile a list of common dietary preferences and conduct a survey to find out how people commonly refer to them. What level of consistency is there? Does it matter if there is no agreed terminology for things, provided we can find some way of talking about them? Would there be any advantage for our ability to conceptualize and communicate if there were agreed words for all of these different preferences and conditions?

Other project ideas

25   Design your own model to show how different components of language processing interact. Are the words selected first and then made into a sentence or is the sentence planned first and then words slotted into it? At what point are the sounds selected? Are they selected as *phonemes* and then given an allophonic identity at a later stage or is all the phonetic information selected at once? Evaluate the model against published data or other models.

26 Take a psycholinguistic perspective on some other area of linguistics that you know well, such as phonetic sequencing, the production and/or comprehension of intonation, the construction and/or comprehension of sentences, functional approaches to language production/comprehension, the storage of idioms and so on. Draw up a model or use one from the literature and then take a detailed look at what the model needs to deal with in the course of constructing or understanding an utterance. Remember that it will be your detailed knowledge of this other area of linguistic theory that will justify the model you produce.

27 Investigate experimentally the hypothesis that science students will perform less well on a difficult linguistic task than humanities students. Justifications for this hypothesis might be, for example, that: any individual is either mathematical or linguistic, and people select careers that reflect their strengths; scientists do not get as much practice in language tasks; scientists are less confident in language tasks. If the results do not support a hypothesis, suggest reasons why.

28 Run an experiment separately on two groups. In both cases, tell them to write down as many words beginning with, say, 'm' as they can think of in two minutes (you can make this harder by specifying that they must be nouns and/or more than three letters long). Then go through the same procedure again (using a different letter) but, before they start, tell one group that an average score on this test is ten words and tell the other group that it is 35 words. Use the literature to decide which of the following hypotheses to favour: (a) when people feel pressured into attaining high standards, they will perform less well; (b) when people feel pressured into attaining high standards, they will perform better; or (c) putting pressure on people does not significantly reduce or increase their ability to access items in the lexicon. Use the results of the first task as a control (see Chapter 12), to check that the two groups are capable of performing to similar levels in identical conditions. Then you can have confidence that any differences in the second task are relevant to your hypotheses.

29 Monitor the progress of two individuals with aphasia who are considered by the experts to have broadly similar symptoms and prognoses, but one of whom gets more help (speech therapy, family involvement and so on) than the other. Use this to examine the role of practice, motivation, and the need to communicate in the recovery of speech

For further project ideas, see Prideaux (1990), Clark and Clark (1977), Greene and Coulson (1995), and Field (2003).

3
First-language acquisition and development

Research in first-language acquisition and development addresses the central question of why and how children succeed in acquiring language. Questions of current interest include:

❏   What do children bring to the process of acquisition?

❏   Are there general patterns (universals) for the acquisition of all human languages?

❏   How crucial is the role of the language the child hears around it, both from carers and from other children?

❏   To what extent do children vary in their language acquisition and usage, and why?

❏   How long does language acquisition take?

❏   Is there a 'critical period', or finite age range, within which acquisition must take place, if it is to occur at all?

❏   To what extent should the acquisition of literacy be seen as part of the language acquisition and development process?

❏   In what respects are the processes of oral and written language acquisition similar?

❏   How does literature written for children reflect their developing knowledge of language?

❏   How does language acquisition proceed in bilingual or multilingual children?

❏   Do the processes at work in second- or foreign-language acquisition in adults resemble the processes of first-language acquisition?

Approaches to research

Many of the above questions are addressed by studying the structure and meaning of the language produced by children at different ages or stages of development. This has made it possible to construct a generalized profile of the stages of language acquisition, and to make detailed comparisons of the child's language and the adult model. Study of the variation between children focuses on the *rate* at which features of language are acquired and the *route* of development – that is, the order in which language rules are acquired and the strategies used to acquire them. Researchers are also interested in how language comes to be used in ways appropriate to social context, gender, and social group, and this entails an examination of the mechanisms by which situation-sensitive usage is acquired, and the relevance of adult role models. Cross-linguistic and cross-cultural comparisons of the acquisition process provide a broader baseline for hypotheses about innate language abilities and universals. Studies of different types of language disability and abnormal delay in acquisition, whether due to internal or external causes, tell us about normal processes by indicating what it looks like when various individual components go wrong.

Terminology

Acquisition is often used to refer to the learning of language structures or rules, especially those of grammar, phonology and so on. (Note that within the context of second-language acquisition research, the term 'acquisition' can have a slightly different meaning, see Chapter 4.) **Development** often refers to the child's *use* of the acquired language rules and structures in a widening variety of language contexts.

Textbooks and major journals

There are many excellent books on language acquisition, so take a look on the relevant shelves in your university library. Lieven (2006a, b), MacWhinney (2003), Steinberg *et al.* (2002, Ch. 1) and Fromkin *et al.* (2003, Ch. 8) provide excellent short general overviews. Less detailed overviews can be found in Crystal (2003b, Section 24) and Crystal (1997, Part VII). Useful introductory books include Foley and Thompson (2003) and O'Grady (2005), and an excellent reader is Trott, Dobbinson, and Griffiths (2003). Detailed accounts of key issues in first-language acquisition can be found in the various papers in Tomasello and Bates (2001) and in Ritchie and Bhatia (1999), where there is also a chapter on methodology. A good starting point for information on literacy learning is Garton and Pratt (1998). For an account of learning to read, see Oakhill and Cain (2006), and also Kress (1997) on early literacy and Kress (2000) on children's spelling. The latter stages of language acquisition, including pragmatic development in adolescents, can provide an interesting focus – see Nippold (2006) for an overview. For project ideas, try Peccei (2005). Useful journals for projects in first-language acquisition include the following:

JOURNALS

Annals of Dyslexia
Applied Psycholinguistics
British Journal of Developmental Psychology
Child Development
Cognition
Developmental Psychology
Journal of Child Language
Journal of Educational Psychology
Journal of Experimental Child Psychology
Journal of Memory and Language

Journal of Psycholinguistic Research
Journal of Reading Behaviour
Journal of Speech and Hearing Research
Language Acquisition
Merrill-Palmer Quarterly
Psychological Review

The CHILDES database

The **Child Language Data Exchange System (CHILDES)** is a computer-based collection of child language data accumulated by individuals and groups of researchers, and available on the Internet at http://childes.psy.cmu.edu/. It is briefly described in Crystal (1997a, 2003b). If you want good-quality data and have not got the resources to collect it yourself, you can use data from CHILDES instead, though you will have to understand the notations that are used. Data collected for one type of analysis can often be used for a quite different one, provided that the transcription has included sufficient detail.

Things to think about

❏   Focus on an aspect of child language that enables you to capitalize on the core skills and knowledge that you are most competent and interested in.

❏   Make sure you have a general overview of the main stages of language acquisition and development, so that you know roughly what to expect and look out for, and where it fits into the broader picture.

❏   Engaging in an analysis of your data from within an established theoretical framework, drawn from such areas as syntax, semantics, or phonology, is important in assuring that you avoid simply listing examples; you should be identifying patterns and commenting on their significance.

❏   Children do not possess adult competence in language use. Child language has its own rules, which may not closely resemble those of adult language, so be careful in identifying things as 'wrong' or 'ungrammatical' – in the child's system they may be correct.

❏   Remember that child language can include writing, which may be studied in its own right or compared with the spoken language of children.

❏   Although the preschool years manifest most development, some structures and skills of oral language, such as passives and relative clauses, do not appear in this period. Intonation patterns are also still developing (see Cruttenden 1979), and broader aspects of communicative competence can also provide a rewarding focus with older children.

Accessing children

Recent legal changes offer greater protection for children, so it is no longer as easy as it once was to get access to child subjects at school or through youth organizations. The new restrictions may be reflected in your university's own ethics policies – you may need to get clearance for working with anyone under 16 – and almost certainly they will determine the way that a school or other organization handles your approach. You will fare best if you use personal contacts. Otherwise, you might approach the school that you attended yourself, or ask current parents, if you know some, to introduce you. Certain procedures, which might include police checks, will still be required, so leave plenty of time for them. Despite the potential complications, approaching a school remains a good way of contacting a large number of children from a wide variety of backgrounds and ages.

Write formally to the head teacher, stating clearly what your work will involve. Explain how the children might benefit, given that you will be intruding on their school time. Indicate what extra work, if any, may be involved for staff. Look for ways of linking your work to an ongoing class project. If you can afford to help out during your visits this may help to make your involvement more welcome. The head teacher will almost certainly require you to seek parental approval, as, in the eyes of the law, children are not old enough to decide what is in their best interests.

Working with children

☐ Children do not necessarily behave in a similar way to adult subjects. Children you know already could find it difficult to adjust to the formal procedures in your investigation, if they have previously seen you only in informal contexts.

☐ When planning activities, remember that children have a shorter attention span than adults. Show your planned activities to teachers or parents in advance, to check that the materials are pitched at an appropriate level.

☐ If using pictures or other types of stimulus to generate language use, a pilot run will help you check that the children can make sense of the images. Drawn images with unusual shading, for example, can distract children into irrelevant questions and comments.

☐ To avoid having some children feeling left out and to ensure good relations with the school, you may have to include children whose data you do not plan to use.

☐ Children are often far more curious than adults about recording equipment. Not only may they be distracted or inhibited by it, they may want to play with it while you are collecting data.

☐ Children tend to move about far more than adult subjects. Can you set up your audio- or video-recording equipment to cope with this?

☐ Parents and teachers may be keen that the children cannot be identified from your recording. Protecting identity is obviously much more difficult with video than audio data. Be sensitive to the justifiable concerns of adult carers about the potential for video material to fall into the wrong hands. Also be aware that some teachers may be nervous of their teaching being videoed.

☐ School environments can be very noisy and prone to unexpected disruption. The time available may prove rather shorter than you expect.

❐   It can be very hard to distinguish between different child voices in audio recordings, even when you know the children quite well. This is especially true when several are interacting. It can even be difficult to differentiate girls from boys. Using a video recorder and getting children to introduce themselves on audio recordings at the start of activities are two ways of reducing the risk of later problems, but most importantly, keep careful notes at the time.

❐   If your work involves an assessment of children's social class or background, be aware that children are not always able to supply reliable information themselves, school records are not always very up to date, and schools and parents might be cautious about releasing such data. Furthermore, socio-economic categorizations based on parental occupations are not always appropriate or accurate.

Central themes and project ideas

There is a huge range of possible project areas within the field of child language, because many aspects of language can be studied at different stages of development. What is provided below is a selection of areas and ideas taken from some of the main branches of research within child language, including studies of prelinguistic development; the development of core structures, such as grammar and phonology; broader aspects of communicative competence, such as conversation and joke-telling; literacy development; and variation in child language.

Longitudinal case studies

Many linguists have undertaken and published case studies of their own children or of a few specially selected children. The emphasis for most has been on finding out more about 'normative' development. Roger Brown conducted a longitudinal study of three children, Adam, Eve, and Sarah (Brown 1973). This work is a primary source of information on analyses and indices of development, such as a child's Mean Length of Utterance (MLU) and stages of grammatical morpheme development. Paul Fletcher studied his daughter, Sophie (Fletcher 1985), providing a 'profile' of her development in areas including syntax and phonology at strategic points in her early life. Michael Halliday studied his son Nigel's early vocalizations and transition into early multiword utterances from a functional perspective (Halliday 1975). His proposed 'developmental functions of language' provide one key framework for the analysis of early utterance meaning.

Conducting a longitudinal case study requires commitment over a considerable period, not just from you but also from the child and its family. If you know you have a project coming up, and you think you might want to write a study of this sort, talk to a potential supervisor early on about starting to collect the data. It is better to collect something you end up not using than to wish later that you had planned ahead.

Projects

30 Follow the language development of two children of the same age, one of whom is an only child and one of whom is the youngest in a larger family. Do language features appear at the same rate and in the same order? How might their profiles of development be determined by differences in their everyday communication needs? Use children from a similar background and of the same gender to minimize other sources of variation.

31 Record a child every few weeks as he/she learns to read. Do the skills develop gradually and/or is there a sudden transition from being a non-reader to being a reader? Ask the child for his/her own thoughts on what reading is, what it is for, and how it is achieved.

Prelinguistic development

Are children working on their language development before they can produce their first word? In recent years many researchers have addressed this question, examining aspects of prelinguistic (i.e. birth to one-word) development. Halliday (1975) looked for evidence of the same sound strings or 'proto-words' being used consistently to refer to the same things. Other researchers, such as Stark (1986), have focused on how prelinguistic sound-making, such as cooing and babbling, lays the foundation for phonological and intonational development. Useful examples of research can be found in Tomasello and Bates (2001).

Project

32 Video a prelinguistic child with its mother. Show the recording to the mother and ask her which of the baby's noises and gestures she believes are intentional communication. Analyse these, looking for patterns and for indications that they are the precursors of language. Include a commentary on any difficulties you encounter with this. Remember to relate your findings to those of other studies, and/or to profiles of normative ages and stages of development.

Over- and under-extension: lexical and semantic development

Young children often use words in a way that suggests they understand them differently from adults. They may use a word to refer to too wide a category of things, such as 'apple' for any round fruit: this is known as **over-extension**. Conversely, they may use a word to refer to too small a category of things, such as 'dog' only for the family's pet dog and not for the next-door neighbour's (termed **under-extension**). This is a rich field for possible projects, since nearly all children, irrespective of their native language, go through periods of apparent over-extension of words (under-extension is less well documented). Several researchers have proposed explanations for this behaviour. One key contributor is Eve Clark, whose early proposal, the **Semantic Feature Hypothesis**, is still perhaps the most influential of all (see Clark and Clark 1977).

Project

33　Collect examples of over-extension in a child's speech, taking care to keep notes of precisely what was being referred to. How easy is it to identify the perceptual boundaries that the child might be operating with, when it assigns the same name to several things? What support is there for the hypothesis that the child's view is the same as the adult's, but it just doesn't have enough words for everything it wants to talk about? (You could get insight into this by seeing how easily the child adopts a new word that breaks up the set.) Aitchison (2003, Ch. 16) will give you some preliminary pointers to what over-extension may entail.

Children's morphology

One of the best-known studies in this area is Jean Berko-Gleason's 'wug' experiment, of which simple summaries are given in Aitchison (1998: 124ff.) and Fromkin *et al.* (2003, Ch. 8). The study demonstrated that children have an internalized rule for the plural, because they were able to give the correct phonological form for made-up words. Children often make apparent errors in the way they form past tenses, comparative adjectives, and plurals, going through a phase of using a regular ending where the adult form is irregular. Since this is a very common phenomenon, it makes it an accessible and popular project area.

Project

34　Draw up an inventory of morphological 'errors' in a child's language production. Categorize each according to whether it is an irregular form for a regular one, a regular form for an irregular one, or an irregular form for a different irregular one. Also ascertain which word classes the errors occur in: verbs (are all tenses represented?), nouns, adjectives (e.g. *the bestest* for *the best*), etc. If the balance is unequal, look for reasons, both within child language development and within the target language that the child is aiming for. Compare your findings with those reported in the published literature.

Development of phonology and intonation

One very productive approach to the language of under-fives especially is to study apparent 'mispronunciations'. These can appear to be idiosyncratic mistakes but, as with inflectional errors, many children display similar patterns, and they are considered to be part of normative development unless they persist for too long. Excellent summaries of the patterns of mispronunciation, which make useful analytical frameworks, can be found in Clark and Clark (1977, Ch. 10) and de Villiers and de Villiers (1978). Smith (1973) is acknowledged as a key source study. For a recent overview, see Stoel-Gammon (2006).

On intonation, Cruttenden (1974) is still a useful study. He used recordings of the football results, studying children's ability to predict the second part of the result on the basis of the intonation used in the first. Seven-year-olds were found to be poor at predicting whether the second part of the score was higher, lower, or a draw whereas, by ten, children were generally far more skilled. Adults usually have few problems with such predictions. Such work suggests that, while intonation is one of the first aspects of language that children focus on and start to master, it is also one of the last to be 'perfected'.

Projects

35 Replicate Cruttenden's study and compare your results with his. If there are differences, what might account for them?

36 Analyse the consistent 'mispronunciations' in words that you elicit from a 2-year-old or 3-year-old child. Identify the phonological processes (substitution, assimilation, syllabic structure) that characterize these mispronunciations (see Clark and Clark 1977, and de Villiers and de Villiers 1978, for systematic coverage of these). Look at the articulations of particular developing phonemes in different phonotactic contexts (word initial, word medial, word final, connected speech, etc.) and compare the patterns of consonants with those given in Crystal (1997: 242). As Crystal's caption indicates, there is substantial variation in the speed of the acquisition of consonants. There can also, however, be some difficulty in knowing whether the child has or has not fully mastered a consonant. Drawing on the experience gained from your analysis, explore various possible reasons why this problem might be encountered by linguists.

Comprehension of complex grammatical structures

Carol Chomsky probed children's comprehension of structures such as active and passive sentences by asking them to perform actions with puppets. Her study also investigated other structures, such as the use of the verbs 'ask', 'tell', and 'promise', in an attempt to shed light on why these features are acquired later than other aspects of language. See Chomsky (1969; also summarized in Garton and Pratt 1998). For a general overview of how syntax develops in children, see Bavin (2006).

Project

37 Taking careful note of Chomsky's procedures and stimuli, devise an experiment of your own along similar lines. Make it close enough for your results to be compared with hers. How do you account for any differences? Write also about the procedural difficulties inherent in this kind of experiment.

Children's metalinguistic awareness

Research in this area has focused on:

☐ children's awareness of what a word, sound and sentence, etc. is, and at what age or stage of awareness each type of structure emerges (e.g. Clark's work, described in Garton and Pratt 1998, Ch. 7);

☐ the role of language games and nursery rhymes in promoting metalinguistic awareness (e.g. work by Bryant *et al.*, reviewed in Garton and Pratt 1998: 160);

☐ the link between metalinguistic awareness and the development of literacy. See Garton and Pratt (1998, Ch. 7) for summaries of example studies and further references.

☐ children's appreciation of verbal jokes and puns. This skill is very much part of a child's broader developing communicative competence, and can be an entertaining area in which to run projects. For children to understand jokes and puns, they often need to understand **sense relations** such as synonymy and polysemy. This may also be linked to a milestone in cognitive development that Piaget proposed that children reach at about the age of 7.

Project

38 Following established research practice, test children's surface and deep understanding of humour by telling them jokes, monitoring the reaction, and then asking the children to explain why the joke was funny or why it was a joke. Crystal (1989: 185 ff.) provides very introductory information on this 'playing with language' and Trott (1996) gives a more detailed overview. Some source studies include Fowles and Glanz (1977) and Shultz and Horibe (1974).

Colour terms

This is an interesting and relatively little-studied aspect of child language development. It can be studied as part of overall lexical and semantic development. For introductory information, see Crystal (1989: 99 ff.) and, for a fuller summary, Trott (1996: 26–30).

Projects

39 Keep a note of the order in which a child acquires colour terms and what objects the child labels with them. Compare your results with the findings of Berlin and Kay (1969), regarding the order in which languages add colour terms to their inventory (for a brief summary of this, see Crystal 1997: 106).

40 Some children go through a stage of using colour terms liberally but apparently quite haphazardly. If you know such a child, make a careful study of this phenomenon: does the child simply not know which colour name is which, is it operating 'over-extension' (see pp. 35–6) of the colour names it knows, or has it failed to grasp the notion of colour-naming at all, so that it doesn't realize what property of an object is being referred to when it is called *red*?

41 If you have access to a child who is bilingual, compare the order in which the colours are correctly learned and used in each language. To do this, you will need to understand both languages yourself or have help from someone who does. It does not matter if the colour terms develop in one language before the other, but include in your account a consideration of what effect knowing (some) colour names in one language might have on learning the colour terminology of the other.

42 Compare colour-term acquisition in two monolingual children acquiring different languages. Use children of the same gender, and whose background and day-to-day experience are as similar as possible. As in Project 41, make suitable provision if you do not know both languages yourself. Compare your results with normative development as reported in the literature. Are there any linguistic or social reasons that you can identify to account for any differences between your two subjects, or your subjects and the reports in the literature?

43 Test a small number of children who have not yet mastered their colour names by playing a sorting game with them, in which they have to put like colours together. Do they choose to put together different shades of blue, separately from shades of green, etc.? Use your findings to address the question of whether children have the colour concepts *before* the words appear (cf. Berlin and Kay 1969, but also Pinker 1994: 62 and 65–6) or whether, as with most words, they have to learn the boundaries of meaning by experience (see 'under-' and 'over-extension', pp. 35–6).

44 Are there differences between males' and females' uses of colour terminology? Use a paint chart with the names of the colours removed, and ask, say, three boys and three girls aged about eight or nine to give each colour an appropriate name. Do both sexes find this task equally easy? What sort of wider vocabulary (e.g. names for things in the physical world) is drawn upon to meet the shortfall in established colour names? Do girls know more of the secondary colour names (such as *vermilion*, *maroon*, and *ochre*) than boys? Warning: be sensitive to the possibility that children will become confused and/or bored if they are bombarded with too many colours for which they do not have names.

Carer language (or child-directed speech)

The role of carer language, or **child-directed speech,** has been a hotly debated issue in child language ever since Noam Chomsky declared adult language to be a 'degenerate' model from which children could never learn all the rules of their language. A key researcher has been Catherine Snow (e.g. Snow 1986). Of interest are the properties of carer language and the extent to which it is necessary, or at least beneficial, to the child's language development. However, it is not easy to establish such a causal link. One approach has been to compare language acquisition in cultures where carers use no special language register with that in cultures where such a register has been identified. Famous studies of this nature are by Ochs in Western Samoa, and Schieffelin in Papua New Guinea (see Romaine 1984, Ch. 6 for a description of these).

Projects

45   If you are fluent in two languages associated with different cultures, observe the
     carer talk used with a child from each. Look for special vocabulary, intonation
     features, repetition, simplified structures (e.g. short sentences), and the overall
     amount of verbal communication offered by the carer. You may find Heath (1983)
     useful, a study of middle-class white and lower-class black and white communities
     in the United States, showing how children are socialized, through the influence of
     adults, into particular expectations and norms of language usage.

46   Do fathers as well as mothers use the special features of carer language? Using
     Berko-Gleason (1975) as a starting point, gather your own data from a family
     where you can record both parents in one-to-one interaction with the child. If
     feasible and appropriate, extend this to study the carer talk of an older sibling. As
     carers may be inhibited to behave normally when someone else is listening, be
     prepared to run the tape for quite a long time. Alternatively, explore the possibility
     of leaving the machine running while you leave or even using a baby intercom to
     listen in during your absence.

47   Observe one or more young children playing with dolls. Do they use features of
     carer language? See Romaine (1984, Ch. 6) for studies.

48   If you can find a pair of mixed-sex twins, record the carer talk that goes on with
     each individually, and the two together. Wells' Bristol Survey found evidence that
     parents talked more to boys during some activities and more to girls during others
     (see, for example, Wells 1986b).

Conversational development

This field tends to overlap with that of the role of carer language (see above), since it is generally acknowledged that children first learn from carers how to participate in conversations. McTear (1985) and Foster (1990) provide coverage of conversational development. Garton and Pratt (1998, Ch. 6) summarize some research (largely from the Bristol Survey) into the differences in conversation that children encounter when making the transition from home to school.

Project

49 Compare the conversational skills of two or more children either of different ages or of the same age but different gender, social background or family size etc. Are there indications that any differences you find are genuinely to do with the *development* of conversation skills, as opposed to more permanent differences in style and/or personality? One type of data that might be particularly interesting is children's telephone conversation skills.

Sources of variation in child language

Since the early 1980s, there has been growing interest in the variation between children in their rate and route of acquisition. This has developed in part as a reaction to the tendency for child language researchers to focus on the 'average' or 'normal' child, as though all children develop identically. Researchers have started to consider a range of sources of variation in terms of how they might influence children's long-term language development and how they could affect the way that children behave as subjects in fieldwork projects. A considerable amount of key research on sources of variation stems from the Bristol Language Survey (see Wells 1981, 1985, and 1986a, b). A useful introduction is provided by Wells (1986b). Romaine (1984, especially Chs 4 and 6) provides coverage on social class, gender, peer group, school and family. Coates (2004, Ch. 9) and Swann (1992) also give excellent coverage on gender.

Project

50 Using a detailed picture book for children (e.g. from the *First Thousand Words* series), test children of the same age, who contrast on one of the variation criteria listed above, on their range of vocabulary. For example, you could test a boy and girl, or two girls from different backgrounds, or two boys, one of whom is in full-time preschool education while the other is not. How easy is it to gain a clear picture of any differences? You could also write about any limitations that you consider intrinsic to collecting data in this way.

Literacy development

For introductory coverage, see the textbook review earlier in this chapter. Read more specifically about research in this area in Garton and Pratt (1998, Chs 7–10), Steinberg *et al.* (2002, Ch. 3), Perera (1979, 1984, 1986) and Smith (1986). For information on dyslexia, see Chapter 2 of this book.

Projects

51   Interview children, teachers and parents about the impact that they consider the *Harry Potter* books to have had on the children's enthusiasm for reading, their concentration and their linguistic development. Do adults and children agree about what it is that makes these books special? To what extent are the benefits of reading them viewed as spilling into a more general enjoyment of reading?

52   Focusing on a child who is still reading short texts in large print, make a list of all the vocabulary in every book that the child reads over the course of a month (or longer if you can). Sort the words according to the frequency of their occurrence in the texts you are studying. Type out sample words and ask the child to read them to you and explain their meaning. What relationship do you find between the child's knowledge of a word and the frequency with which he/she has encountered it?

53   Investigate the relationship between a child's abilities in reading and spelling. Find examples of words that the child spells incorrectly or inconsistently, and find out whether he/she also struggles to read them. Are there any words that the child can spell correctly but finds difficulty in reading aloud and/or understanding? Use a psycholinguistic model of the relationship between reading and writing (see Chapter 2) to help explain the patterns you find. Warning: some word meanings (including many very common words, e.g. *the*) are very difficult even for an adult to explain: don't expect your child subjects to do anything that you would struggle to do yourself.

54   Select some reading books aimed at children of different ages and analyse the grammatical complexity of the sentences, using Nippold's (2006: 317) examples as a guide. Are the structures uniformly more complex as the target reading age increases or do other factors come into play as well, such as the subject matter of the book?

55   Interview some authors of children's fiction. What do they consider to be the most important considerations when writing a book for a certain age of reader? How do they successfully operate within these constraints? Show some of their works to children of the intended age, in order to evaluate how effective the author is in achieving his/her objectives.

56   Go into local libraries and bookshops and ask to be shown books suitable for a boy aged 7, a girl aged 10, and so on. Whenever you find helpful assistants, ask them to explain to you how they can look at a book and know who it is suitable for. In particular, try to get them to tell you what features of the language they look for. In this way, identify the various features that adults appear to use in deciding what is suitable for a child of a particular age and compare them to the features that children themselves identify when browsing through books.

Developmental problems

A number of conditions are either characterized by, or else can lead to, a delay or overall reduction in the scope of language acquisition. They include autism, blindness, deafness, dyslexia, specific language impairment (SLI) and Down's Syndrome. Usually, you will only take on a study of someone with such a condition if you already know them, and you need to maintain particular sensitivity towards the subject and his/her family during your investigation, remembering always that the standard expectations of a child of that age may not be appropriate.

Projects

57 Conduct a case study of a child with a particular disability affecting language (such as a hearing impairment, stuttering or autism). Can you establish what, exactly, the difficulties are, and which aspects of language are not causing any difficulties at all? You will need to read up about the disability in question before you start the case study, and be warned: you may find that relevant books on the subject are quite technical or that the approach to language is different from the one you are familiar with from your previous studies.

58 Find a child with very poor speech production and research what carers say to the child. Does the fact that the child's speech is difficult to understand affect the quality of the input that he/she receives? Using published studies of the way in which language acquisition proceeds, consider the potential long-term effects on the child of not receiving the same kind of input as other children.

Later language acquisition

Language acquisition continues into adulthood. According to Nippold (2006), 6-year-old children have less than one-third of the vocabulary that they will know by the end of their teenage years and create sentences that are only 60 per cent the length of those of adults and less structurally complex. The ability to understand and use metaphors, idioms and proverbs also develops late, as does the capacity to appreciate the subtleties of pragmatics and to develop an argument. The way that narratives are constructed also changes over time (Pearson and de Villiers 2006). By focusing your research on older children or young adults, you can avoid some of the basic procedural complications that often arise with the very young.

Projects

59 Find a dictionary of proverbs and select examples that are particularly graphic and metaphorical. Show them to 12-year-olds and ask them to guess what they mean and how they might be used. Examine the responses you get: how similar are they

and what do they reflect about the world-view and experiences of that age group? For comparison, give the same proverbs to some informants in their sixties – how do you account for the similarities and differences you find?

60   Ask children of different ages, and also adults, to look through a joke book and select the three jokes that they think are funniest (use a book that has a variety of different types of joke). Are there any patterns regarding the kinds of jokes that are considered funny at different ages? Aim to explain the patterns in terms of the development of pragmatic understanding.

61   Show a silent cartoon film to children of different ages and then record them telling the story back to you. Use a story they have not come across before, as children are very good memorizers! Analyse the sophistication of the child's narrative of the story and how the events are connected. See Pearson and de Villiers (2006: 691) for a useful framework.

Other project ideas

62   Conduct an observation study of how children interact with each other when they are engaged in activities at home or at school. Example: how they use language co-operatively in playing a game or undertaking a classroom task.

63   Observe the differences between parental and teacher strategies in telling stories with children or in controlling children.

64   Make a study of children's command of language **register**: how does the way that they talk to each other differ from the way they talk to the teacher?

65   Do a cross-sectional study of children at different stages of their development, aimed at creating a general picture of sequences of development. (Note that this entails the assumption that child A will behave like child B when it is child B's age, so no account is taken of variation between individuals.)

66   Run an experimental study of comprehension, perhaps repeated over a period of time. For example, you could test subjects' comprehension of dimensional adjectives by showing them a set of five illustrated cards and asking them *show me the picture where the fence is taller than the tree*. (See Cruttenden 1979, Section 4.5.1, for a summary of, and references to, studies on dimensional adjectives.)

67   Ask a child to identify a much-loved story book and then ask him/her to tell you the story without reading the text. How much of the text does the child reproduce word for word? What sorts of words, phrases, and sentences seem most likely to have been memorized in the course of reading, and why?

4

Second-language acquisition

There is considerable interest in the processes by which we succeed or fail in learning a second (or third, fourth, etc.) language. The insights we can gain from research into this area can tell us more about the nature of language, how the brain stores language, and how language learning takes place. Research into second-language acquisition asks questions such as:

- ❑ Is classroom learning a valid way to gain communicative language skills?
- ❑ Is there a fundamental difference between being taught a language and picking it up from the environment?
- ❑ Which language-teaching methods work best?
- ❑ Is second-language acquisition intrinsically the same as or different from first-language acquisition?
- ❑ How does the brain organize the storage and accessing of more than one language?
- ❑ Why are some adults more successful at language learning than others?
- ❑ Are children inherently better at language learning and if so, why?
- ❑ Does residence abroad make a qualitative difference to language skills?
- ❑ How can we accurately gauge the linguistic knowledge of learners?
- ❑ Are there any consistent patterns in the order in which learners master language features?
- ❑ How effective are immersion programmes, self-teach courses, and other specialized approaches?

Terminology

In your reading on this area, you need to be aware that the same terms may be used by different authors with slightly different meanings. Here is some of the most common terminology. The **mother tongue (MT)** is the language acquired in early childhood from parents and spoken in the home environment; it is normally synonymous with **first language (L1)**. Although these terms may seem easy to define at first glance, there are many situations in which it might be difficult to identify which language deserves either or both of these labels: for example, when each parent speaks a different language, when two or more languages are commonly used in the family or immediate community, when the child is regularly exposed to a second language outside the home, or when the child (or adult) is more comfortable with and fluent in a language learned later and/or has forgotten his/her earliest acquired language. Such situations are by no means uncommon – in world terms, monolingualism is not the norm. **Bilingualism** and **multilingualism** are also difficult to define, because there are so many different situations and possible states of knowledge. Even if individuals know two languages (bilingualism) or more than two (multilingualism), they may have equal fluency and ability in them or some (however minimal) ability in one language together with fluency in one or more others. They may have the ability to switch easily between languages in speech, or may be able to understand but not speak some of them. Li Wei (2000) and Edwards (2004) both provide useful information.

Foreign-language (FL) learning occurs when the language is taught in the L1 environment, often through the medium of the L1, such as when French children learn English at school in France, through the medium of French. A **foreign language** 'plays no major role in the community' (Ellis 1994: 12). **Second-language learning** occurs where the language being taught is that of the host community, such as in the case of Chileans arriving in Britain and learning English either informally or in classes. The term **second language (L2)** is also used in a more general way, as a cover term for second and foreign language, and it may also be used to refer to a third or fourth language. The term **second-language acquisition** is used to refer to both acquisition and learning (in Krashen's sense – see below), and you will find this abbreviated to **SLA, 2LA,** and **L2A**. There are many situations in the world where the distinction between **foreign-** and **second-language learning** is not so clear-cut, especially where the language being learned has some sort of special political or social status or significance, as with English in India or South Africa, for example. **EFL** and **ESL** refer to English as a Foreign and as a Second Language, respectively. The terms **TEFL** (Teaching EFL) and **TESL** (Teaching ESL) have largely been replaced by the term **TESOL** (Teaching English to Speakers of Other Languages).

Acquisition *vs* **learning** is a distinction made by Stephen Krashen at the beginning of the 1980s. In Krashen's terms, **acquisition** is the subconscious assimilation of the language without any awareness of knowing rules. This is how the child gains its first language, and what children and adults may be capable of achieving for a second language, if exposed to it in a natural way and enabled to pick it up subconsciously. **Learning** is a conscious process, achieved particularly through formal study, and resulting in an explicit knowledge of rules.

Language skills are normally defined as the skills of listening, speaking, reading and writing. Some formal classroom activities will encourage the learner to focus on one or two of the skills, others focus on integrating the skills within a communication activity.

Textbooks and major journals

Useful starting points for information about this area can be found in any of the handbooks and readers published recently (for example, Bhatia and Richards 2003,

Carter and Nunan 2001, Davies and Elder 2003, Doughty and Long 2003, Kaplan 2005, Lowie *et al.* 2005). Kachru *et al.* (forthcoming) links into relevant global issues, as does Block and Cameron (2002). Guidance on carrying out research in second-language acquisition can be found in Brown and Rodgers (2002) and Ellis and Barkhuizen (2006). Dornyei (2002) offers specific information on using questionnaires in 2LA research and Dornyei (2001) covers research on motivation. Useful journals for projects in second-language acquisition include the following:

JOURNALS

AILA Review (www.aila.soton.ac.uk/aila_rev01)
Applied Linguistics
Applied Psycholinguistics
Computer Assisted Language Learning
ELT Journal
International Review of Applied Linguistics in Language Teaching (IRAL)
Journal of Applied Linguistics
Language Learning
Language Teaching (an abstracting journal with a feature article in each issue)
Language Teaching Research
Modern English Teacher
Second Language Research
Studies in Second Language Acquisition
TESOL Quarterly

Things to think about

❏ Overall, language learning is a slow process, and you may not have a long enough time period to conduct a study that involves steady progress. However, you can certainly observe specific learning events, and if you introduce new material to learners you can track their knowledge of it.

❏ 'Think-aloud reporting' is a technique whereby the researcher asks learners to verbalize their thinking processes as they complete a task. You can find out more about this in Tirkkonen-Condit (2006).

❏ Think carefully about which language you will use in your dealings with subjects. Tempting as it is to use the language *you* know best, bear in mind that this may cause difficulties for non-native speakers. If using a questionnaire it may be better, in some circumstances, to use the native language of the subjects. However, be careful not to make assumptions about what language that is, or their level of literacy in it.

❏ For more on the potential pitfalls of SLA research, see Seliger and Shohamy (1990).

Central themes and project ideas

Developmental sequences and the process of acquisition

Is there a fundamental difference between the processes of first- and second-language acquisition? It is well documented that children acquire certain morphological features of L1 (such as verb endings, and plural and possessive forms) in a fairly consistent order (e.g. Brown 1973; de Villiers and de Villiers 1973). Many studies have looked for a similar order of acquisition in the second language. For an overview of this research, see Ellis (1994, Ch. 3), Lightbown and Spada (2006), and most other introductory texts.

Projects

68　Ask for access to the work of some language learners over, say, the past two years. Look for evidence of the successful and unsuccessful incorporation of, say, verb forms into their free writing (a) immediately after the form has been taught; (b) several weeks after; and (c) several months after. If they are learning English, compare the order of acquisition with that given by Ellis (1994), Lightbown and Spada (2006) or some other authoritative source. If they are learning another language, find out if similar sequences have been identified (there are references to work on German in Ellis 1994: 103ff.). Remember that a single example of a form being used correctly is not necessarily evidence that the learner has mastered it. You could base this project on oral and written data to compare the same students' acquisition of the same feature in speech and writing.

69　Interview one or more teachers about their approach to teaching, say, verb forms, the plural or the possessive. Are they aware of the research into the order of acquisition? For help with the possible answers to this, look at Ellis (1994, Ch. 15), Alderson (1997), or Doughty and Long (2003), who explore the possibilities that SLA research is of no, of some, or of paramount importance for the teachers' presentation of language in the classroom.

70　Compare the sequence of presentation of language forms in one (or more) TESOL textbook(s) with the acquisition sequences reported by Ellis (1994). See also Hawkins and Lozano (2006) for an overview of developmental sequences in 2LA.

Comparison of L1 and L2 acquisition

Research into the similarities and differences between L1 and L2 acquisition goes further than just the developmental sequences described above. Much has been written about the learning environment, the quantity and quality of the input, the expectations and the actual output, the attitude and tolerance level of the listener to errors and dysfluency, the time period over which the language is learned, and so on. A number of ideas could be developed from reading about **universal grammar** in more detail in, for example, White (2003), Cook (1993, Ch. 9) or Doughty and Long (2003).

Project

71 Compare carer-talk (**motherese**) addressed to an L1 learner, with foreigner-talk. What are the similarities and what are the differences? Compare them for: range of vocabulary, use of any special words, the complexity (or absence of it) of the grammar, any non-adult or non-standard grammatical forms, pronunciation, intonation, volume, range and so on.

Language-learning targets

Many people leave school saying that they 'know' another language, meaning that they can just about buy a postcard or a glass of beer using it. For others, knowing another language would mean that they could speak and write fluently about a wide range of subjects and could follow the speech and writing of others with no difficulty. In other contexts, it might mean being able to discuss the rules of grammar in great detail, whether or not that knowledge could be applied in comprehension or production. If we want to include all native speakers within the group who do 'know' the language, what constraints does that put upon the definition? What sorts of targets or goals do learners have?

Projects

72 Use evidence from errors in the speech or writing of advanced non-native speakers to identify some of the more subtle aspects of full competence in a language. Pawley and Syder (1983) may give you some ideas.
73 Compare the views of some learners and their teacher (interviewed separately) about what 'knowing' a language means. If the responses do not fully correspond, consider what implications this might have for the success of the teaching and learning process in that class. Remember to consider the effect on some people of consistently failing to meet the goal they have set themselves.
74 Monitor the range of input encountered by one or more intermediate learners, looking at (a) variation between native speakers (within a group or family, national and international); and (b) contemporary change (for example, in the vocabulary and expressions of adolescents). How do learners handle such variation?
75 By careful observation of your own day, or by 'shadowing' a foreign student, compile guidelines for what English a foreign student most needs for successful communication in your college or university environment. Variations on this, if you have access to the appropriate environment, include: a nurse or doctor in a hospital, a businessman visiting another country in order to make a formal presentation about a product or service he hopes to sell, and so on. You may find it valuable to engage in some role play with a

friend, to explore some of the finer points of these scenarios. Munby (1978) may provide some insights.

76 Carry out a survey of English-language teaching schools and units, to see how they go about testing the level of their students at entry. Are they satisfied with the accuracy of the tests (i.e. do they have to redistribute the students across ability levels a week later because the tests did not correctly sort them into groups)? A critical evaluation of entry tests is given in Wesche *et al.* (1996).

Motivation

What role does motivation play in language learning and what will motivate someone to learn? What sort of control might a teacher have in supporting and increasing motivation in a class? These questions are of immense importance in studying second-language acquisition. For an overview of the issues and how to research them, see Dornyei (2001).

Project

77 Interview language learners from the top and bottom grades in a language class, and ask them what they like and don't like about learning the language and why. Ask them what would increase and decrease their motivation. Do you think that reduced motivation in learners results in lower performance levels or that lower performance levels result in reduced motivation? Draw up some recommendations for teachers and learners about practical ways to increase and sustain motivation.

Grammar-based and communication-based teaching

Some teachers work on the assumption that, without a thorough grounding in the grammar, semantics and phonology of the target language of English, the student cannot be expected to know and use the language. Their lessons will therefore focus on teaching grammatical structures, introducing lists of new vocabulary and correcting the students' pronunciation. Such an approach to language learning is widespread in many countries and it contrasts with approaches that focus primarily on communicative competence. In the latter, students are expected to use the language to interact (e.g. in role plays) and to share real information. There will be fewer activities that involve the more mechanical manipulations of language forms that appear in a structurally based lesson. The Natural Approach (Stephen Krashen), Suggestopaedia (Georgi Lozanov), Community Language Learning (Charles A. Curran), Language from Within (Beverly Galyean), Total Physical Response (James Asher) and Task-Based Learning (Carter and Nunan 2001; Doughty and Long 2003) have all been developed as alternatives to 'formal' teaching, and each makes substantive claims for its own validity.

Projects

78 V. Cook (2001) considers explicit teaching and the learning of the formal components of the language and suggests comparing a range of textbooks to see the different ways in which the language can be made explicit. You could do this for English or for another language that you know, or you could look for variation across different languages within a single published series, such as Linguaphone, Hugo, Teach Yourself, or one of the BBC series.

79 Obtain several different beginners' courses for a language and persuade subjects to spend a set number of hours over a week studying the language, using the course material you assign to them. At the end of the week, interview the subjects as a group and individually to find out, for example, how easy, interesting or useful they found the approach, whether they think they learned anything, and whether they would feel motivated to carry on.

80 Make a single visit to each of several language classes (with different teachers) and assess each on a continuum for formal grammar instruction, communicative activities, use of L1 to explain things, and so on. Supplement this information with interviews with the teacher and a couple of students from each class. Ask them what they felt the balance was in the lesson you observed, as a way of assessing the correspondence between their views and yours (consider the significance of a mismatch between views of teacher and student(s) in the same class). Check whether the teaching content and/or approach is laid down by the institution and if so, whether it is what the teacher would use by choice. To what extent can this, or any teaching, be labelled as fully 'communicative' or 'grammar-driven' and why? Classroom observation is difficult to do well and you may find Spada and Fröhlich (1995) useful in developing your approach.

81 Make several visits to one language class where there is at least some explanation of grammatical detail given in L1. Make a note of all the sentences that contain technical terms (recording the lesson will make this easier). List a selection of the sentences (don't just list the words out of context, as that makes the test much more difficult) and ask members of the class to write down what each one means. Use the scores to assess the extent to which the students are successfully grasping the grammatical information and consider whether it is a prerequisite for learning a grammatical point that you understand all the techical terms used to describe it. Try to avoid implying that the teacher is somehow failing – explaining language is very difficult!

82 Interview a group of learners about their goals in studying the language (such as what they will use it for). Widen this into a discussion of whether teachers need to be aware of what the learner expects or dreams of, and what they can do about it if they are. In a separate interview with the teacher, find out what he/she *thinks* the learners want the language for. Assess the extent to which the learners' goals map onto the style and approach of the teaching they are receiving and the sort of work they are being asked to produce.

Vocabulary acquisition

A wide range of studies has been carried out on the processes and the significance for overall learning of vocabulary acquisition. Among the questions that have been addressed are: Does it help or hinder learning if you present vocabulary out of context? Does it help learning if you teach the key vocabulary *before* you read a new passage, or should you let the learners read it first, and then have the new words explained? How many words do you need to know in order to function adequately in a language (for example, to hold a conversation, read a newspaper, or follow a TV drama)? Should you teach or learn words with related meanings together (such as opposites, synonyms, members of a set) or is that confusing? When can you say that you 'know' a word? What is the best way to memorize words? How can you test how many words a learner knows? Does it matter which words you learn first? How can you tell how difficult a passage is going to be for a learner to read? Answers to these, and other related questions, are considered in Nation's (1990, 2001) research.

Projects

83   Interview learners about their attitude and practical approach to vocabulary learning. Use this information to evaluate critically assumptions made in the research, and make suggestions for how teachers might help learners more.

84   Using data from willing 'guinea pigs', write a critical evaluation of the Linkword learning system developed by Mike Gruneberg as the *Instant Recall* technique (e.g. Gruneberg 2002a, b). You can read more about the use of mnemonic techniques in vocabulary learning in Nation (1990: 166ff.).

85   Get a class of language learners to memorize a set of words (and their translations) from a language they do not know. Test them and identify the most successful learners. Get them to tell the class what their techniques are. Go through the same process again with a new set of words, telling the poorer performers to try one of the successful techniques. Compare the performances across the two tests to see if adopting the 'successful' techniques has had an effect. Widen this into a discussion of the usefulness of teaching learning *techniques* as well as the language itself.

86   Use one of the tests at the back of Nation (1990) as the basis for your own investigation. Alternatively, if you have very high competence in another language, try producing one or more of the tests in that language and chronicle the problems you encounter.

Different concepts expressed in different languages

German has two words that both translate into English as *but*. In translating the sentence *Jane went to the pictures but I stayed at home*, the German word *aber* would be used for *but*. However, in the sentence *Jane didn't go to the pictures but stayed at home*, the word *sondern* would be used. In Welsh (and many other languages), there is no single pair of words for *yes* and *no* – you need to know what the verb is, what tense it is in and where it comes in the sentence before you can choose the right word. Researchers have been interested in investigating whether such differences between languages make them more difficult to learn, or whether all humans share an underlying sensitivity to differences in meaning, even if not all languages show them.

Project

87   With the help of a bilingual informant, identify words in one language that do not have simple corresponding translations (words relating to culture, religion, and food are often good candidates). Get a group of subjects who do not know the foreign language to learn the words on this list, plus, interspersed, a balancing number of words which *do* have a direct translation. Compare their success in remembering the words: is it easier to learn a word that you can 'hook' directly onto an L1 word?

The learner's approach and experience

What makes a successful language learner? Ellis and Sinclair (1989) look at this question and you can gain an overview of work in the field from Richards and Lockhart (1994: 63–6). Stevick (1989) presents seven case studies of language learners, each of whom has a different approach. Bailey and Nunan (1996) provide a collection of papers on teaching methodology, but from the perspective of the learners and teachers rather than the theorists. One of the most influential studies of the 1970s was that of the *Good Language Learner*, conducted by Naiman, Fröhlich, Stern, and Todesco (1978/1995). A compilation of personal accounts by outstanding Chinese learners of English (*21st Century China Daily* 2005) gives fascinating insights into successful learning strategies for oral performance, especially text memorization. It is a classic account of the strategies used by successful foreign-language learners, and it could form the basis for a good replication study.

Projects

88   Do a case study of a good language learner and see how easily (if at all) he/she fits into one of Stevick's or Naiman *et al.*'s categories, by carefully identifying and categorizing his or her approach to different aspects of the learning process.

89   Pre-test some willing language learners on the vocabulary in a passage that they have not seen and keep a note of the material that they do not know. Give them the text to memorize for recitation. Afterwards, record them reciting the text, and interview them regarding the difficulties they had. Test them on the words they did not know before they saw the passage – has memorizing it led them to learn the meanings of the words or have they bypassed that learning? You could compare the results of this experiment with those of a similar group who were simply introduced to the text, without having to memorize it. Do your findings suggest that memorization could be used as a learning tool?

Interlanguage, error analysis and contrastive analysis

Interlanguage, a term coined by Selinker (1972), is used fairly loosely by many to mean, variously, what the learner can do at any given point after beginning L2 but before perfecting it, the total profile of all the learner's performance stages from beginning L2 to perfecting it, the underlying knowledge that produces the imperfect performance, and a system essentially the same for all learners, featuring rules and patterns consistently found at any given stage, irrespective of the L1 and the learning method (see also Ellis 1994: 710). In Selinker's original definition, interlanguage is the result of having to use a learning system that is not language-specific. For him, its features result from a combination of **language transfer** (elements of L1 are incorrectly imposed onto L2), **overgeneralization** (using an L2 rule in inappropriate conditions), **transfer of training** (an artefact of the teacher's style, creating an apparent rule where there is none), **learning strategies** (choices made by the learner to achieve short-term learning goals, such as simplifying the verb system) and **communication strategies** (a focus on getting the message across, even at the expense of total accuracy) (Cook 1993: 18–19). For an overview of interlanguage, see Tarone (2006).

Error analysis was for many years the standard approach to identifying the features of an interlanguage. **Contrastive analysis** takes direct account of how the L1 and L2 differ in their expression of an idea or their construction of a grammatical relationship and predicts certain errors directly emanating from using the L1 patterns in L2. For an account of error analysis, see Cook (1993: 19 ff.) and Ellis (1994, Ch. 2). Swan and Smith (2001) is useful for finding out what major types of interference can be expected from learners of English with different first languages.

Projects

90   Compare the errors made in English by native speakers of two or more languages that you know in such areas as vocabulary use, grammatical forms and pronunciation. Do they make substantially different errors? Are you able to account for the errors in terms of features of the L1? Do the patterns correspond with those documented in Swan and Smith (2001)?

91   Collect and sort the corrections made by a teacher in class: which errors are allowed to pass? Interview the teacher to find out why and in what circumstances they choose to focus on certain errors and not others.

Language assessment and testing

There are almost as many forms of language test as there are approaches to language learning, because it would not be fair for students drilled in grammar and translation to be tested only on their communicative skills, and vice versa. In actual fact, it is often the examination tail that wags the teaching dog, and much classroom practice is determined by the testing methods used in the external examinations.

Projects

92 Find two classes of equivalent level, working towards roughly equivalent exams for different examining boards or agencies. Is it possible to identify any strong patterns in the teaching that reflect the exam format? What effects might such restrictions have upon balanced learning? If you can, find out what motivates the different examining agencies to present their tests in the way they do (it may not be to do with language-related considerations at all: perhaps, for example, some sorts of answers are quicker to mark than others).

93 Explore some of the formal and communicative tests of English for speakers of other languages (e.g. those produced by the University of Cambridge), asking how far they are genuine tests of language ability. Ask experienced teachers for their opinions on how easy it would be for a candidate to learn how to pass the exams while lacking aspects of the ability in that language that is assumed to go with such a performance.

94 Get hold of some tests for foreign learners of English (as above) and give them to native speakers to do. You could use people with different levels of education and of different ages, including children. How do they perform? What would the implications be of (a) consistently very high scores; and (b) a range of scores, some of which are below those of non-native speakers? What account should be taken of age and level of general education in *non*-native speakers?

Bilinguals, multilinguals and polyglots

Bilingualism is an enormous area of research in its own right. As much of the work does not directly relate to the acquisition of the languages, we shall not cover it here. However, there does exist work on how already knowing more than one language affects your subsequent learning of languages. Many *polyglots* (speakers of several languages) say that language learning becomes easier the more languages you learn, because you get the hang of how to do it and can make generalizations and predictions based on your previous experience of what languages can be like. Yet many learners experience interference between their foreign languages. Why that happens is perhaps a question for the psycholinguist, but how it affects the learning experience is a question relevant to SLA research. For a general overview of bilingualism, see Li Wei (2006) and Bhatia (2006).

Projects

95 Interview a group of polyglots and childhood bilinguals. Are their experiences of interference between the languages (in retrieving words, say) the same or different? Use your findings to construct a model of how the different people might store their languages in the brain and access them. Compare your models with those described by Li Wei (2006: 2–6).

96 Devise an experiment that will elicit cross-language interference. For example, you might get subjects to translate words alternately, and at speed, into their L2 and L3, and see how often they come out with the right word in the wrong language. How do your findings relate to the predictions that the models described in Li Wei (2006: 2–6) would make?

Language teaching policies

Most countries have experimented with different foreign-language teaching policies over the years. In the UK, attempts to teach French to all can be traced back to the 1960s. Burstall *et al.* (1974) report on why they were unsuccessful. Halsall (1968) compared French teaching in Holland, England and Flemish-speaking Belgium. She concluded that 'there was . . . on average, a real inferiority in the standards achieved for French in the English secondary modern school at the 3rd and 4th year levels' (p. 89). A useful source of insight into the factors that might account for this (such as motivation, amount and type of input and attitudes at home) is Clark (1987, Ch. 5), which documents practice and attitudes towards foreign-language teaching and learning in Scottish schools. A few UK schools experimented with teaching a curriculum subject such as history or geography through the medium of French or another language, with impressive results. For specific accounts of such attempts, see Hawkins and Perren (1978, Chs 2–5).

More recently, the European Union has been maintaining its proactive position on language learning. *Promoting Language Learning and Linguistic Diversity: An Action Plan 2004–2006* (European Communities 2003) clearly states that, 'It is a priority for Member States to ensure that language learning in kindergarten and primary school is effective, for it is here that key attitudes towards other languages and cultures are formed, and the foundations for later language learning are laid.' The Action Plan continues, 'Member States agree that pupils [in secondary schools] should master at least two foreign languages, with the emphasis on effective communicative ability: active skills rather than passive knowledge. "Native speaker" fluency is not the objective' and, as far as Higher Education is concerned, 'All students should study abroad, preferably in a foreign language, for at least one term, and should gain an accepted language qualification as part of their degree course.'

Projects

97 Interview a group of native English-speaking, and non-native overseas students about their language-learning experiences in school. How much time was given to the language? How much homework did they get? How much support did they get from home? What did they think they would use the language for? Make sure you are comparing like with like: visiting students are, by definition, motivated to try out their (above-average?) English, so at least compare them with home students who are studying a foreign language.

98 In the UK, all 7–11-year-olds must have the opportunity to learn a foreign language by 2010. Investigate, either directly or via media and other reports, the preparation of this initiative, and the issues arising from it. If you have access to a school that is offering a foreign language to that age group, study the approach taken and assess its efficacy. How do the expectations of the teachers match up to what is known about children's inherent ability to learn languages effectively?

99 Interview school students and try to ascertain what motivates them to choose to study one or another foreign language. Have they dropped a language and if so, why? What do their parents think of language learning? If you have access to individuals from more than one country, incorporate a comparison.

100 Hawkins (1987, Ch. 3) poses the question 'Why French?' and explores the complex issue of how French came to be, and has remained, the first foreign language offered in most British schools. Re-examine his arguments in the light of subsequent political change or consider which languages are most appropriately taught in multi-ethnic schools. Rees (1989: especially 85–91) is a valuable source of information about attitudes to, and the feasibility of, offering a wider range of languages in schools.

101 Develop a strategic plan for supplanting the customary first foreign language in schools in your country (e.g. French in the UK) with another language. You should consider the significance of the language you choose (should it be a language of commercial importance such as Japanese or Chinese, political importance such as Arabic, cultural importance such as Italian, or a language with a large worldwide population such as Spanish?). Work through the practical implications, including what happens to all the teachers whose specialist language is no longer needed, where the new teachers will come from, the possible effects on culture and balances of power within and beyond your country, and so on.

102 Make a study of foreign-language teaching in the former Eastern-bloc countries since the collapse of communism. Focus on the marginalization of Russian as the first foreign language (outside Russia) and of other East European languages (inside Russia), and the rapid introduction of English. How has this been achieved? Are the standards achieved in English comparable with those previously achieved for Russian or other languages? You could try making contact with teachers of English in these countries via the Internet, or via a TESOL unit that is involved in training overseas.

103 Investigate the history and current status of Welsh teaching in Wales, Irish teaching in Ireland, or the teaching of another indigenous minority language. If possible, visit some schools and interview teachers and pupils with the minority and the majority language as their mother tongue. If you can't travel that far, write to them, or make Internet links.

Effect of the year abroad

Students who are sent abroad for a year's study expect, and are expected, to improve their language skills in the host language, but there has been surprisingly little research into the nature and amount of improvement achieved. Milton and Meara (1995) review some studies and report their own, in which the greatest improvement was made by those with the poorest skills at the outset. Students who were already competent benefited much less, if at all, linguistically.

Project

104 Record an interview with an overseas exchange student at the beginning of his/her visit and again some time later. In both interviews, talk about the same subject, so that it is easier to compare the two performances. Choose a subject about which he/she already has some knowledge at the time of the first interview. Analyse the language of the two interviews for fluency, breadth of vocabulary, variety of grammatical structures, length of conversational turn, idiomaticity, ability to make jokes and witticisms, and so on, and list the types of error and their frequency. Use this data to assess the general improvement of the student during the stay. You could also ask him/her in the second interview what he/she feels about the level of improvement and how it seems to have been achieved (for example, by socializing, studying, or watching TV). In the light of Milton and Meara's findings, this study may work best with an individual who is not highly competent on arrival.

Role of the social and political status of English as L2

English occupies an extraordinary and complex position in the modern world. Its precise status varies in different places and is subject to constant change. It is not always easy to see who or what has elevated it to its position and what maintains it: is it culture, policy or something else? Crystal (2003b) has a section entitled 'World English', in which he considers the different international varieties of English and asks whether the English language is under threat or is a threat to other languages. Crystal (2003a) is dedicated to this subject. Hartmann (1996) contains a range of papers on aspects of the role and status of English in the European Union, including its use as a *lingua franca*, the adoption of English loan words into other languages, and the phenomenon of bilingualism with English in different EU countries. You can search the Internet for policy documents and a range of views on the place of English and other languages in Europe. The same can be done for other languages in other countries, e.g. Spanish in the United States. For a history of English-language teaching, which indicates how the status of English has been reflected in the changing demand for it abroad, see Howatt (1984).

Projects

105 How has the current language situation (including foreign-language provision and proficiency) arisen in a particular country of your choice? South Africa, India and

China would make interesting case studies. You need to think carefully about how you will gain the necessary information. A government office or embassy will give the official reasoning, but you may want to discuss the issues with citizens of that country as well.

106 Explore the reasons why English language is, or is not, on the school syllabus in a particular country. This type of project could simply take a historical perspective and explain how the country in question has reached the situation in which it now finds itself; or you could attempt to predict what language provision will be most appropriate for the country in the near future.

Other project ideas

107 Conduct some tests, or interview teachers, or both, to investigate whether girls are better at learning foreign languages than boys.

108 Through observation of non-native speakers in real interaction, analyse how the learner's social behaviour in the learning situation correlates with his/her overall achievement, fluency and/or accuracy.

109 Consider, in a theory-based project, to what extent learning Orwell's Newspeak (described in an essay at the back of his novel *Nineteen Eighty-Four*) would be the same as, and different from, learning an L2.

110 Compare three beginners in a foreign language: one in a regular class, one working with an individual tutor (contact could be made via a local Home Tutor scheme) and one teaching himself/herself. Apart from monitoring and comparing their progress (remember to devise tests that do not favour one or the other's approach), consider what advantages and disadvantages each method of learning has, as regards changes in motivation, commitment and interest, availability of feedback, accuracy of what is learned, number of hours put in and how regularly, and so on.

111 Use the various accounts of successful learning in Stevick (1989) as the basis for a critical appraisal of a model of how languages are learned.

For further inspiration, read Ellis (1994, Ch. 1), and follow up an idea that interests you by finding his more detailed account elsewhere in the book – or explore any of the issues raised in Bhatia and Ritchie (2003), Carter and Nunan (2001), or Doughty and Long (2003).

5
Structure and meaning

In this chapter we look at research that might fall under the headings of pragmatics, syntax, semantics, morphology. Each of these areas extends considerably beyond what we cover, however, and you may want to seek further information in specialist textbooks, some of which are listed in the next section.

The sorts of questions that you might want to ask in a project on structure and meaning include:

❒ How does a speaker convey messages indirectly, i.e. ones that are not explicitly carried in the words themselves?

❒ How does a speaker express subtle differences in meaning by shifting elements of the sentence around, or by choosing one word rather than another?

❒ How do we express politeness through structure?

❒ What makes jokes funny?

❒ Why are some sentences ambiguous?

❒ What restrictions are there regarding which words can go with which others?

❒ What does a word mean and who decides?

❒ How do intonation and punctuation contribute to meaning?

❒ What is 'correct' grammar?

❒ How are words constructed?

❒ What role does the hearer play in making sure the speaker's utterance is correctly understood?

❒ How do languages (and varieties of a single language) vary in the way they express meaning through words and through strings of words?

Textbooks and major journals

Halliday and Matthiessen (2004) is a thorough introduction to Functional Grammar, an approach to analysis which many students and researchers find valuable in relating structure to meaning. Dixon (2005) explores meaning through grammar, and Hewings and Hewings (2005) have project ideas on grammar. Saeed (2002) provides a thorough introduction to semantics though if you have not studied semantics before, Kearns (2000) might be an easier initial resource. A good introduction to metaphor is Knowles and Moon (2005), and for morphology try Booij (2005) or Carstairs-McCarthy (2002). For pragmatics, Huang (2006) and Mey (2001) provide comprehensive introductions and Grundy (2000) gives useful guidance on executing projects. Carter *et al.* (2001) show how authentic everyday text can be analysed from a range of perspectives.

Journal articles on any of these areas can be quite difficult to read but they do indicate the questions that the experts want to answer and their questions may inspire similar questions for your project. Useful journals for projects on structure and meaning include the following:

JOURNALS

Corpus Linguistics and Linguistic Theory
English Language and Linguistics
English Today
Humour
Journal of Linguistics
Journal of Pragmatics
Language
Linguistic Inquiry
Linguistics and Philosophy
Linguistic Review

In addition, we recommend that you check the journals lists in other chapters in this book, if your interest in structure and meaning coincides with, say, language and gender, history of English, or language development. Research in such areas often deals with structure and meaning in a more accessible way than does the research that focuses directly on semantics, pragmatics, and syntax.

Central themes and project ideas

Pragmatics

Much of our verbal communication is expressed in rather indirect ways, creating a potential obstacle course for the hearer. For example, arriving at someone's house on a muddy day, we might be expected to interpret *I'll see if I can find my spare slippers* as an invitation to take our shoes off at the door. However, such indirect communication is risky for the speaker: we might genuinely not pick up the hidden message or we might deliberately choose to ignore it. In our day-to-day interaction, there is more than an exchange of words: there is a social dance, and we, as the listener, may choose to keep in step or to clumsily upset the rhythm of the communication by not listening to the music. Pragmatics deals with the hidden messages.

In **Speech Act Theory** (Austin 1961, 1962; Searle 1965, 1975, 1979), the way in which apparently straightforward utterances perform complex interactional tasks is revealed. For example, **performatives**, easily identified by the possibility of inserting the word *hereby*, have a permanent effect upon the state of the world (e.g. *I name this ship HMS Endurance*; *I bet you £5 he loses the match*; *I promise to return the book*). In an important application of Speech Act Theory, Shuy (1993) explores the forensic role of the linguist in ascertaining whether or not an individual has committed a crime that hinges on a performative speech act. The subtlety of such research lies in the fact that it is rare for an illegal offer such as a bribe to be made explicitly and, in the absence of a recording that contains the words 'I'm offering you a bribe', it is obviously difficult to be sure that the speech act (verbal agreement) was actually carried out.

Grice's (1975) theory of **Conversational Implicature** takes account of the need for the speaker and the hearer to enter into a pact regarding how things will be said and interpreted if communication is to be successful and efficient. Grice's four **maxims** characterize this co-operation: the hearer will assume that the speaker is only saying things that are relevant to the current state of the conversation, giving neither too little nor too much information, speaking truthfully and avoiding ambiguity and obscurity. The speaker may deliberately flout a maxim in order to deceive the hearer (e.g. by telling a lie), something that is made easier by the hearer's expectation of co-operation (i.e. assuming the truth will be told). Hearers or readers will work very hard to find relevance in an utterance, as can be seen from our ability to interpret an exchange such as: *A: Is there any more butter? B: I didn't leave work till seven*. Besides Grice's own (1975) paper, you can read about conversational implicature in Mey (2001), Grundy (2000), Thomas (1995), and Levinson (1983: 97–166).

Relevance Theory (Sperber and Wilson 1995) is based on the belief that humans pay attention to the information that they perceive to be relevant. Their account solves the problem of how communication succeeds even though speaker and hearer do not know how much information about the situation the other has. Relevance Theory is not easy to get to grips with. Rather than reading the whole book, try Sperber and Wilson's (1987) précis of it, Mey (2001, Ch. 4), Grundy (2000), or Yus (2006).

Projects

112 Examine the text of a play for evidence of implicit messages, and consider what the playwright is deliberately conveying about the attitudes and personality of the characters.

113 Write two scripts for the same sequence of events, one that is totally explicit and one that expresses the same information by implication, shared assumptions, and so on. Get three people to judge each one for naturalness or plausibility, and to describe their reaction to the characters.

114 Examine one or more comedy TV sketches that rely on pragmatic manipulation for their humour (*The Two Ronnies* is particularly good for this).

115 Take a five-minute sequence from a TV comedy show and write a commentary, to run alongside the script, that describes what the audience is intended to understand, even though it is not explicitly stated. Use the script and commentary to identify how the language in the script, along with other signals such as glances

and gestures, studio laughter and music, variously signal information to the audience, and what this tells us about what you need to know about culture, language and behaviour in order to find that comedy funny.

116 What we say when we want to get something done provides interesting paradigms, in which a decreasing scale of directness may reflect increasing levels of politeness. For example, all of the following could be used as a request for a book: *Give me that*; *Could I have that, please? Would you mind passing me that book? I haven't seen that book*; *That book looks interesting.* Examine data from, say, episodes of a soap opera, to evaluate how the level of directness reflects the relationships between the characters, as independently demonstrated by their behaviour and the content of their utterances (e.g. Do two people who dislike each other use more direct framings? Do two people of unequal status contrast in their politeness markers when talking to each other?).

117 Analyse different types of joke (puns, shaggy-dog stories and so forth) for ways in which they flout Grice's maxims (e.g. consider what the person hearing a joke is expecting).

118 Record a group of people carrying out a particular task and compare that recording with a scene from a soap opera where the characters are accomplishing the same task (e.g. telling somebody what to do). Is the scripted exchange more direct than the authentic non-scripted?

119 Record a lesson and anayse how a teacher gets the class to do what he/she wants them to do. How directly are the instructions given and how do different modes of address impact on the reactions of the class?

Metaphor

While we are accustomed to seeing metaphor as a feature of literary language, it is clear that we also use it in everyday life. We talk about the *journey through life*, about *battling something out*, or about *sailing through an exam*. Financial reports talk about one currency *weakening* or *strengthening* in comparison to another. Research on metaphor obviously needs to do more than just list examples, so you need to find out about the major theoretical approaches to understanding it (see, e.g. Cameron and Low 1999). Among these is the **constructivist** approach, which you can read about first-hand in Lakoff and Johnson (1980). They propose that, rather than being an abstraction away from a more fundamental, literal way of seeing things, metaphor is the very basis of the way in which we make sense of the world, and, in effect, is what our 'reality' is based upon. A useful overview of theories can be found in Gibbs (2006). For concise definitions of **metaphor** and other devices, see Crystal (1997a: 70; 2003b: 421).

Projects

120 Identify the metaphors in a passage from a novel and systematically replace each with a more literal equivalent. Show the new passage to informants and ask them

to rate it for readability, interest and style. Then show them the original and ask them to rate that. Is it possible to say that the use of metaphor always produces better prose?

121 Analyse how reports in the media use metaphor. Choose a particular event and identify the metaphors used. How do metaphors create particular images for the reader or hearer, and are these images sustained with associated metaphors, or simply used and then dropped?

122 If you are familiar with Old or Middle English, compare the metaphors used then with ones used in a similar (i.e. literary) context today. Crystal (2003b: 23) gives some examples of metaphors in Old English, including *hronrād* (*whale-road*) for *sea*, and *bānhūs* (*bone-house*) for *human body*. One way to test how similar our 'feel' for metaphors is to that of years ago is to see whether modern informants can make sense of a modernized version of the old ones. If the choice of metaphors then and now is essentially similar, what does that tell us? If old and modern metaphors seem quite different in kind, why might that be?

123 Consider the claim that 'most lexical items [are] dead metaphors' (Sadock 1979: 48) by conducting an etymological study of English vocabulary. For example, Partridge (1977) gives the origin of *lord* as Old English *hlāfweard* (*loaf-guardian*) and that of *lady* as *hlāfdīge* (*loaf-kneader*). To keep a focus, pick one sub-area of vocabulary for the study, such as words for people or tools. Remember to link your findings back into a theoretical discussion of the nature and function of metaphor.

124 Search through books about how to be a successful creative writer, for guidelines on the pros and cons of using metaphors and advice on what to do and what to avoid. Do the books agree and are the examples convincing? Can you identify underlying common beliefs about what makes a metaphor effective and desirable? Where you can, do you view the beliefs to be built upon current fashion or more fundamental linguistic principles?

125 Lakoff (1992) outlines very clearly how metaphor was used to frame reports of the 1990–91 Gulf War. His observations include: *the State as a person, war as a competitive game, international politics as business*, and *war as medicine*. Using his framework, analyse the framing of a more recent conflict to evaluate the extent to which the metaphors are the same or different, and why that might be.

Sentence structure

The precise way in which words are strung together can subtly affect the meaning. For example, word order can change the topic (focus). Compare: *There's a tiger on the church roof, It's a tiger that's on the church roof* and *It's the church roof that a tiger's on*. Omitting information can also have a marked effect on the slant of the message. Compare: *The soldier fired his gun at the protester at point-blank range; The gun was fired at the protester at point-blank range; The gun fired at the protester at point-blank range*, and *The protester was shot at point-blank range*. To understand this kind of variation, it helps to identify the **roles** of the different participants in the events. Here, the soldier is always the person firing the gun (**actor**), even when he is not mentioned and some other noun phrase is the subject of the sentence. The gun is always the **instrument**, irrespective of whether the phrase *the gun* is subject, object, object of a preposition, or not mentioned at all. The protester is always the **goal**, i.e. the one who is shot. A useful introduction to semantic roles is Bloor and Bloor (2004). There are also some examples, with discussion, in Pinker (1994: 114). For some insight into the subtleties of our linguistic understanding compared to that of a logical machine, see Pinker (1994: 78–81).

Not all differences in meaning are explicit on the surface, however. Syntactic theory examines the structures that underpin sentences and attempts to account for a range of phenomena, such as unexpectedly ungrammatical sequences and ones that are apparently similar but where structural differences exist, like: *The pupils are usually easy to help* and *The pupils are usually eager to help*. Here, it seems as if there has been a straightforward replacement of one adjective with another, but this is not so, as we can see if we ask *who does the helping?*

Syntax also addresses issues of ambiguity, as in *Biting insects can be unpleasant*. You can learn a lot about the nature of English by trying to make up further examples of this kind. One particular type of ambiguity is the garden-path sentence, where there is, in fact, only one grammatical reading, but we are fooled by the sequence of words into looking for a different one (e.g. *The soup boiled vigorously spilt over*; *The ball bounced past the goalpost burst*). These are grammatical only if you read them as a (legitimately) shortened version of sentences with *that was* after the subject noun phrase. Again, trying to make up your own examples of garden-path sentences will soon indicate to you how they work. You can read about them in Pinker (1994: 212–17) and in Kess (1992: 129 ff.), where you will also find accounts of psycholinguistic experiments using them. They are also briefly mentioned in Chapter 2 of this book.

Projects

126 Compare newspaper accounts of an event (something with strong political implications is best, such as a scandal at the heart of a political party), using publications that are likely to take sides. Look for different ways in which the same story can be told so that a different emphasis (e.g. about blame) is achieved. For guidelines on how to do this, see Freeborn *et al.* (1993, Ch. 9).

127 In newspapers that take opposing stances, compare the editorial opinion in the leader columns. Choose editorials on emotive events about which contrasting views are possible, such as assisted suicide or immigration policy, rather than catastrophes or atrocities that everyone will condemn.

128 Examine the writing of a 9-year-old, an 11-year-old and a 13-year-old for evidence of a developing ability to manipulate the structure of English for the purposes of subtle expression. You could achieve this by asking each of your subjects to write on the same topic, and imposing certain conditions. For instance, can they tell the story of a day in the life of a person without giving away the person's gender, or that he/she cannot speak the language, or is living on another planet?

account for how or why the English language divides things up this way (does it reflect the language itself? human perception? history? culture?). Is there a conscious aspect to these sets or do native speakers have no idea about them? Show some native speakers the lists and ask for their reactions.

135 Remove the terms from Table 5.1, and see how many of Farb's terms native speakers can fill in. Are there patterns regarding what people know and don't know? Why might some terms be more central to our common vocabulary than others? Use a word frequency list (see Chapter 1) and/or a corpus search (Chapter 18) to check whether it is the least-used words that are least well-known. If it is, consider whether infrequency causes unfamiliarity or the reverse.

136 Compare the frequency distributions of words in comparable texts from different dates in the twentieth century. You can conduct an electronic comparison using Nation's *Range* software (Nation 2001). Leech *et al.* (2001) also provide useful data as a starting point.

137 Construct a list of common collective nouns (e.g. *flock of sheep, pride of lions, shoal of fish*). How have they come about, and how long have they been in use? (Use the full *Oxford English Dictionary* or a good etymological dictionary – references are given in Chapter 10.) Why do we need such terms (if at all)? Under what circumstances might newly coined ones end up coming into common usage?

138 Compared with some other languages, English has very few kinship terms. What is the sociocultural significance of a lack of different words, for example, for *mother's sister* and *father's sister* in English? Make a comparison with other languages that you know and read more widely about languages that you don't know, to establish the motivation for the creation and retention of these terms. You could extend your research by asking informants to talk about their families, to establish how the practicalities of designation are handled. For instance, is it common for the maternal and paternal grandparents to be differently referred to, and if so, is there any pattern across families? Do people see any need to indicate, when referring to aunts, uncles, and cousins, which side of the family they are from?

139 Investigate the meaning that informants give to words such as *barely* in a sentence like *He barely has ten books on his shelf*. How many has he? More than ten, fewer or exactly ten? Another interesting word is *orphan*. Precisely who counts as one? Can you cease to be one? If you were brought up by foster parents while your own parents were still alive, who would have to die for you to become an orphan? Use examples like this to explore the agreement, or lack of it, between native speakers about precise definitions, and to discuss whether or not it matters.

140 Explore the meaning of the word *edition*, carefully identifying its range of uses (including *special-edition* chocolate bars and cars). Ask informants what the word means (a) in isolation and (b) in its different contexts. How easy is it to pin down a central core to its meaning, and how does that relate to the history of the word's use? Find other words used in an extended way, probably also in advertising or marketing, and investigate them similarly (e.g. *'fresh' orange juice/cream; light/lite; bio*). How effectively can these uses be explained using Rosch's prototype theory (described above)?

Morphology and etymology

The morpheme is the smallest unit of meaning. Some morphemes (**free morphemes**) stand alone, such as *dog, smile, black, from, also*. Others are **bound**, needing to combine with other morphemes, e.g. *-s* (plural), *un-, -ish, pseudo-*. You can find examples of the prefixes and suffixes of English in Crystal (2003b, Ch. 14). English is a particularly fascinating language to study, because its history of borrowing from other languages has left it with an enormous collection of morphemes, not all of which still have meanings that are recognizable without recourse to a dictionary. Because of this history, for English the studies of morphology (how we make up words today) and etymology (how words have come to have the form they do) are closely allied. For more information and suggestions for projects on etymology, see Chapter 10.

Projects

141 Look through teenage magazines for words that are new to the language or interview some children about the current playground vocabulary, what it means, and how they use it. Investigate the way in which these words have been constructed and/or where they have been borrowed from. If they are borrowed, have they had their meaning changed? When and how have they first appeared? Do they express an idea for which there was previously no word? If not, what was wrong with the old word? Is there any way of telling which of the words will last, becoming fully established in mainstream English, and which will soon fall into disuse again?

142 Look through magazines from the 1950s or 1960s and try to identify words that were new then. Divide them into two categories – those that have survived and those that have not – and look for reasons why each word may have undergone its fate.

143 Find out about the construction of vocabulary in a sign language used by deaf people. What happens when a new sign is needed? Who introduces it and under what circumstances? How does the sign language express things like past tense, plural or the conditional? Interview signers who also know English about the way in which the two languages are the same and different.

144 Take a passage from a novel or a document and attempt to rewrite it using only monomorphemic words (i.e. words that cannot be broken down any further into meaning components). What problems arise with: availability of vocabulary, deciding whether a word is monomorphemic or not, style, and so on?

145 Anderson (1988: 185 ff.) explores the restrictions on English vocabulary formation, which outlaw *He sang *goodly; She stared in *amazion; The bruise began to blacken and *bluen; Delia Smith is a good *cooker* (the asterisk indicates that the word does not exist). Use this as a basis for an analysis of idiosyncratic vocabulary in the work of a poet such as Gerard Manley Hopkins or e. e. cummings. What determines whether words of this kind are seen as humorous on the one hand, or beautiful and creative coinages on the other?

146 Make a list of words that, if split, have a different meaning, such as *altogether/all together; into/in to; however/how ever; everyone/every one; layby/lay by*. Ask informants to pin down the differences in meaning. Research the history of the words, to find out whether the opposition has always existed. Pay attention to the syntactic classes of the words and the structures in which they appear. For further examples, see Greenbaum (1991: 200).

Punctuation

Punctuation plays various roles in clarifying meaning. Putting a word in inverted commas, for example, can indicate that the writer considers it unfamiliar, inappropriate, and so on. Commas are used to indicate the structure of the sentence, sometimes clarifying potential ambiguity, and, without punctuation, a string of words may be complete nonsense. One well-known example concerns what two students wrote in a translation exercise: *Jones, where Smith had had 'had', had had 'had had'. 'Had had' had had the teacher's approval.*

Projects

147 Remove the punctuation from some texts and get informants to put it back. To what extent do they agree? Categorize the conventions into those that genuinely make the meaning clear and those that could be dispensed with. Do your informants have most difficulty with those aspects of punctuation that play the least role in clarifying the meaning? Survey their attitudes to and problems with 'correct' punctuation.

148 Truss (2003: 9) provides examples where the meaning of a text can change completely, simply by changing the punctuation. One of her examples is *A woman, without her man, is nothing* as opposed to *A woman: without her, man is nothing*. Track down and/or create similar examples and use them to work out which aspects of English vocabulary and structure are most vulnerable to this kind of potential ambiguity. Give your examples, with no punctuation in at all, to some informants and ask them to add punctuation. Does one of the two options tend to be more commonly selected than the other? If so, which, and why?

149 Research the history of punctuation in English, both in books about the history of the language and by looking at original texts from Old, Middle and Modern English. Was there ever no punctuation at all? Which usages have existed longest? Has their scope of application changed?

150 The poet e.e. cummings makes very limited use of punctuation. Show some of his poems to informants and compare their reactions and their understanding of the meaning. Does the poet's approach permit subtle expressions of meaning that would be destroyed by using punctuation more conventionally, or is it just a gimmick?

151 Is the apostrophe disappearing from written English? Truss (2003: 37) claims (with many others) that 'it's on its last legs' and bemoans 'showbiz promoters [who] stick apostrophes in names for purely decorative purposes'. Collect examples of the use of apostrophes in a wide variety of texts (e.g. shop names, market-stall labels, hoardings, menus) and decide where the apostrophe is being used meaningfully, where decoratively, and where for some other reason.

'Correct' grammar

In order to understand the issue of *correctness* in grammar, it is necessary to differentiate between **linguistic** and **social** judgements. A descriptive linguistic approach recognizes that many of the features that are considered 'incorrect' in English are in fact simply *non-standard* and within their own variety they are entirely grammatical and consistent. However, the existence of a 'standard' English indicates that there is a variety of the language that is socially and culturally more acceptable than the others. Forms that do not adhere to it are often seen as 'incorrect'. See Freeborn (1995) for a review of the arguments regarding what constitutes 'good' and 'correct' English and for examples of how actual text does not always conform to the 'rules'. Freeborn *et al.* (1993, Ch. 1) and Crystal (2003b: 366–67) also discuss the question of correctness, and Wray (1996) explores the conflicts between prescriptivism and descriptivism that arise when academic linguists have to correct the work of their students. Cameron (1995) gives a spirited account of the debate in her chapter 'Dr Syntax and Mrs Grundy: the great grammar crusade'. On the other hand, Marenbon (1994) suggests that descriptivism and prescriptivism are mutually supportive: 'by describing how a certain language is spoken or written, the grammarian prescribes usage for those who wish to speak or write that language' (p. 20).

Projects

152 Compare the grammar of two strong dialects of English (such as Scots, Geordie, Black English Vernacular, Indian English) or compare one of them with standard English. What things can be expressed by one and not the other? For some ideas on this, see Labov's paper on non-standard Black American English, originally published as Labov (1969) but also available in many collections of classic papers in sociolinguistics. Consider the implications for the expressive potential of an individual of accepting or rejecting his/her variety as a legitimate form of English in its own right.

153 Research the history of a prescriptive feature of English grammar, such as not splitting infinitives, not ending sentences with a preposition, or use of apostrophes. Use textbooks on the history of English (see Chapter 10) and original sources where possible. Categorize a collection of conventions (along with some examples of them) into two sets: those that reflect a long-standing convention and those that are a recent imposition. Mix the two sets together and ask native and non-native speaker informants for their views on how important it is to adhere to the rule and how long they think it has applied to English. Do your results suggest that

a rule has more, or less, credibility if it is believed to (or actually does) reflect a long-standing tradition?

154 Do school pupils, teachers, school governors and employers in business and in the public services share the same opinions on what good English is? Show the same stimuli to pupils and one of the other groups above and compare the responses. For example stimuli, see Freeborn *et al.* (1993: 11–12).

155 Examples such as *I would of done that* or *she was been silly* are often marked as errors in student essays. Find more examples and explain how the non-grammatical forms might have been produced. Interview teachers about the prevalence of such errors and ask them how they try to help their students not to produce them. Then tell the teachers that, according to some theories of language change, it is only a matter of time until these 'errors' become acceptable. Ask them to categorize the examples for the likelihood that they will be acceptable within the next 20, 50 and 100 years and ask them under what circumstances they believe that the drift towards acceptability might and might not occur. Compare their responses, to establish whether teachers hold common views about correctness and their role in promoting it.

156 Use a corpus search to discover the ways in which the reflexive pronouns (e.g. *myself, yourself*) are used. Pay particular attention to usages such as *I spoke to yourself about it* and *a person cannot help themselves*. Consider what is being expressed and what other options there are. Try to establish whether the usages are new or have always been there. If the latter, why are they not considered 'correct'? Read about the dynamics of language change and acceptability, to predict what might happen next.

157 Find examples of *alot, aswell,* and other non-standard spellings of this kind. Collect data by borrowing essays from a local school or your fellow students. Which word strings are now being perceived as single items and which remain consistently separate? Use basic phrase-structure analysis (such as Burton-Roberts 1997, Thomas 1993) to establish whether there are structural reasons for this. For some background and example data, see Wray (1996).

158 Explore the role of dictionaries as prescribers or describers. By comparing their forewords, their format and what information they include, find out who they are targeted at and what their aims are. Interview native and non-native speakers of English about how and why they use dictionaries, whether they always believe what they find there, and what they do if they can't find the word or meaning they are looking for.

Other project ideas

159 Investigate the form and usage of idiomatic and 'rule-breaking' expressions such as *He was sleeping like the proverbial* or *I've just had himself on the phone*. Explore the nature of their form and usage, taking account of the syntax (including any

restrictions they violate) and the pragmatics (shared information, about whom or in what circumstances they would be used, the effect of using them rather than an alternative and so on).

160 Take a selection of jokes from a joke book or website and catalogue them for humour based on pragmatics, ambiguity (phonological, lexical, and structural) and non-linguistic factors such as situation. Give the jokes (intermixed) to groups of subjects and get them to rate them for funniness. Do 10-year-olds give consistently different ratings from adults for the different types? What about men and women? Nash (1985) and Chiaro (1992) provide a good introduction to the pragmatics of humour and ideas to follow up for projects.

161 Take Monty Python's *Parrot Sketch*, or a sketch of similar anarchic complexity, and categorize the lexical, structural and pragmatic sources of its humour.

162 Explore the origins of idiomatic expressions such as *spitting feathers* or *raining cats and dogs*. Ask informants what they think the expressions mean. We found most people think that *spitting feathers* means very angry but one informant is adamant that it means very thirsty. How might such differences come about?

163 Track changes made to entries in Wikipedia (http://en.wikipedia.org/wiki/Main_Page) by watching the pages themselves and also the discussion pages associated with the entries. Use this information to comment on how meaning and accuracy are negotiated, with particular attention to how people cope with multiple beliefs about 'facts'. Consider the extent to which meaning and information are being created or revised rather than simply discovered, and how this process relates to more traditional ways of presenting information. To get yourself started, look at the 'recent changes' list (http://en.wikipedia.org/wiki/Special:Recentchanges) and follow up several topics for a few days, until you see which ones are most active and most interesting.

164 Ask musicians who do not know the Italian language to identify, from a list, common Italian musical terms that they are familiar with and would not need to look up if they occurred in a piece of music. Examples might be *andante, staccato, forte, largo*, and *legato*. Then, for each term, ask your informants to explain the meaning and how they would obey the instruction in a piece of music. Compare the explanations: do all musicians share a common understanding of a term? Is a term differently interpreted according to the instrument? Now look up the terms in a good Italian-language dictionary, to discover what the words literally mean (for instance, *legato* means 'bound together'). If possible, check with a native speaker of Italian whether the terms still have their literal meaning in everyday Italian or whether they are now solely musical terms. Use your results to map out the ways in which the original meaning of the Italian words can shift when used by musicians who do not know the language.

165 Conduct an analysis of the hand signs described in the science-fiction novel *The Foreigners* by James Lovegrove (2001). How different are they to words, and how plausible is Lovegrove's proposal that humans could use them to communicate with aliens? Get some friends to learn the signs (and perhaps invent some more of

your own) and then try to communicate messages using only the signs. Write
methodically about the problems that arise and how the group attempts to solve
them.

You can find lots of information that will inspire ideas for projects by reading Chapters
8–16 of Crystal (2003b).

6
Style in spoken and written texts

In any successful communication, whether we are giving the message or receiving it, we are sensitive not only to the content but also to the way in which the message is encoded. The encoding is dependent on very subtle features of what the speaker wants to achieve. How might you ask someone to open the window for you? A simple request? An indirect request? Or by simply pointing? Each of those ways will be appropriate in some situations and less appropriate in others. As communicators, we learn to be aware of the response that each might provoke from the message receiver. Now compare the way you might write an essay on a linguistic topic with the way you might organize a web page on the same topic. The possibilities of the medium and the expectations of the reader will be different in each case, leading you to make different choices of linguistic and paralinguistic features.

The characteristic structural and stylistic features of texts are well worth exploring and, since language is all around us, there are many types of text to choose from. You might like to consider legal texts or literary texts, or the instructions for assembling or using a gadget. You might take an interest in specialized technical texts (on any topic that interests you) or simplified texts (how has the text been simplified and for what audience?).

In this chapter we suggest projects that focus on the lexical, syntactic, and structural choices in text construction. If you are doing work in **text analysis**, **discourse analysis**, or **stylistics**, you should find information and ideas here to help you.

The questions that one can ask about a spoken or written text include:

❐   What makes a text a *text* rather than just a set of sentences?

❐   How does a spoken text differ from a written text on the same topic?

❐   How does changing the language used in a text change the message?

❐   (How) have stylistic conventions changed over the years?

❐   What makes some texts easier to understand than others? Can the study of style help us to produce texts that are more comprehensible?

❐   Do different types (genres) of text have discernibly different styles?

❐   What is the effect on the reader of a text *not* being in the style normally associated with it?

❐   Can a stylistic analysis reliably determine the authorship of a text when that
    authorship is in doubt?

❐   How do poets, advertisers, politicians and other professional 'wordsmiths' exploit
    style to create an effect?

The answers to such questions rely on the analyst's examination of patterns in the words
and structures, as well as its presentation (spelling, punctuation, font size, use of
illustrations and so on).

Writing is a person's opportunity to have *his/her* say in a monologue. Although, of
course, a writer aims to create a reaction from the reader, a single written text is not really
a dialogue, because the reader cannot feed responses directly back to the writer in time to
influence what is written next. A spoken monologue is somewhat similar and can be
subjected to many of the same questions as those listed above.

However, *interaction* is different. It is the creation of text, in which what one person
produces is influenced by what one or more others say. We mostly think of speech in this
regard but in fact, writing can also be interactive. For instance, a series of letters between
two correspondents would display some of the same patterns as a conversation, as each
writer reacts to the other. The same goes for on-line discussions, which, though not by any
means identical to spoken conversations, imitate them in some regards, while also
retaining some features only found in writing.

The feature of interaction in spoken and written texts introduces other interesting
questions, such as:

❐   How are the participants working out when it is their turn to contribute?

❐   How are they signalling that they have finished their turn or have more to say?

❐   How are they indicating that they understand, agree, or disagree with others'
    contributions?

❐   How are participants moving from one topic of conversation to another?

❐   How are they bringing the interaction to a close?

❐   To what extent are the different participants picking up topics or lexical or stylistic
    features from each other and re-using them, and what effect does that create?

As you will no doubt have realized, many of the ideas that we describe in this chapter
coincide with topics in other chapters. In relation to language and gender (Chapter 8),
you could examine male–female differences in interaction or in the creation of written
text. In a study of second-language acquisition (Chapter 4), you could examine how
stylistic features in speech or writing are adopted from the first language, so that the
second language sounds un-nativelike in subtle ways. In an investigation of how children
acquire language (Chapter 3), you could examine the process by which the skills of text
assembly or of conversational behaviour develop.

Textbooks and major journals

The broad scope of this chapter means that there are a great many books that you can
turn to. In the area of discourse analysis, Schiffrin *et al.* (2003) offers an excellent

grounding and is sure to inspire project ideas. From the structural perspective, Hillier (2005) analyses a wide range of texts within a Hallidayan framework. Carter (2004), Have (1999) and Cameron (2001) focus on oral-language use. Crystal (2001) addresses some of the varieties found in electronic use of language. Useful journals for projects on spoken and written style include the following:

JOURNALS

British Journal of Social Psychology
Communication Monographs
Discourse and Society
Discourse Processes
Journal of Communication
Journal of Politeness Research: Language, Behaviour, Culture
Journal of Pragmatics
Research on Language and Social interaction
Text and Talk (previously *Text*)

Central themes and project ideas

Texts are created for so many different purposes, and in so many different forms, that there are several approaches that one can take to researching them. We have divided the themes according to the *level of analysis*. This enables you to consider the options for how you engage with the construction and function of a text, either alone or as part of a comparison. Text comparison is a very fruitful approach, and it is possible to focus both on how even quite similar texts can differ and how very different texts still have similarities.

But what types of text are there, that you might consider working on? Each text type has characteristics that you can exploit in your investigation. An oral text (that is, spoken language) will have different features from an equivalent written text: consider the difference between someone reading a story out of a book as compared with telling a story directly in the oral medium. Within the oral medium, a television discussion will differ in certain kinds of ways from a radio one: to get a feel for how, try listening to a television discussion without looking at the pictures. In the written medium, linguistic researchers are currently very interested in the way that certain features of spoken language might be 'leaking' into new forms of written text, such as web logs and text messages. For each of these types of text – and there are many more subtle divisions within them – you can ask certain basic questions about the sounds or letters, the words, the grammar, the meaning and the interpersonal function. Furthermore, you can ask those questions of just one text type, or use the analysis as a means of comparing one text type with another.

Sound patterns within texts

In some texts, the sound patterns created by the writer are clearly the most important feature. Although we associate rhyme, alliteration, assonance and consonance with poetry, advertisers or politicians also frequently use such devices as a way of making a slogan or soundbite more memorable. Whether you are describing a Shakespeare sonnet or a soap-powder advert, the formal description of the phonetic patterns will use the same approach and terminology. Stress and intonation are also often used to great effect.

Nursery rhymes often follow strong metrical patterns, the heavily stressed rhythms making them easier to memorize. *Twinkle twinkle little star* is a good example of a nursery rhyme with a particularly strong metrical rhythm. In *Three Blind Mice*, on the other hand, we see reflected the wider potential of the stress-timed pattern of everyday English speech, with different numbers of unstressed syllables packed in between equally spaced stressed ones. **Iambs**, **dactyls** and other metrical patterns and rhyme schemes are explained in most of the introductory books on literary stylistics (such as Leech 1969) or in the dictionaries of literary terms (such as Gray 1984). Cummings and Simmons (1983) show a detailed analysis of sound patterning in poetry and prose by Hopkins, Dylan Thomas, Birney, Frost and Arnold. Freeborn (1996) also gives some examples of sound patterning in a range of verse and prose texts, including Chaucer's *Canterbury Tales*, *Remember* by Christina Rossetti and Dylan Thomas's *Under Milk Wood*.

A writer may use onomatopoeia: the choice of words could imitate the noise of walking through crisp leaves in the forest in autumn or the sound of a snake slithering through the grass, for example. These effects can be captured in analysis by using phonetic or phonemic transcription to highlight common sound features that may be obscured by the complex spelling system of English. Indeed, even more general assonance and rhyme in a text benefits from this treatment: the words *all, haunch, lawn, broad, floor, more, pour, sure* appear to have little in common when spelled, yet a phonemic transcription reveals that, in many varieties of English, they all contain the same vowel.

Projects

166 Look at the work of one or more poets (such as Gerard Manley Hopkins or Benjamin Zephaniah) to see what makes their work sound so different from that of other poets.

167 Focus on an advertising campaign that uses sound. For example, Perrier used a play on the word *eau* (French for 'water') to illustrate occasions when their product could be consumed, including: *Sleau lunch* (with a picture of a snail), *A reau at the regatta* (during the Henley Regatta), and *Eau, I say!* (during Wimbledon, where one commentator was known to exclaim 'Oh, I say!' to a good shot). This last example demonstrates very clearly what is often called intertextuality: our interpretation of any one text may require a knowledge of other texts or situations. A new twist to this intertextuality came from a 'piggyback' advertising campaign (where one advertiser exploits the idea of another) by Nestlé-Rowntree. An advertisement for Polo Mints used the slogan *The mint with the heaule* with a picture of the mints looking like the bubbles in a glass of Perrier. Look for examples of wordplay and piggybacking in advertising: what options are there for different mediums? That is, what can a written advertisement achieve that a spoken one could not, and vice versa?

168 Record some political speeches at election time or at the annual party conferences, or consider party political slogans. Examine specifically the sound patterning that is used and how it reinforces the meaning. Look for ways in which subtle cues in the language help to differentiate the political persuasions of the different parties and/or how linguistic choices are made in order to appeal to particular sections of the electorate.

Lexical choice within texts

To work in this area, you need to be familiar with the field of semantics. Carter (1998) and Kearns (2000) provide good introductions to areas such as connotation and denotation, and to semantic relationships like synonymy, antonymy and hyponymy. Crystal (2003b) has a whole section on the lexicon and English vocabulary, including discussions on 'loaded' vocabulary (p. 170) and 'doublespeak' (p. 176).

A lexical analysis of style will ask: Why have these particular words been chosen and not others, and what are the connotations of the chosen words? For example, if *white* is mentioned, is it being used simply to indicate the colour of a physical object, or also to imply a sense of purity? (If the latter, there is a heavy cultural dependency, as white has different symbolism in different parts of the world.)

In newspaper reporting, the lexical choice of the journalist can indicate the ideological standpoint from which he/she is writing. Is a gunman described as a *terrorist*, a *guerrilla* or a *freedom fighter*? Was a victim *shot by a marksman* or *picked off by a sniper*? In fiction, the author's perspective and opinion of characters are often indicated through the choice of nouns, verbs and adjectives with positive or negative connotations. Consider this description of Zoltan Kaparthy's dancing, in the musical *My Fair Lady*: *Oozing charm from ev'ry pore, he oiled his way around the floor*. Carter and Nash (1990) focus on how individual characters are presented in Galsworthy's *The Man of Property* by analysing the way a dinner-party conversation is narrated. In an essay at the end of his novel *1984*, George Orwell explains in some detail how lexical choice can be manipulated as a tool of political and personal repression.

In Chapter 8 of Freeborn (1996), you can find a discussion of the notion of 'styleless prose', or that style which the semiologist Roland Barthes described as 'neutral writing'. Freeborn uses parts of Orwell's *Animal Farm*, Seth's *A Suitable Boy* and Camus's *The Outsider* to explore this from a grammatical and lexical perspective, and concludes that, while the stylistic details can differ greatly from one text to another, there is style in all texts.

Projects

169 Compare two translations of the same original text. By making different choices, the translators can create distinctly different texts. You can do a study of this sort even if you don't understand the original language: it is possible to compare the implications of the lexical and syntactic choices made by two translators of the same original text without any reference to that original, providing you don't want to make any judgement about which version is 'better'. To gain an idea of how two translations might differ, look at Short and Leech (2006), where, in 'Passages and Topics for Further Study', two translations of the first paragraph of Kafka's *The Trial* are juxtaposed.

170 Compare the way that writers achieve different effects from the same word. Choose something that is neutral enough to carry positive or negative connotations, e.g. *family*; *rain*; *compromise*. Add a dimension to your study by taking certain examples from across your texts and asking people with different backgrounds, ages and attitudes for their views on the use of the words. This will give you insights into how the reader as well as the writer can play a part in constructing meaning.

171 Are the words used in a given text largely of Latin or of Anglo-Saxon origin? Books on the history of the English language (see Chapter 10 for references) will give you some insights into the significance of this distinction, as well as how to spot the difference. Are the words in a text morphologically simple or complex, and what is the effect of this on the reader? Freeborn (1996) considers the effect of lexical choice by looking at different versions of part of the Sermon on the Mount from the Bible, and by looking at two translations of an extract from *The Swiss Family Robinson*. He also compares three versions of the first verses of St John's Gospel from different periods.

172 Find two or more texts on the same subject and see how *few* words they have in common and how they cover the same ideas in different words. For example, compare a poetical and a prose description of a tiger.

173 Find examples of words that have a particular meaning and resonance in advertising. Examples are *crispy*, which is used as a desirable attribute for processed food that is high in fat, and *creamy*, which is intended to give the impression of a luxury product (soup, soap, etc.). Try replacing the words with others that have a similar meaning (e.g. for these examples, *crisp*, *hard*, etc. and *thick*, *viscous*, etc.). Work out the boundaries of the words' use – which products are and are not so described – and, by interviewing informants, assess the precise connotations and images that the words create.

174 How do puns work? Collect examples of puns and show how the pun depends on multiple meanings for an individual lexical item. Carter (2004: 91) gives some examples. Ask informants to rate puns as to how funny they are, and analyse the funniest and unfunniest to see what it is about them that has this effect. Do adults and children have similar views?

Grammatical structure within texts

Specific effects can be achieved by using short sentences with a simple clause and phrase structure on the one hand, and long and complex sentences with many embedded clauses and phrases on the other. A structure may be repeated for effect, while a passive construction may enable the agent to remain unnamed. Useful guidance on basic clause and phrase structure can be found in Bloor and Bloor (2004) and in Freeborn (1995). You can find out how to apply this knowledge to text analysis in Freeborn (1996), as well as in Carter (1982, 2004), Fairclough (2001) and Fowler (1991). You should also read Chapter 5 in this book.

Questions you can ask when approaching text analysis from this angle include:

- ❑ Are the sentences of equal length and complexity throughout the text?
- ❑ Is the clause structure always neutral (unmarked), or have particular elements sometimes been emphasized by being placed at the beginning of the sentence or deliberately held back until the end?
- ❑ Have any structural patterns been created by cohesive devices such as repetition or ellipsis, anaphoric or cataphoric reference?
- ❑ Are any of these patterns then deliberately broken to create a particular effect?

Creating and then destroying a structural pattern is a technique employed by many writers to highlight a particular point, as this extract from *Yes, Prime Minister* (Lynn and Jay 1987: 107) illustrates:

The Times is read by the people who run the country.
The Daily Mirror is read by the people who think they run the country.
The Guardian is read by the people who think they ought to run the country.
The Morning Star is read by the people who think the country ought to be run by another country.
The Independent is read by the people who don't know who runs the country but are sure they are doing it wrong.
The Daily Mail is read by the wives of the people who run the country.
The Financial Times is read by the people who own the country.
The Daily Express is read by the people who think the country ought to be run as it used to be run.
The Daily Telegraph is read by the people who still think it is their country.
And the Sun's readers don't care who runs the country providing she has big tits.

Projects

175 Reading schemes for young children or EFL/SLA learners are often graded in terms of the structures used in the text. Examine the books in such a scheme. How precise is the grading? What effect does the limiting of available structures have on the flow of the text?

176 There are many simplified versions of classic texts for learners of English as a Foreign Language. How has the original text been modified in terms of structure? Ask some native and non-native speakers of English to compare the two and say which they prefer and why.

177 Compare old and recent versions of the Bible or a church liturgy. What differences are there in the grammar and form – or are the changes all lexical? Have the changes made the text more accessible?

178 Are business letters today written following the same grammatical conventions as, say, in the 1930s? Do the differences extend to personal letters and to public letters (e.g. to newspapers)? You can gain a sense of the differences by trying to rewrite a modern letter in 1930s style and vice versa.

179 Collect a series of different types of joke that rely on a formulaic structure and examine exactly how the discourse structure remains the same even though the detail differs. You might use *knock knock* jokes, or comic aphorisms such as *One sandwich short of a picnic, One can short of a six-pack,* and *Is the Pope a Catholic? Does a one-legged duck swim round in circles?* Ask members of the older generation to help you collect similar lists that have been popular in the past, such as *Old lecturers never die, they just lose their faculties, Old farmers never die, they just go to seed.* Once you have a type, you can search for further examples on the Internet (e.g. www.ahajokes.com/off40.html). Focus your analysis on questions such as: What makes a good and bad example of the set and why? How easy is it to create new items for the set? You could explore the second question by asking informants to do exactly that. What rules can you identify as implicitly underlying their choices?

180 As for Project 179, but focus on the extent to which children are able to understand the content and structure of such jokes. Try 8-year-olds and 11-year-olds. Check out Chapter 3 for guidance on developmental issues.

Interpersonal function of texts

Linguists recognize that not everything about a text is contained in its words and structures, because texts are received as well as produced. Thus, it is possible to ask what the effect of a text is (and is intended to be) on its readers or hearers. Why was the text produced in the first place? Sometimes this will be obvious, but quite often, particularly in advertising and in propaganda, the superficial aim of the text disguises a deeper message. For example, an advertisement that appears to be explaining how little servicing a particular car requires is, of course, actually trying to sell the car. A newspaper report of an event and an entry about the same event in a personal diary or a web log will read quite differently because they are written for different audiences, as will an account of that same event provided in a radio or television interview. G. Cook (2001) gives you some idea of how to approach advertisements as samples of individual texts, as well as indicating some of the more generic features of advertising. For ideas on how to tackle the analysis of propaganda, see Chilton (1985).

Projects

181 Choose a specific brand-named product and compare the way in which it is advertised in different places (print, radio, television, the Web). You will find most variation where there is fierce competition between brands and where the product is not in itself geared to a niche market. A good example is mobile phone advertising. How is the same product described differently for different readers in

the different media? Consider the extent to which the same individual is addressed differently according to the medium – does this somehow imply that he/she is perceived as having different interests or priorities simply by virtue of opening a magazine as opposed to a web page?

182 Compare texts in a single medium, on the same topic and for the same purpose, but from different countries. You could look at advertisements for the same product (say, the same make of car) or feature items in an internationally marketed magazine such as *Cosmopolitan* or *National Geographic*.

183 In a report in the UK daily newspaper, *The Guardian* (13 August 2005), a paragraph about Omar Bakri says:

> *To his enemies, he is the Preacher of Hate, the benefit-scrounging suicide bomber's cheerleader and a test of Tony Blair's resolve in the battle against terrorism. To his small band of followers, he is a distinguished Islamic scholar, a devoted family man persecuted in the same way as was the prophet Muhammad.*

Collect reports and discussions from different sides in some major or local political conflict and compare their use of language in accounts of the same event or issue. Decide which medium to draw from: newspapers, journals, radio, television and the Internet are all possible. You might want to draw on materials with an international circulation or audience such as *Time* and *New Statesman*, BBC World Service, CNN and so on. Remember to consider the collusion of readers and listeners/viewers in deliberately choosing to access one source rather than another, because they know or sense what ideology will be reflected. Keep focus in your project – a small quantity of text analysed carefully may gain you more credit than a superficial description of a larger amount.

184 Using the public library archives, compare the coverage of an event (such as an election or a disaster) 30 or 50 years ago with the coverage of a similar event much more recently. Look not only at the reports during the day or two after it, but also the coverage in the longer term. One comparison might be the disaster in 1966 in Aberfan, Wales and the shootings in Dunblane, Scotland in 1996, and Columbine High School in the USA in 1999, all of which resulted in the death of many children in their school building. How have styles of reporting changed, and how are the changes best characterized linguistically?

185 Travel texts can be a fruitful area for linguistic analysis. Compare descriptions of a specific location or hotel as found in a holiday brochure, a guidebook, or a diary, and on a postcard home.

186 For a piece of household equipment (such as a hi-fi, microwave, personal computer, mobile phone, or iPOD), compare the description in the manual with the one in the sales literature that is trying to persuade you to buy the item and, if appropriate, with the technical description for the engineer or installer.

187 Compare the style in which recipes for the same dish are written in a range of cookery books. Alternatively, choose any other activity that interests you and analyse any texts relevant to it. Aim to identify features that can be changed as an

in fact, for an actor to sound entirely 'natural' when speaking from a script. There are a number of reasons for this, including:

☐   the way a script is constructed: many of the features we associate with conversation are simply not found there;

☐   the purpose of a script: there is an external audience that needs to be given sufficient contextualization to understand what is going on;

☐   the non-spontaneity of a script: much of what makes spontaneous speech sound the way it does is that it is constructed at the time, while scripted speech is not. This affects the interaction between speakers too. In a script, each actor knows precisely when the next person will speak, whether there will be an interruption, and if so, who will win the turn and so on. This is entirely unlike most natural conversation, where these 'battles' have to be fought out at the time.

Some directors make a point of not using written scripts, but plan the 'route' of the conversation with the actors and allow them to ad lib until they have settled on a comfortable expression of the ideas.

Projects

203 Compare a scripted conversation from a radio play or a TV soap with a real one on a similar subject and taking place in a similar environment, perhaps from a fly-on-the-wall documentary. Write about the differences in the appearance of your two transcriptions and compare the way in which turns are taken and relinquished and topics are managed, and how those present contribute verbally outside their own turn.

204 Ask some actor friends to learn an extract from a play and to experiment with different ways of performing it so that it sounds as natural as possible. Allow them to try changing the words, improvising, and so on. Record their 'performances' and transcribe them. Ask some independent 'judges' to rate the recordings for naturalness. What characterizes the versions that are judged most natural? How might scriptwriters help the actors to perform more naturally? Include a commentary on the problems that arise in attempting to define and quantify naturalness in conversation.

205 From a film or a television or radio drama, focus on a stretch of conversation that seems particularly naturalistic. Assess what it is that gives it the appearance of naturalness, and identify the ways in which it is still not like real conversation. Are these 'shortfalls' intentional or accidental? In either case, why might they be unavoidable? Good places to look for improvised or semi-improvised dialogue are the films of Mike Leigh and some Woody Allen films. The comedians French and Saunders also sometimes improvise around a previously written script. You could also analyse the television show *The Office* from this perspective.

Radio and TV interviews

Since interviews tend to have a fairly predictable question-and-answer format, they can be an interesting opportunity to observe other aspects of conversational behaviour, particularly in relation to interruptions on both the interviewee's and the interviewer's parts.

Projects

206 Collect three or four conversations with the same political figure or personality, each conducted by a different interviewer. Compare not only the interviewing styles themselves, but also the ways in which the different interviewers draw different conversational behaviour out of the interviewee. Perhaps he/she is more argumentative in one interview than another, or interrupts more, or takes longer turns.

207 Collect a number of interviews (radio or TV) conducted by the same interviewer and compare the style of questioning used with different interviewees. What might be determining the contrasts? For instance, is it the way the interviewees present themselves, or whether or not they are being viewed as responsible for some problem as compared with offering a solution to it? Other issues that you might consider include: Does the interviewer remain neutral through the questioning or does his/her opinion(s) become apparent and, if so, how? Does the interviewer's style change from radio to TV?

208 Drawing on a live radio news and current affairs programme such as the BBC's *Today* on Radio 4 (www.bbc.co.uk/radio4), compare the way in which a chosen presenter copes with interviewing (a) a seasoned interviewee such as a politician; (b) a specific 'expert' who has been thrust into the media as a spokesperson for a current news item; and (c) a member of the public who probably has no experience of public speaking and no expertise to offer, but who has a 'bystander' or 'aggrieved victim' story to tell. How does the interviewer's management of conversational features vary in terms of such matters as aggression, insistence on pursuing a theme, putting words in the interviewee's mouth, and in opening and closing the whole event?

Electronically conveyed texts

There is considerable interest in how electronic communication is achieved linguistically. Although some kinds of communication are genuinely new in the electronic medium, most of what we do in email, phone texting and message posting on websites is simply a version of what we have always done, just using a new means. The language used in this new medium is therefore often a hybrid of the old and the new. For instance, the fact that we have a greeting at the start of an email and a signing-off at the end is an indication of the email's letter-writing origins. On the other hand, the embedding of a website address and the use of emoticons (smileys, etc.) to indicate attitude are not features of conventional writing. Now is a good time to research electronic communication, because a great many people who use it can remember the time before it was available and have memories about how they learned it, how it has changed, and so on. One way to observe recent developments is to compare older and newer publications about computer-mediated language. For instance, to what extent are the observations presented in Leech *et al.* (1995) still true?

Projects

209 Analyse emails, in relation to the following questions:

- ❏ How do writers choose to open/close the email? Do they use 'Dear *name*' or just start the message? How do they sign off? How do the emerging conventions compare and contrast with those of letter writing?

- ❏ Do writers use complete sentences or something resembling note-form? If the latter, how do they abbreviate the sentences? How do they ensure that the reader understands their meaning?

- ❏ Does the text of the emails resemble oral language or written language? How do you know?

- ❏ How is the formality dimension handled in emails (since many are somewhat formal, particularly in a work context)?

- ❏ How do email writers achieve some of the pragmatic purposes of language, e.g. does an emailed apology (or request or invitation) look/sound more like a spoken apology (request, invitation) or more like a written one? Is the same amount of background information provided in the email as in speech or in a letter?

- ❏ When writers use emoticons in emails, what is their role? Do they replace text in carrying meaning, do they add meaning that could not be expressed easily in text, or are they simply decoration? How do you know?

210 Look at a range of web pages on a single topic of your choice and compare how the language used on the websites differs from that in written documents on the same topic. In your view, are websites simply a new forum for providing the information previously, and alternatively, held in books and magazines? Does the evidence suggest that the linguistic nature of web material will gradually become more like that in books and magazines or less like it?

211 The language of texting is changing very fast and is having an effect on traditional paper-printed language (cf. Project 213). Gather a collection of text messages and analyse them in the terms outlined in this chapter: grammatical structure, lexical choice (including spelling and use of abbreviations and contractions and/or levels of formality).

Other project ideas

212 Look at the feedback provided in student assignments where the lecturer has chosen to comment on language use. What elements of language use are focused on in the feedback? Is the tutor adopting a prescriptive or descriptive approach? On what grounds might you agree (or not) with the tutor's comments on the student's language use? For detail about language attitudes, including prescriptive influences in teaching, see Edwards (2006).

213 Do you agree with the comment that 'mobile fone spk has gn 2 far' and that 'txt spk oftn apprs "inappropriately" in xms' (Bloomer *et al.* 2005: 217)? Ask people of different ages, educational background and gender their opinions on the present and future use of text language as a replacement for standard written English, and use their views to inform your own balanced debate of the issues. Include an evaluation of which situations txt lng might never be appropriate for, as well as those where it might soon be acceptable.

214 There are several means by which punchlines in jokes can be signalled as such, including text structure, timing, emphasis and intonation. But what about in comic songs? In a song, the text is constrained by the rhythm and often by rhyme patterns too, timing is dictated by the music, emphasis is difficult to separate from the natural rhythm and may be hard to achieve on a low or high-pitched note, and intonation is heavily constrained by the melody. Collect recordings of comic songs from the twentieth and twenty-first centuries (there are many classic performers to consider, including George Formby, Arthur Askey, Flanders and Swann, Jake Thackeray, and Victoria Wood). Analyse the means by which the punchline is made prominent, if it is. Play selected extracts to informants and ask them to judge how funny they find the line. Do you see a relationship between delivery and the effectiveness of the joke or are other factors in play as well?

7
Sociolinguistics

Sociolinguistics studies the relationship between language and society. Trudgill provides a good summary of some aspects of its coverage:

> Whenever we speak, we cannot avoid giving our listeners clues about our origins and the sort of person we are. Our accent and our speech generally show where we come from, and what sort of background we have. We may even give some indication of certain of our ideas and attitudes, and all of this information can be used by the people we are speaking with to help them formulate an opinion about us.
>   These two aspects of language behaviour are very important from a social point of view: first, the function of language in establishing social relationships; and, second, the role played by language in conveying information about the speaker. (Trudgill 2000: 2)

Sociolinguistics has been a thriving area within linguistics since the 1960s and there are now numerous sub-areas within it. It would be impossible to summarize them all in a single chapter, but you will gain a feel for the subject here, and should follow up leads in the books recommended below. In addition, remember the chapters in this book on language and gender, accents and dialects and style, all of which border on and link into this area. Chapters 13 and 14 are also important reading before you embark on a project in sociolinguistics. Themes and questions in sociolinguistics include:

❒   How and why do accents and dialects develop?
❒   Is there a link between a speaker's use of regional accents or dialects and his/her social characteristics (e.g. age, gender, social background and ethnicity)?
❒   What is the relationship between 'standard' and 'non-standard' accents and dialects?
❒   How do we decide what is a dialect or accent and what is a language?
❒   What do people's attitudes towards accents, dialects and other aspects of language use tell us, and why are some accents, dialects or languages, and their speakers, perceived in particular ways? How accurate are these perceptions when compared with other types of evidence?
❒   How does language change across time and geographical areas?
❒   How and why does language vary from one social context (situation) to another?

❏ What happens when languages come into contact, or when speakers of a country need to use more than one language on a regular basis (bilingualism or multilingualism)?

❏ How do 'pidgins' and 'creoles' come into existence? Are they more like dialects or languages?

❏ Why do speakers sometimes change their accent, dialect or even the language spoken when in conversation with others, and what sorts of changes do they make?

❏ How do speakers signal their identity in the language they use, and why do people who live in specific communities sometimes speak in a similar way?

❏ What is the link between language and disadvantage (e.g. the language of minority groups) or language and power/powerlessness?

Terminology and central concepts

Within sociolinguistics there is a division into **micro** and **macro** research. **Microlinguistic** studies 'typically focus on very specific linguistic items or individual differences' in language use and look for 'wide-ranging linguistic and/or social implications (e.g. the distribution of *singing* and *singin'*)' (Wardhaugh 2006: 17). They often involve the detailed study of interpersonal communication. **Macrolinguistic** studies, on the other hand, 'examine large amounts of language data to draw broad conclusions about group relationships' (Wardhaugh 2006: 17–18) and relate these to social factors. Aspects of bilingualism, multilingualism and language planning are issues that often fall under this heading.

The roots of sociolinguistics lie in the work of key figures such as William Labov, often referred to as the 'father of sociolinguistics', who has conducted studies in **modern (urban) dialectology**. Some of the techniques used in sociolinguistics for collecting data (such as questionnaires and interviews) stem from the older field of **traditional dialectology** (**rural dialectology** or **dialect geography**). However, traditional dialectology largely ignored social variation: few young or female informants were used and town-dwellers were excluded, since their dialect was thought to be too new or inconsistent to reflect the older forms of 'pure' dialect that researchers assumed existed. Language change was to some extent the enemy of traditional dialectologists rather than their focus, since it 'muddied the waters' in their search for older forms.

An essential characteristic of language is **variation**. While some approaches within linguistics (such as Chomsky's) expressly do not focus on *variation* in language, but rather on its structural properties and rules (linked to 'linguistic competence'), *socio*linguistics studies how speakers use language *appropriately*, in terms of what Dell Hymes first called **communicative competence**: 'when to speak, when not, and ... what to talk about with whom, when, where, in what manner' (1971: 277). In other words, sociolinguists stress that language varies not only in the sense that words can be combined together to form an infinite number of sentences or longer discourses, but also **systematically**, according to a range of factors such as age, sex, background of speaker, and the situation or social context where the language is used (see below).

Language variation can be approached from a number of angles, including: what the variation consists of, which groups display it, in which situations it occurs, and the approaches that can be taken to its analysis. Language features that vary in precise form from speaker to speaker are known as **linguistic variables**. The detailing and analysing of linguistic variables require tools such as orthographic and phonetic transcription, and draw on the research techniques of conversation analysis, phonetic, phonological and structural analysis, discourse analysis and so on. The *causes* of variation are known as **extralinguistic variables** and where there is a relationship between linguistic and extralinguistic variables, this is sometimes referred to as **co-variation**.

We can identify three main types of extralinguistic variable: speaker, group and situation. The sorts of speaker characteristic that are a backdrop to variation include age, gender, ethnic origin, social background, regional origin, level of education, occupation and religious persuasion. If variation exists between the language varieties of two or more groups, the sociolinguist needs to identify a pre-existing group membership. He/she might decide there are grounds for saying that these people belong to this group and as a result speak differently. Alternatively, there may be evidence that people belong to a group only by virtue of the fact that they speak differently.

Group variation can shed light on **language change**. Labov tried to demonstrate that, contrary to earlier beliefs, it is possible to see language change in progress, if you know where to look. The variability in language use found within a community of speakers and uncertainty about what constitutes 'correct' or acceptable usage often give clues to what aspects of language may change in the future.

Situational variables are observable where the same person speaks differently in different environments. Studying language from this angle often means thinking about the role or function that language is playing in a situation. This, in turn, means that you can gauge the status and mutual familiarity of speakers and their reasons for needing to communicate, from the style or **register** that they use. Consider, for example, how a politician might speak to his parliamentary colleagues and to prospective voters. The linguistic variation might be seen in the manner of address, including the use of colloquialisms, jargon, and regionalisms, in the selection of topic and examples, and in the level of detail.

Textbooks and major journals

Holmes (2001) and Romaine (2000) are introductory textbooks that will set the scene. Coulmas (1998), Eckert and Rickford (2002), Paulston and Tucker (2003) and Coupland and Jaworski (2006) are readers or edited collections containing classic papers that have shaped the field and/or specially commissioned articles from prominent contemporary researchers. Stockwell (2002) provides many valuable resources that could inspire projects, as may the discussion questions in Coulmas (2005). For methodological guidance, Milroy and Gordon (2003) will be useful.

Check for a sociolinguistic perspective on child language, second-language acquisition, conversation and so on. For journals relating to those areas, see the relevant chapters in this book. Useful journals for projects in sociolinguistics include the following:

JOURNALS

English World-Wide: A Journal of Varieties of English
International Journal of the Sociology of Language
Journal of Politeness Research: Language, Behaviour, Culture
Journal of Sociolinguistics
Journal of Social Psychology
Language and Communication
Language and Intercultural Communication
Language in Society
Language Variation and Change
Multilingua

Central themes and project ideas

Quantitative approaches

One of the key features of linguistic variables is that they can often be counted or **quantified**. For example, a group of speakers' pronunciations of /t/ in words like *better* and *bottle* can be scored according to whether they use the 'standard' [t], the 'non-standard' glottal stop [ʔ] or something in between. Scores for different sexes, social backgrounds, or age groups can then be compared to see whether there are consistent patterns of usage by different groups. Features in the speech of the same person in different situations can also be counted and compared. Labov devised a means of eliciting five different **speech styles** in interview situations. He elicited a careful or formal style by asking subjects to read 'minimal pairs' (pairs of words which differ by just one key sound – see Chapter 16), and gained increasingly less formal styles from, respectively, read lists of words, read passages, careful and casual conversation.

The **Labovian paradigm** is the name given to Labov's framework and classification. It provides a methodology for sampling speech styles and is heavily associated with the quantitative studies of accent features that he conducted in the United States, especially in Martha's Vineyard and New York City (Labov 1972). Trudgill's (1972, 1974) work on Norwich speech adopted the same paradigm. Trudgill gathered subjects' responses to recordings of particular words, pronounced with accents ranging from RP to broad local ones, and compared these to the tally of features in their own spontaneous language. He was able to demonstrate that women often 'over-reported', claiming that they used pronunciations that were nearer to RP more frequently than they actually did, whereas men often 'under-reported'. Trudgill concluded that the men and women had different notions of 'prestige language'.

When deciding which features to study, check in the published literature for information on the most characteristic features of that accent or dialect. For example, Trudgill (1974) looked at *-ing* in Norwich speech (see above) and Cheshire (1978) looked at forms of *do* (among other things) used by Reading teenagers. A good source for pronunciation features in various accents of British English is Hughes and Trudgill (2005), and for non-British English, Trudgill and Hannah (2002) or Melchers and Shaw (2003) (see Chapter 9). Vowel pronunciations (**continuous** variables) are more 'fluid' and can therefore be very difficult to distinguish and score for. Consonants, especially where you are simply listening for their presence or absence (as in /h/ dropping on words like *hammer*), are often easier to handle and score. Reduce extralinguistic variation by using subjects who are as similar as possible in all respects except for the one you are interested in.

Projects

215 Select one or more features in a variety that has previously been researched and conduct a replication study to see if the same patterns still hold. If they do not, consider social and other reasons why this might be the case.

216 Undertake a study of the pronunciation and/or dialect features of a group of speakers, eliciting samples of language from them, using methodology similar to that of Labov or another researcher (see Como 2006 for an overview of approaches). This should yield information on how the speakers actually use language. Then, by replicating an aspect of Trudgill's work (see above), investigate the speakers' attitudes to the accent, to ascertain whether these are linked to current changes in the local accent or dialect.

217 Compare two varieties of international English, taking account of the social and historical forces that have brought about the differences. To what extent has the 'new' variety of English taken on systematic new forms that are causing it to diverge from British, American, or other varieties of English? Are these divergences more marked in younger or older speakers? Are they more marked in men or women? For information on features of international English, see Trudgill and Hannah (2002) or Melchers and Shaw (2003). Jenkins (2003) and Edwards (2004) also cover English in the international context.

Social networks

One of the criticisms of Labov's work was that he concentrated too heavily on collecting data from rather superficially defined 'social class' groupings. The concepts of 'social groups', 'speech communities', and, moreover, 'social networks', were borrowed from the social sciences by sociolinguists such as Gumperz (e.g. 1982). Gumperz's aim was to find ways of showing how language use was linked with membership and allegiance to certain clearly defined social *groups* (such as adolescent peer groups, unusually tight-knit communities, and so on), rather than 'classes'. Speakers often, consciously or unconsciously, use language to convey their social identity, so members of a group may sound alike in their speech. Sounding alike also helps groups to seem distinctive when compared with others. The concept of social networks is explained very simply in Coates (2004, Ch. 5). More detail is given in Wardhaugh (2006, Ch. 5), and especially Milroy (1987; Milroy and Milroy 1978), whose study of Belfast pronunciation was based on the social network framework. Where large-scale studies, such as Labov's New York City work, lose the profiles of individuals in the group scores, this approach allows a much closer examination of the individual and is far more ethnographic in nature.

Projects

218 Labov (1972), Cheshire (1978, 1982) and Milroy (1987) all observed how language can be used, even at a subconscious level, as a 'badge' of belonging. Focusing on a group in your own life (or known to someone close to you), collect data that can enable you to judge whether commitment to the group affects individual members' language. You may be able to judge how central a member someone is by the strength or frequency with which the group's speech forms are used (e.g. catch phrases, special vocabulary or grammatical structures). Many types of groups may be appropriate for this kind of study, but groups that share an ideology or specialist knowledge, or who have a strong motivation for seeming 'different', should be particularly fruitful. Possibilities include sports and hobby clubs, and religious, political and environmental action groups.

219 Make a study of a family that is well known to you. Examine specific language features used by different members of the family and compare them. To what extent can differences be attributed to different group membership? Are there any *similarities* that might relate to the family being a group in its own right?

Qualitative approaches

Qualitative approaches, by definition, involve description and analysis rather than, for example, the counting of features. They often have much in common with linguistic work on discourse and pragmatics (see Chapters 5 and 6). The emphasis is on exploring the types of strategy that particular speakers use in specific contexts with particular people. For example, how does a hospital consultant or GP (a 'high-status participant'), inform a patient that he/she must take more exercise or stop smoking? Is it achieved by negotiation (e.g. *Could you try to take some exercise? Do you think your smoking is affecting your health?*) or more directly (e.g. *You need to stop smoking and lose weight now*)?

This kind of research often involves longer-term observation, very detailed and close perusal of the data, and relatively small numbers of subjects. Findings can therefore only be said to hold true for that particular group until comparative work can be undertaken with other groups. Some researchers feel that purely qualitative approaches lack the rigour of research supported by frequency figures. They feel that, without such figures, no generalizations about trends in language usage can be made. Others, however, feel that the process of eliciting data suitable for counting and comparisons may prevent truly 'natural' and spontaneous language from being produced (the 'observer's paradox' – see Chapter 1).

It is possible to combine elements of all the approaches. Cheshire, in her social-network research with teenagers in Reading (Cheshire 1982), not only examined the frequency of certain types of language structure (such as *you was* as opposed to *you were*) but also explored how these forms were used by individuals on particular occasions. Cheshire was able to show a connection between one speaker's use of vernacular forms and his/her central position in one of the teenage gangs.

Projects

220 Document the key daily routines in the lives of recent immigrants to your country or region. What part does language (in general, or one language in particular) play in these routines? Are special registers (or styles) of language used for particular activities (such as religious worship, speaking to elders)?

221 Focusing on **diglossia** (the use by a whole community of different languages or distinct language varieties in different situations), make a study as described in Project 220, but looking at the way in which your subjects switch between languages during their day according to where they are and what they are doing.

222 Investigate the phenomena of **code-switching** (where bilingual speakers switch between their two languages on the basis of topic and/or addressee) and **code-mixing** (where they mix languages within a single conversation or even a single sentence). What appears to determine when they use each language? For further information, see Appel and Muysken (1987), Romaine (1995) or Li Wei (2000).

223 Make a study of how a language or a language variety under threat from a dominant surrounding language or variety interfaces with that dominant language or variety. For example, if you know Welsh, use data from Welsh TV and radio programmes to examine borrowing from English. What kinds of words are borrowed from the dominant language and why do you think this happens? Your study could incorporate both quantitative and qualitative techniques.

224 Study the linguistic behaviour of individuals who operate together in more than one domain with different power relationships. For instance, you might look at the interaction between a shopkeeper who is also a non-stipendiary church leader and one or more individuals who are both customers and parishioners. Alternatively, you could study how a schoolteacher interacts on parents' evening with a parent who is also his/her heating engineer or pharmacist. You will need to observe interactions in both contexts to establish how variation in the power dimension is expressed. For information on language and power, see Thomas and Wareing (1999) and Fairclough (2001). Specifically in an institutional setting, see Thornborrow (2002).

Other project ideas

225 Focusing your project on language change, collect samples of written and/or spoken English, and look for aspects of usage about which people seem unsure (what might be termed 'inconsistent usage'). Obvious examples are constructions such as *would of, could of* instead of the standard *would have, could have*, and the linking of words in writing, as in the case of *aswell, alot* (see also Project 157). How frequently do the constructions appear in your sample? Who uses them? Are they more common in written as opposed to spoken language? Why might they be occurring, and is there any reason to believe that they indicate language change? Your study could incorporate both quantitative and qualitative techniques.

226 Embed some examples of non-standard usage in sentences or paragraphs and present the texts to a range of 'judges' selected carefully with respect to such characteristics as age, gender, background or regional origins. Ask if the language samples are acceptable to them and if not, where the problems are and how they would resolve them. How similar are people's attitudes and identifications of what is problematic? Decide in advance whether you want your data to be quantitative, qualitative or both, and use the appropriate techniques (see Chapters 13 and 14). For examples of similar types of study, see Freeborn *et al.* (1993, Ch. 1).

227 Over a period of at least several months, examine the linguistic behaviour of a recently arrived non-native speaker in an English-speaking area. What patterns emerge regarding the situations where English is used? Does your subject cope with the distinction between colloquial and formal language?

228 Undertake a primarily qualitative study of the language used with elderly people. To what extent does it resemble the 'carer talk' used with children (see Chapter 3) or 'foreigner talk'? Does the selection of this 'register' seem necessary for successful communication in the situations where it is used? You might ascertain this by finding out whether *all* people speaking to an elderly person appear to see the need for features of this register to make themselves understood and whether elderly people seem to understand less well when the features are not used. What does your study tell you about how elderly people are viewed by society? For fuller discussion of language and the elderly, see Coupland *et al.* (1991) and Nussbaum and Coupland (2004).

229 Make a study of language and power by observing the forms of address or politeness strategies used in one of the following situations: a university tutorial setting; transactions at a bar, shop or some other form of agency. What range of linguistic structures or strategies is used? Are there any patterns regarding which types of people are most polite? Determining factors might be: age, apparent social status or occupation, gender and so on. If you have the means of recording and analysing them, extend your study to include intonational features or paralinguistic features such as gesture or facial expression. Your study could incorporate both quantitative and qualitative techniques.

230 Explore the ways in which dress affects the way people speak to someone. Visit several times a range of shops selling a particular product (e.g. jewellery, cars or bikes, furniture, antiques) but, each time you go, wear different styles of clothing (smart and elegant, casual, scruffy). Keep notes on key features in the language used in addressing you: are you given a title such as 'sir' or 'madam'? How direct are enquiries? How solicitous and complimentary are staff towards you when you

take interest in a particular product? Spread your visits out over a month or so, so that there is less likelihood of being recognized by the sales assistants. You might want to persuade a friend to 'act' as the customer so that you can observe closely what happens and then make notes later.

231 Investigate the attitudes of some carefully selected subjects towards language varieties by surveying their reactions to particular accents. This could involve using the 'matched guise technique' (see Chapter 13).

232 We know that many people have a 'telephone voice'. People often adapt their pronunciation to fit particular situations and/or to blend in with other speakers. The latter, in particular, is **convergence** – part of what linguists call **accommodation**. The opposite of this is called **divergence** – when someone changes their accent or dialect (or even their language choice) on a specific occasion in order to distance themselves from the people they are among. Collect samples of a subject's language from several situations in which contrasting varieties of English are used by the other speakers involved. Observe the extent to which your subject converges with or diverges from the language of the others present. One way to do this would be to ask someone to tape their telephone conversations for a week, using their home answering machine. (Allow your subject to delete any conversations that they consider too personal or private in nature.) Avoid revealing until afterwards the true focus of your interest in the data, as knowing what you are looking for may affect the way your subject speaks. Look for things like style-shifting between the subject's initial phone-answering style and his/her subsequent accent and dialect use, as he/she accommodates to the language variety used by the caller. For more information on accommodation, see Bell (2006).

233 The language used to talk about taboo topics can be very interesting. How are death notices or obituaries written and how do they differ from each other? Are they written in all cultures and if so, are they written in the same way?

234 What euphemistic terms are there for discussing taboo topics? In what social contexts are the euphemisms used as opposed to the direct terms? To what extent are the euphemisms metaphors and what is the source of the metaphor?

235 There has been a lot of work done on linguistic politeness but what about linguistic rudeness? You might like to explore the language use of fictional characters such as Basil Fawlty (from the BBC sitcom *Fawlty Towers*) and compare it with everyday rudeness. Anne Robinson often appears rude to contestants in *The Weakest Link* on BBC TV. What is it about her use of language that makes her appear rude?

236 In discussions of religion, how do believers and non-believers signal their position through language? Bring together socially some people who do not know each other and engineer a discussion of some religious or spiritual issue (e.g. reincarnation; religious foundation schooling; whether empty churches should be sold off as houses, etc.). Record the conversation and identify how individuals use language to position themselves and check where others stand.

237 Over the course of a week or two, attend the meetings of a number of organizations that you are not a member of, such as a hockey-club training, a

church service, an environmental action group meeting, an evening class or a discussion group. What language is used that is unfamiliar to you as an outsider and do the members make assumptions about your own use of that language? How does their use of language with you minimize or maximize your identity as an outsider?

8

Language and gender

Gender is just one of many variables that linguists consider when they examine the conscious and unconscious choices that we make in relation to our linguistic behaviour. We have singled it out for its own chapter because it is a particularly fruitful topic for researchers and a good focus for a project. Among the questions addressed by research into language and gender are:

- In what ways do males and females use language differently (e.g. grammar, pronunciation, vocabulary choice, amount of talk, topics selected for talk, strategies selected in conversation, use of taboo words, politeness, accuracy in written language)?
- Are the patterns equally observable in all societies?
- Do males and females speak differently in single-sex groups and mixed groups?
- What are people's attitudes towards male and female language, how do they relate to the genuine observable differences found through research, and are they changing?
- How are males and females portrayed as communicators in literature, commercials, comedy and so on?
- What happens to individuals whose language does not fit the popular stereotype of how a man or a woman should behave?
- What is the role of gender differences in linguistic change?
- What is linguistic sexism, where does it exist, and why?
- Can political correctness change people's attitudes and behaviour regarding language and sexism?
- How do children learn to speak and write appropriately for their gender?
- How does the linguistic signalling of sexual orientation relate to gender stereotypes?

Terminology

In the context of language and gender research, gender is not just a synonym for sex: 'Sex refers to a biological distinction, while gender is the term to describe socially constructed categories based on sex' (Coates 2004: 4). That is, 'Generally speaking, gender-linked patterns of language-use arise not because men and women are naturally different, but because of the way that difference is made significant in the organization of social life and social relations' (Cameron 2006: 733).

Textbooks and major journals

Introductions to language and gender include Litosseliti (2006), Coates (2004) and Talbot (1998). Eckert and McConnell-Ginet (2003) develops ideas beyond the introductory level. Holmes and Meyerhoff (2003) and Coates (1998a) are readers containing many useful key papers. Coates's (2003) account of male talk balances the recent focus on women talk, including in her own earlier book (Coates 1996). Curzan (2003) takes a historical perspective. Sunderland (2004) examines the features of discourse about gender. Cameron and Kulick (2003) include consideration of gay language, and Leap and Boellstorff (2003) focus on gay language worldwide. For project ideas, try Goddard and Patterson (2000) or Sunderland (2005).

Because of the broad scope of the area, there are many journals where papers on language and gender issues might appear. Gender is often the focus of a special issue, as with *Journal of Pragmatics* volume 38, issue 1 (2006), on gender and humour. Useful journals for projects on language and gender include the following:

JOURNALS

Applied Linguistics
Gender and Language
Journal of Language and Social Psychology
Journal of Pragmatics
Journal of Sociolinguistics
Language and Communication
Language and Education
Language in Society
Merrill-Palmer Quarterly
Psychology of Women Quarterly
Women's Studies International Forum

Central themes and project ideas

Due to the popularity of projects in language and gender, certain topics have been 'done to death'. Look for a focus that can add something new, no matter how small, to the field. Discussion with a tutor should help with this.

The gender variable in linguistic research

In spite of their training, many linguists in the past were not curious about gender differences in language, sometimes because they allowed themselves to be influenced by popular opinions on female language (see *Attitudes towards male and female language* below). Coates (2004) gives a good overview of some of the main themes, particularly in

Chapters 2 and 3. Chambers and Trudgill (1998) give coverage on the methods of traditional and urban dialectology.

The first studies of gender differences in language were formal studies. Formal studies place emphasis on quantitative techniques, relatively small units of language (sounds, words), large groups of subjects about whom comparatively little is known, and relatively small samples of speech collected from a fairly restricted range of situations, using structured questions in an interview format. Formal studies are now less popular than studies focusing on interaction between speakers of one or both genders.

Projects

238 Look in detail at some of the material from a major linguistic survey, such as the *Survey of English Dialects*, and examine the extent to which the questionnaires reflected issues of interest or relevance to women. Many university libraries have copies of the full survey and related publications.

239 Contact researchers who have worked on published surveys that have taken gender as a variable. Try to establish where their motivation for studying gender comes from and how they view early work in the field. Study their results in order to gauge the extent to which the gender variable has been a fruitful focus for our understanding of language more generally.

240 Survey recent books and journal articles to find out what the most popular issues in language and gender research currently are. You could combine this with a survey of the questions and approaches followed in these studies. Write a critical comparative evaluation of the issues and how they are researched, aimed at establishing the extent to which gender, as just one variable, has gained disproportionate attention or simply what was needed to redress a previous imbalance.

Attitudes towards male and female language

Gender-based attitudinal research involves looking not so much at real language use as at society's perceptions, attitudes, and stereotypes of it: sometimes termed 'folk-linguistic beliefs'. If attitudes and stereotypes are not based on truth, how and why have they arisen? Do they exert any influence on how males and females acquire or use language?

Use Coates (2004, Chs 2 and 3) as a starting point for information on gender-related language attitudes in Western society. Niedzielski and Preston (2003) cover language and gender from the folk-linguistics perspective.

Projects

241 Using Coates (2004, Chs 2 and 3) as a reference resource, survey key writings of prominent authors, commentators and early linguists, to investigate the kinds of opinions that were held concerning male and female language. Supplement this with general reading from books about language written in the nineteenth and early twentieth centuries. Identify one or two specific linguistic features from these sources and carry out your own survey of current attitudes towards them.

242 If you have contacts with native speakers of other languages, especially if they are from markedly contrasting cultures, probe their perceptions of male and female language, at the same time asking about wider beliefs in their culture. This may involve using some kind of structured interview technique or questionnaire (see Chapter 13 in this book).

243 What do children think of adult male and female speech, and at what age are their perceptions strongest? Again, Coates (2004) can provide some orientation. Source studies include Edelsky (1976).

244 On the basis of what the research literature identifies as strongly and mildly indicative features of male and female written language, assemble some short tests and give them to male and female informants. Can they tell which are which? Ask them to write commentaries on their decisions so that you can see what they are homing in on.

245 How is male and female speech portrayed in novels, cartoons, or TV and radio drama? Investigating these issues can be an oblique way of asking questions about society's attitudes. One source reference for cartoons is Kramer (1974). Smith (1985) has summary coverage of relevant issues.

246 Replicate or adapt Trudgill's (1972) study of male and female speech. He found that women tended to think they used standard forms more than their real language data showed they did, whereas men did the opposite. The roles of males and females in society have changed since then – will that lead to different results? For similar ideas, but with a different slant, see Projects 216 and 248.

Gender differences in accent and dialect

Several key studies, such as Labov (1966) and Trudgill (1974), have identified certain groups of women as the driving force behind pronunciation change within their communities, and have provided insights into the different models of prestige which males and females adopt, as well as helping to shape a picture of how and why accents change. Cheshire (1978) studied non-standard verb forms used by three adolescent peer groups (two male, one female) in Reading, 'hanging out' with the groups and becoming accepted by them. Cheshire saw how the girls and boys became socialized into their adult roles and linguistic patterns. This type of approach, because it takes the emphasis away from gender differences and places it on gender 'behaviour', legitimizes studies that look at only one of the sexes. See also 'Gay language' below, where research into the dialect *Polari* is mentioned.

Projects

247 Conduct a study of your local dialect, paying attention to the gender dimension. Replicate or adapt the methodology of one of the key studies, and write about the particular problems encountered in making the adaptation and/or in collecting representative data from both sexes.

248 Much of what we know about male and female dialect patterns stems from work done more than 30 years ago. Social conditions have changed markedly since then. Conduct your own survey of male and female language and compare your findings with those of an older study in the same locality. You will need to gather information on any changes in lifestyle, employment, population (immigration and emigration, for example) that might have led to changes in the roles of males and females with a corresponding change in their language.

Differences in conversation and style of language use

Studies following this theme tend to focus on differences in **communicative competence**, i.e. broad features of language use, including the issue of *appropriate* language use (Coates 2004: 85ff.). One central question is that of whether males and females have different models of communicative competence, such that there are identifiably male and female 'styles'.

One of the pioneer studies in this area was Lakoff (1975). She proposed a set of so-called **women's language** features. Although Lakoff's list was based largely on her intuitions and informal observations of friends rather than on systematically gathered evidence, it was for many years a starting point for other studies that set out to find empirical evidence for or against the existence of these features. One informative 'spin-off' study is published as Chapter 7 in Coates and Cameron (1989). Other key sources include Kramarae (1981), Maltz and Borker (1982/1998) and Thorne and Henley (1975).

Lakoff's work has encouraged and inspired research in several areas. One is gender patterns in conversational styles and strategies, including turn-taking, topic selection and control, minimal responses (also known as backchannel behaviour or sympathetic circularity), interruption and overlapping speech, and the initiation and ending of conversation. Studies have tended to find that women are far less domineering in conversation and tend to favour co-operative or supportive participation. Coates (2004) provides an excellent starting point on these issues. Coates (1996) gives a more detailed account of women's talk, while Johnson and Meinhof (1996) and Coates (2003) examine men's talk.

Politeness also reveals gender patterns. Although 'politeness' clearly involves more than saying 'please', 'may I', and so on, writers differ in what they put under this heading. Holmes (1995) considers 'hedges' and 'tag questions', apologies and compliments as politeness features, whereas Coates (2004), for example, sometimes classifies them differently. Findings on these features have usually suggested that women use more politeness strategies than men. As regards **talkativeness**, Western society often stereotypes women as the more talkative gender. However, research has frequently indicated that this is not the case. Summaries of key studies on these issues can be found in Coates (2004: Ch. 6) and Spender (1998). Coates and Cameron (1989: Ch. 8) and Johnson and Meinhof (1996) cover 'gossip' from female and male perspectives respectively, and Talbot (2003) examines it as a gender stereotype. See also Coates (1998b). **Swearing and taboo language** is another of Lakoff's themes where folk-linguistic beliefs seem to be undermined by research findings. Both genders seem to swear more in single-sex company than in mixed, but there is only limited evidence to support the view that men swear more than females overall (see Coates 2004: Ch. 6).

Projects

249 Are there gender differences in forms of address? Brouwer *et al.* (1979) investigated politeness and forms of address used by males and females at the ticket office of Amsterdam Central Station. Both ticket sellers and customers were studied. Find an environment where you could collect data from a large number of transactional exchanges (do you know anyone who owns a shop or works in a bar and can give you permission to observe or record exchanges?). You might find yourself looking at a relatively small range of speech features and variations, but your work would have a clear focus and the features would be easy to count. Remember to consider the ethics of recording in specific environments (are you likely to capture material which you shouldn't record without the speaker's consent?) and problems with background noise if you are using a tape recorder (see Chapter 11).

250 Observe a mixed group of friends, and examine the frequency of swearing, the 'strength' of the terms used (this could be evaluated by a questionnaire to the subjects after recording), and the word classes that swearwords typically occupy (such as noun, verb, or adjective). Are there male–female differences in any of these criteria? McEnery (2005) is a good source of information.

251 Is it true that female students swear a lot, relative to male students? Do a gender-controlled survey of what your informants consider to be swearing. When might they use swearwords and of what strength? Ask them to characterize their own swearing behaviour and that of other people in your survey (assuming they know each other). Are there male–female differences in the way that people admit to swearing, and characterize swearing in others? Remember that neither a person's own evaluation nor that of others actually tells you how much a person really swears – to find that out, you would need to observe their discourse.

252 To examine single- and mixed-sex conversational strategies, try the following procedure. Ask a small group of mutual friends, half of them male and the other

female, to your house for a meal. Ask the females to arrive earlier than the males (or vice versa) and record their conversation. When the other gender group arrives, record some mixed-sex conversation and, at some point, arrange for the first group to leave the room. You can then record the second group talking. This methodology has the advantage of using the same informants for each gender in both the single- and mixed-sex interactions, and gives you data sets from the same time and context. Remember the ethical issues involved in recording people's speech – you will have to tell them afterwards what you have done, and give them the option of withdrawing from the study. To help them agree to stay in it, reassure them that you will replace names in your transcripts, and remove anything that might be hurtful or embarrassing (e.g. what was said about someone when they were out of the room).

Gay language

Studies of gay and lesbian language are increasingly common. See Coates (2004: Ch. 12) for an overview, and Livia and Hall (1997) and Baker (2005) for studies. At the interface of gender and dialect studies, Baker (2002) tells the story of Polari, a secret language among male homosexuals in the twentieth century.

Projects

253 Do your own study of Polari, using Baker's (2002) book and his web resources at www.ling.lancs.ac.uk/staff/paulb/polari/home.htm. Assemble examples of sentences containing words from Polari and ask informants to explain their meaning. Look for patterns regarding the words that are generally known and those that are not. Do gay informants know more Polari words than non-gay informants do?
254 Adapt Project 252 to focus on gay discourse.

Explanations of difference

There have been various explanations of gender differences in language, starting with claims (since refuted) about the mental or cognitive inferiority of women. Subsequent explanations were less judgemental but suggested that biologically programmed tendencies or properties might account for the differences (see Coates 2004: Ch. 3). However, researchers generally agree that most differences (those relating to language acquisition are one possible exception) are culturally determined (Cameron 2006: 733).

Accounts in the 1960s and 1970s focused on women's status in society. Trudgill (1972) suggested that women's greater tendency to use prestige forms was the result of the profile of their lives: they were less likely to be able to signal their status via their occupation, so they signalled it through the way they spoke. Lakoff (1975) suggested that women's social inequality made them unassertive, and her work has become associated with so-called 'dominance' explanations. Some women reacted to this viewpoint by trying to eliminate the 'female' characteristics from their language style and by striving to be more assertive, which often meant copying male speech strategies. O'Barr and Atkins (1980/1998) used data from courtrooms to suggest that Lakoff's features related not to gender but to status, and proposed that they be renamed **powerless language**. However, subsequent research has challenged this (see Coates 2004: Ch. 6).

In the 1980s, there was some re-evaluation of the features of **women's language**. Coates, for example, has stressed the co-operative (rather than weak or unassertive) nature of female style (see Coates 2004: Ch. 6; Coates 1996; Coates and Cameron 1989; Cameron 1995). This links with accounts of how children are pushed towards different interactional styles by socialization in predominantly single-sex groups (see Maltz and Borker 1982/1998). In making sense of all these explanations, one very useful framework to be aware of is Tajfel's theory of inter-group relations and social change (e.g. Tajfel and Turner 1986).

Projects

255 Investigate the language of an informant who has an untypical male lifestyle (for example, acting as prime child-carer). Does he display any of the characteristics of the typically female co-operative style? If so, is the style 'female' at all, or just the product of a social role, and is he displaying female language because of his role or does he find the role more comfortable than most men because of his 'female side'?

256 Examine the discourse of a female informant who has reached a powerful position in a male-dominated work environment. Collect data from situations in which she is heavily outnumbered by male colleagues of equal or higher status and also from professional interactions with women only. Do your results suggest that she is 'in disguise' when she interacts with men? Or is it the power dimension rather than a gender one that is operating?

Language and sexism

Sexist language can be found in adverts, film dialogue, posters, comedy, many types of written document and conversation. Some sexism is inherent in language, such as the generic *he* in English. Graddol and Swann (1989: 110) point out that English 'has no direct feminine equivalent of *virility*' to reflect female sexual potency. Some research investigates how derogatory or potentially patronizing terms are applied to women. One antidote to sexism in language has been political correctness, in which deliberate linguistic choices are made to raise awareness of entrenched biases.

Projects

257 Investigate the origins of forms of address used to males and females. Ask informants for their perceptions of the connotations of different forms and compare their responses with what you have discovered about the forms' histories. Map out trajectories over time for how individual forms may have changed their meaning. Read about language change to establish what the role of political correctness has been, or may yet be, on the use of the forms.

258 Investigate the assumptions made about gender for people in certain jobs. Examples would be a nurse, cleaner, mechanic, hairdresser, brain surgeon, judge and so on. Does the vocabulary of English offer the possibility of non-sexist job descriptions?

259 Ask two groups of different ages to provide specific types of terms for men and women (for example, relating to sexual promiscuity or untidy personal appearance). Does your data bear out the claim that there are more derogatory terms for women, and that they are considered 'stronger'? If there are differences between the two age groups, what is the significance of these?

260 If you have a working knowledge of another language, focus on one of the above issues from the perspective of speakers of that language and compare the results with patterns identified in English that you have found in textbooks.

Gender-differentiated language in first-language acquisition

Much of the research into the acquisition of structures has focused on the rate of development of grammar, phonology or lexis. Early work either assumed or suggested that girls acquire language faster and better than boys, perhaps because of earlier maturation. However, later research has questioned whether girls' acquisition patterns are markedly superior at all. For a summary of views, see Coates (2004: Ch. 9) and Wells (1986b). Research on **communicative competence** concerns how girls and boys learn what it means to speak and write appropriately for their gender in a given society. Edelsky (1976) investigated how children perceived stereotypes of male and female language and how these perceptions might influence them (see Coates 2004; Swann 1992). There is some evidence that girls become aware far earlier than boys of the need to 'style-shift' towards standard pronunciation in formal contexts (Romaine 1984: Ch. 4).

Other studies have focused on how parents speak to children of each gender and the way they encourage girls and boys to speak to others. One question has been whether parents provide a good model of the language they require from their children (e.g. does the father constantly tell his son not to interrupt his sister and then interrupt her himself?). Wells's (1986b: 124) study on when and with which gender parents will initiate conversations found a focus on 'helping/non-play' activities with girls and on 'playing with an adult' contexts with boys. Recent studies on **socialization** have suggested that girls and boys are socialized in single-sex peer groups and that this is a key means by which they learn how to talk like boys and girls. Coates (2004: Ch. 9) reviews studies suggesting that adult female 'co-operative discourse' can already be seen in the ways in which girls' peer groups are structured and in the activities they engage in.

Projects

261 Conduct a case study of a pair of mixed-sex twins. By studying brother and sister, you eliminate extralinguistic variables, such as differences in social background and family structure. If, in spite of both subjects belonging to the same family, there are differences in their stages of language development (see Chapter 3), accent and dialect, or conversational style, is it reasonable to attribute these to the gender differences? What else might have caused them (e.g. parental models, friends, other models from TV)?

262 Compare male and female children of the same age, background and educational level describing a picture or retelling a story they have previously watched on video. Do the girls exhibit the sorts of style features found in adult female language? Is the boys' language different in specific ways and if so, how would you evaluate the differences?

Language, gender and education

Are gender differences in children's oral and written language the result of boys and girls being treated differently by teachers? Conversely, do teachers treat boys and girls differently because the children use language differently in the first place? Related issues are: whether teachers exercise as much equality as they intend to or as they believe they do; strategies that boys use to get more conversational turns than girls in classroom settings; and the implications, for their educational achievement, of girls' tendency to be more quiet and passive than boys in the classroom (see Coates 2004; Swann 1992). White (1986) explored the ways in which some girls' literacy skills, combined with more modest career expectations, were leading them into low-status secretarial jobs rather than other professions, and the extent to which girls' literacy skills led them away from science-based topics at school, college or university (see Swann 1992). Many changes have taken place in educational curricula since then, with an upgrading of the value of 'female' oracy skills like co-operative discourse features. This fact makes the education domain an excellent choice for research on language and gender.

Projects

263 Study the types of reading material (such as fiction or non-fiction, and sub-genres within these) used by a mixed group of children. How far can you identify patterns of preference, according to gender, for particular types of material? Can these be linked in any way to styles of language (such as descriptive, imaginative, or factual)? What might the implications of your findings be?

264 Investigate how a group of girls and boys feel about the writing tasks they are asked to do at school. Which tasks do they enjoy most, and why? Collect samples of their writing and analyse the styles, or the presentation, punctuation, spelling, use of non-standard grammar and so on. Do any trends emerge?

265 Since computers became a normal part of the work and home environment, the traditional 'secretarial' career for women has changed its identity. Interview older women in typical office support jobs (your university or college is one place to look, but you could also approach private businesses) about the role that text writing, note-taking and transcription play nowadays, in comparison with when they began their career. To what extent is there any indication that the jobs that women do in these posts are best suited to women?

9

Accents and dialects of English

Accents and dialects are the focus of interest for various groups of linguists. The main two groups are sociolinguists studying how people use pronunciation, vocabulary and grammar to express and retain social identity, and phoneticians and phonologists, who study the sound systems of accents. Although this chapter focuses on varieties of English, most of the methods would be the same if you were collecting information about another language. The sorts of questions that you might ask in research into accents and dialects include:

❐ Where are the geographical borders between different pronunciations of the same word?

❐ Where are the geographical borders between different words or expressions for the same entity, action and so on?

❐ Are such borders consistent across a large set of words or expressions, or must they be differently drawn for each?

❐ How are past settlements of communities reflected in the pronunciation, vocabulary and grammar of a local variety?

❐ How are social and cultural differences in society expressed through language?

❐ What level of variation can be observed in an individual's pronunciation, vocabulary and/or grammar in different social situations?

❐ What differences are there between the pronunciation and vocabulary of men and women using the same regional variety?

❐ In what ways do TV and film actors exaggerate, under-represent or successfully reproduce a given regional accent?

❐ How do the grammatical forms of a given dialect differ from Standard English, or from another variety, and why?

❐ How mutually comprehensible are dialects and accents from different places?

❐ To what extent is dialect used, and should it be used, in schools?

❐ What subtle differences in pronunciation and vocabulary mark out subgroups within a single local community?

Research on accent and dialect often requires a baseline for comparison. It is entirely feasible to compare any variety with any other. However, you may well find it easier to compare the variety that interests you to the national 'standard', or another variety that is frequently described in books. A good place to start is Trudgill and Hannah (2002).

Describing pronunciation will require phonetic script. Phonemic transcription will probably not be sufficient to capture the detail you need and in any case, it builds in assumptions about the phonological system that may not apply to the variety under investigation. See Chapter 16 for guidance on transcription.

If you are short of actual data to analyse, there are several ways to obtain some. You could enquire at your local library about recordings, either made for the sake of the language itself or for some other purpose such as an oral-history project. Alternatively, find out about sound archives in national libraries or in museums of local culture and life. However, check first whether you will be able to make a copy to take away, as this isn't always permissible. Local radio programmes and national radio phone-ins are another good source of data. Television news bulletins where onlookers to an incident are interviewed can provide usable, though short, soundbites. Excellent data for studying non-native accents can be gathered from television and radio current-affairs programmes, where politicians, sportspeople and so on are interviewed.

Terminology

The terms **accent** and **dialect** are often used rather imprecisely, even interchangeably. According to the glossary in the *Encyclopedia of Language and Linguistics* (Brown 2006), a dialect is 'a variety of language associated with a particular regional and/or social background, marked by features of grammar, vocabulary, and (for some linguists) accent' (vol. 14: 35), while an accent relates to 'features of pronunciation associated with a speaker's regional or social background' (vol. 14: 2). In other words, dialect is a broader concept than accent, covering also words and grammar. Linguists avoid the suggestion that some people have an accent and dialect while others do not: '*all* of us speak with an accent, and *all* of us speak a dialect' (Trudgill 1999: 2).

Textbooks, reference sources and major journals

Crystal (2003b, Chs 20 and 21) gives a brief well-illustrated account of regional and social variation. Bauer (2002) offers insight into why regional and international varieties exist. Elmes (2005) is an accessible introduction to regional variation in English. Hughes, Trudgill, and Watt (2005) offer specific descriptions of regional varieties of British English and this book comes with a CD-ROM. Foulkes and Docherty (1999) describe urban British varieties and Gordon *et al.* (2004) do the same for New Zealand English. Trudgill and Hannah (2002) and Melchers and Shaw (2003) cover international varieties of English, with audio recordings available. Jenkins (2003) is a useful resource book on world Englishes. For a considerably more in-depth look at varieties of English from the point of view of phonology, morphology and syntax, there is the two-volume edited collection (including CD-ROM) by Kortmann and Schneider (2005). The older three volumes of J.C. Wells (1982a, b, c) also remain a classic resource. A detailed survey of Scots can be found in Corbett *et al.* (2003) and one of Irish English is found in Hickey (2004). There are specialist publications for specialist jobs: dictionaries and books on place names and surnames, dialect dictionaries, and dictionaries of slang, jargon and euphemism. A very handy book for British varieties is Upton and Widdowson (1996), which provides maps from the *Linguistic Atlas of England*, showing the distributions of sounds and vocabulary in different regions. An excellent resource regarding how ordinary people perceive their varieties is the two-volume *Handbook of Perceptual Dialectology* (Preston 1999, Long and Preston 2002).

For examples of how data can be collected, look at the publications spawned by the major national surveys, including the *Survey of English Dialects* (Orton *et al.* 1962–71), *The Linguistic Atlas of England* (Orton *et al.* 1978), *The Linguistic Atlas of Scotland* (Mather and Speitel 1975), *A Word Geography of the Eastern United States* (Kurath 1949) and *The Atlas of North American English* (Labov *et al.* 2006). Samples of the data in these are given in Crystal (2003b, Ch. 20). Information on other languages is given in Veith (2006).

Sources such as the above will help you identify lists of words and forms that you can use as stimuli. For information on particular varieties, use local libraries and bookshops, which will often have books or pamphlets not easy to come by outside that area (for example, the Yorkshire Dialect Society publications). Bear in mind, however, that not all of these will be taking a strictly 'linguistic' approach. Classic sociolinguistically focused accounts of specific varieties include the work by Labov on New York and Martha's Vineyard (Labov 1972) and Black Vernacular English (Labov 1969), Trudgill (1972, 1974) on male–female differences in Norwich, Cheshire (1978, 1982) on Reading, and Milroy (1987) on East and West Belfast. Much of this work is reviewed in Chapter 7 in this book. Ideas for interesting topics can be found in Görlach's (1991, 1995) collections.

Useful journals for projects on accents and dialects include the following:

JOURNALS

American Speech
Dialectologia et Geolinguistica
English and Germanic Studies
English Studies
English World-Wide: A Journal of Varieties of English
Folklore
International Journal of the Sociology of Language
Journal of English Linguistics
Journal of the International Phonetic Association
Journal of the Lakeland Dialect Society
Journal of the Lancashire Dialect Society
Language and Speech
Linguistics
Orbis: Bulletin International de Documentation Linguistique
Scottish Language
Social and Cultural Geography
Transactions of the Yorkshire Dialect Society
Word

Which accent/dialect to choose

One important question to consider is whether you are going to study a variety that you use yourself. The advantage of studying your own variety is that you are yourself a source of data. This means that if a form or a pronunciation is missing, you know what it is and can confidently add it to the list. Working with a variety that is not your own can make it difficult to identify the pattern underlying a set of features, because it is hard to judge what another example would do. (This problem can be eased by using published work on the same or a similar variety to get some ideas.) Other advantages are that you can plan with more confidence how to elicit the forms you need and that when interviewing informants you are not putting them off by using a different pronunciation or vocabulary.

However, there are some serious disadvantages too. You may not have an identical variety to that of your informant, and you may unwittingly remove some of the more subtle layers of data by influencing the informant into your way of speech. Studying a variety requires some perspective and it is very hard to get this when it is very familiar to you. It may be difficult for you to tell which words are part of the standard variety, a 'national slang' or specific to your own variety. We can tend to be quite blind to aspects of our own speech, so you may miss some detail. You can reduce the risk of this by getting a friend who does not use that variety to listen to your data and check your assumptions. A variety you know very well, but which is not your only variety, may provide a compromise, offering the advantages of both scenarios above.

It is accents and dialects that bring us to the realization that there is no single version of English that can be considered *the* reference point. The concept of **World Englishes** focuses on the fact that English 'belongs' to many different people around the world, all bringing to it certain distinctive characteristics. Within the worldwide community of native speakers we find the use of national and regional varieties. There are also many millions of speakers of other languages who have learned English, whether in their early years as the language of education, or later, for use in business or leisure pursuits. In some countries English is one of the official languages, so there is a recognized national variety taught by local teachers, as with India, parts of Africa and parts of Malaysia. Elsewhere, such as in France, Spain and Poland, English is a foreign language. In addition, there are speakers whose native language is not English but who live in an English-speaking environment, like Punjabis in Britain, Greeks in Canada, Hispanics in the USA and so on. There are, in short, many opportunities for studying the accents and dialects of English, wherever you live. If you are interested in researching varieties of a language other than English, start off by finding out about the range of places and circumstances in which the language is spoken around the world, in order to keep your horizons broad.

Obtaining data

It is much easier than it used to be to obtain good-quality audio data, since many recordings are now available on the Internet. Digitally broadcast radio, such as the BBC, offers its material on line and for MP3 download: see www.bbc.co.uk/radio. For accent analysis, even very short extracts can be sufficient. The International Corpus of English website www.ucl.ac.uk/english-usage/ice/ provides links to ICE team sites around the world, on many of which sound files have been made available. Although only a few seconds long, they could be a useful resource for a single or comparative study. The BBC Voices website has a large collection of audio recordings of local UK accents, www.bbc.co.uk/voices/wil/. For longer texts in international and regional accents, try the Audio Archive, http://alt-usage-english.org/audio_archive.shtml#spoken. The extensive set of international readings of a single passage, available in the Speech Accent Archive at http://accent.gmu.edu/browse_language.php could provide the basis for your own comparative study, using the same text. Since phonetic transcriptions and key observations about the accents are also given here, you will be able to relate your own transcriptions to those in the Archive. Other useful websites for resources include: www.americandialect.org/, www.aussieslang.com/ and www.courses.fas.harvard.edu/~ling80/tool/wwwlinks/.

What to look for in an accent

If you are interested in pronunciation, structure your study by listening out for specific sounds and transcribing them in some detail. A list of English phonemes, based on British Received Pronunciation (RP), is provided in Chapter 16. Use this to write down your own examples phonetically next to the appropriate phoneme. Try to find several examples of each phoneme, in case it is pronounced in different ways in different environments in that variety. As your chosen variety may have a different set of phonemes from those of RP, do not be surprised if some categories collapse together and others divide: that is something that you can write about in your study. Kreidler's (2004: Ch. 4) representation of English variety types, as determined by their phonemic inventories, may help you. Hughes, Trudgill, and Watt (2005) also provide a wordlist suitable for eliciting all the phonemes of RP.

What to look for in a dialect

In order to analyse a dialect, you need an understanding of basic grammatical categories, both so that you can accurately describe what you find and so that you know what sorts of phenomena to look for. You may find it helpful to write a 'translation' of your material in Standard English alongside the original, so that the differences become clear. You must categorize your data according to word classes, and really get to grips with morphology (word forms and endings) and grammar as well as vocabulary. The relationship between grammar and vocabulary on the one hand, and pronunciation on the other, is not always clear-cut. Some words which seem to just be 'lazy' pronunciations of the standard form are actually very different, with a separate history. For example, 'em in sort 'em out appears to be a shortened form of them, but it is not (Brook 1978: 105). If you have enough data, you should be able to construct tables of pronoun and verb forms. Use the lists of standard forms in Table 9.1 to help draw up a corresponding set of dialect forms.

Table 9.1 Standard forms

Part of speech	Form
Subject	I, you, he, she, it, we, they, who, which
Object	me, you, him, her, it, us, them, who(m), which
Possessive	my, your, his, her, its, our, their, whose
	mine, yours, his, hers, its, ours, theirs

Pronouns and possessives

Some languages and indeed, some varieties of English may have additional forms that you need to check for, including: a difference between singular and plural *you* forms, a difference in politeness and/or intimacy in *you* forms, a difference between plural forms referring to two and to more than two, a difference between *we* forms which include and exclude the addressee, and separate *they* forms for male and female. For further details on pronouns, see Trudgill (1999: 87–101). Remember to note carefully the pronunciation of all pronoun forms, along with the context in which they have occurred.

Verbs

Besides variations in the meaning or inventory of verbs from place to place, the key things to look for are the different tense forms (present, past, past participle), especially those of the common irregular verbs such as *be* and *go*. If you find an unusual form of a verb, check the rest of its forms. Dialect forms are likely to differ from the standard by having a different strong past tense form, or else a weak (*-ed*) form instead of a strong one, or vice versa. Different varieties can also sometimes use the verb tenses differently. For example, a British southerner would say: *The burglar broke into the house and he ransacked the place*, while further north you might hear: *The burglar has broken into the house and he's ransacked the place*, using the present perfect rather than the simple past. There may also be contrasts in the use of conditionals and subjunctives: where a speaker of standard British English says *If I had seen him I would have chased him*, an American might say *If I would have seen him I would have chased him*.

Nouns

You should find the richest pickings of regional vocabulary here, particularly, of course, where a word is needed locally for something that does not exist elsewhere. (For illustrations of regional variation in nouns, see Crystal 2003b: Ch. 20.) Some terms require local or topical knowledge to explain: according to the *Dictionary of South African English* (1996), Township vernacular contains the words *Mary Decker* (a fast police vehicle) and *Zola Budd* (a slow one), named after an American and a South African who were rival athletes in the 1980s. As this example indicates, an interesting question can be how long certain words will remain in a variety after the local conditions that created the opportunity no longer exist. In addition, look out for non-standard plural forms of familiar words.

Negative forms

Languages have many ways of forming negatives but, even within English grammar there is regional variation. Some people say *Don't you?* and others say *Do you not?* Some varieties use **double negatives**, e.g. *I ain't seen nothing.* Trudgill (1999) is a very useful source of insight into this.

Tags

Tag questions are a hallmark of English. Compare: *It's raining, is it?*, *It's raining, isn't it?*, and *It's not raining, is it?* Different varieties use tags in different ways. In South Wales you might hear: *So you've moved into your flat, is it?* Other varieties replace the standard tag forms with a general *yes* (*yeah*) and *no*: *So it's raining, yeah?* Consider what your variety does: it might make the basis of an interesting study.

Adverbs

Differences between varieties in their use of adverbs can be quite striking when heard for the first time. The following example illustrates how an analysis might progress. In Yorkshire (and some other places), it has been common for a long time to hear *He was well happy* and *They were well tired* for *He was very happy* and *They were very tired.* What is the underlying pattern? One might hypothesize that Yorkshire English simply uses *well* wherever Standard English would use *very*, but this is refuted by the fact that Yorkshire English does not say *You're the well person I was looking for.* To understand how Yorkshire English works, it is necessary to examine the way that Standard English itself distributes *very* and *well* (e.g. *She had been well taught*; **She had been very taught*; *The tyres were well worn*; *The tyres were very worn* – the asterisk indicates that the sentence is ungrammatical). If it is the case that *very* is used with adjectives and *well* with verb forms, then where does *He was well pleased* fit in? It turns out that there is a subtle relationship between adjectives and past participle forms in Standard English and, returning to the Yorkshire variety, this leads to the following question: does the difference between the two varieties lie in the meanings of *very* and *well* themselves, or in the underlying categories of the words they are modifying?

Possible angles and project ideas

You can, of course, just focus your work directly on the variety. However, it is often useful to get an 'angle'. This gives you something to aim at and provides a motivation for exploring some aspects more than others. Most importantly, it can help you avoid simply ending up with a list of forms you have found, without anything very much to say about them.

Comparing the speech of three generations

This is a study of how a variety is changing at the moment. Providing you can get access to compatible recordings of three individuals from the same regional and social background, and at least a generation apart, you can potentially uncover interesting differences that may characterize change within their variety across time. However, remember that other variables may explain the differences that you are attributing to age. For example, it has been suggested that males tend to display more pronounced regional characteristics than females (see Trudgill 1972 and the discussion in Aitchison 2001: 71–3). Avoid this variable by studying only one gender. Alternatively, perhaps the informants have had different amounts and types of contact with outsiders (such as travel or work experiences). Perhaps they watch different quantities of TV or different programmes, and/or are differently influenced by them. Remember here that it is clearly not reasonable to say that the youth are exposed to youth culture through TV and yet to deny that older generations are also exposed to external cultures. You need to take a sensible sociolinguistic approach to the whole question of identity (see Chapter 7).

Projects

266 If you have family members who have lived for several generations in the same area, compare the language of a grandparent, parent and sibling or cousin. Bear in mind the following advantages and disadvantages of this sort of study. There is a good chance of getting good-quality data without very much effort and the research is fairly well controlled, provided the only major difference between the informants is age (not place of birth or residence, social class, extent of travel, gender, level of education and so on). However, while you bring an insight and intuition to a description of your own family's variety, it can also be quite difficult to detach yourself from it and see it for what it is (see earlier discussion). Furthermore, the chances are that there is little, if any, published material about the variety used in your town or village. This is not disastrous, but it can leave you out on a limb, particularly with those observations that you find hard to interpret. For guidance on sociolinguistic factors that may be relevant to this, see Projects 218 and 219.

267 Rather than studying your own or a friend's family, find recordings of three generations of a famous family (the British Royal Family is one obvious choice), and compare their accents.

268 Or, using videos of classic films and TV programmes, study the accents of members from three generations of one of the great acting families such as the Redgraves. Of course, you must restrict yourself to material in which the actors are not adopting an accent different from their natural one.

Comparing the accents of different non-native speakers

Second-language-acquisition research proposes that a person's accent when speaking another language is largely determined by the phonology of his/her native language (see Chapter 4). This being so, in theory predictions can be made on the basis of a given language, about the likely characteristics that will become evident when speaking an L2.

Project

269 Select a non-native accent of English from the list in the Speech Accent Archive at accent.gmu.edu/browse_language.php. Find out about the phonological features of the native language of the speakers and use this information to explain the key characteristics of the accent that the informants have in their English.

Explaining why a variety has come about

This is a study of the accent or dialect of a place, incorporating its history. Clearly, you are going to have to rely on reading for a considerable chunk of your work. This is fine, providing that the language of the place you choose has been fairly extensively studied before. Do check first that that is so. Unless you are looking at a variety with a high profile like Geordie (Newcastle) or Scouse (Liverpool), you may have considerable difficulty in finding more than the odd page in a few books about the history of the place, let alone its language. Writing about the history of settlement in a place is not the same as writing a linguistic history and, if you are not careful, you will end up with a political or social history of the area that you cannot easily relate to the modern variety of English except to say that the dialect 'probably reflects the history of settlement in the area'.

Projects

270 Focus a study on one of the historical centres of immigration, such as inner London, Liverpool, New York, Melbourne, or an industrial city that drew many rural populations to it in a short space of time. The later the settlement, the better documented it is likely to be. There may be useful local records about the origins of settlers in the USA, Canada and Australia, if your study is focused there. To identify linguistic signs of the settlement in an urban accent, compare it with the less-influenced surrounding variety. Can you spot specific features that might reflect the variety (or foreign language) that was spoken by the immigrant population?

271 Find a locality that has a specific story of recent unusual settlement. For example, Corby in Northamptonshire (in the southern Midlands of England) received a sizeable settlement of Scots workers when a steel plant was relocated there. Collect data from the original settlers (if any survive), their descendants, and individuals (or their descendants) who were part of the receiving community. Compare the varieties used for signs of a retained social identity and/or linguistic integration.

The political dimension of a variety

This approach takes a sociolinguistic or historical perspective, focusing on the status of a variety within a community. Read Chapter 7 in this book for background on the social aspects of accent and dialect use. For ideas on the specific social impact of certain dialects, look at Burke and Porter (1994), where the papers include a study of the significance of dialect at the beginnings of the trade union movement, Quaker language, an account of the research done by a seventeenth-century dialectologist and how language is affected by political conquest.

Projects

272 Gather data on attitudes to non-Standard English in the education system. This is a large and lively issue, so use newspaper archives to assemble recent views and reactions to reports and events. You could make recordings in a school in an area where the variety is particularly strong, to see how 'standard' the English is in different contexts, such as formal teaching, discussion and group work, sports or gym, recreational time, staff meetings and in the staffroom at breaks.

273 Write a carefully considered account of the differences there might be in the accents and dialects of a country if some political event or policy or the status quo had been different: for example, if York had been the capital of England in the Middle Ages, if Edinburgh, rather than London, had developed as the centre of British culture, or if Australia had been settled largely by Scots rather than English emigrants. In every case, you will need to assess the long-term effects of the political domination of a variety. Some study of the way that standard and non-standard varieties of English came about will help to give you insight (for references, see Chapter 10).

Accent and dialect in literature

This is a study of an accent or dialect as depicted by a certain author, and it offers an interesting slant on accent and dialect work because authors are not dialectologists and their purpose is not linguistic. When examining accents in literature, take a linguist's eye to what is, in effect, a literary device. You may well find that the author permits him-/herself certain liberties in 'spelling' words 'phonetically' (for example, keeping silent letters in a word to help indicate the meaning, as in y *knaa* for 'you know', where the 'k' is actually silent). Use phonemic script to clarify your understanding of what is depicted in 'spelled' forms. You can read more about this topic in Beal (2006).

Projects

274 Do an analysis of, say, the London accent of one or more of Dickens's characters, the West Country accent or dialect in Hardy's novels, or the speech of the yokels in Shakespeare. Evaluate its accuracy against published descriptions. Assess the extent to which the differences are simply a function of the time lapse between the

literary description and the more recent linguistic account. Alternatively, draw on a linguistic description that is contemporaneous with the work of literature, to remove this variable.

275 Compare an author's depiction of an accent or dialect (as above) with your own data from the same area.

276 Compare an actor's rendering of a local accent with the real thing (try to use an actor who is not from that area). A notorious example is Dick van Dyke's attempt at a Cockney accent in the film *Mary Poppins*. At the other extreme, Meryl Streep is one actor who has tackled many accents with success. What tends to make an actor's rendition more or less convincing? Does a bad attempt tend to exaggerate, under-represent, misplace or incorrectly define features?

277 Find a book with lots of colourful characters in it, including some from different places if possible, and get an extrovert friend to read extracts aloud onto tape, with different voices for each character. Transcribe the examples of each character's speech and identify the markers that the reader has used to make the voice sound distinctive. You could also see how the presentation of that voice changes over time, if the reader has provided several examples of the same character. What has been used to indicate an unpleasant personality, female speech (if your reader is male) or male speech (if female), various regional accents, sadness, annoyance and so on?

Update study

This is a comparison of a published description of a variety with data of your own and it has the makings of an excellent project. Instead of simply making observations that, while valid in their own right, may not fit easily into a wider pre-established context, you can anchor everything that *you* find into something that has been found, or not found, before. It is best if you can replicate as many aspects of the original work as possible – ask the same questions in a similar way, use a similar questionnaire, record in a similar environment with people of the same age, sex, and background as the original etc. Beware of becoming too simplistic and narrow when you have a good single source for comparing your data. Read other descriptions of the variety and see in what ways your chosen study differs from others of the time: if there wasn't full agreement at the time about what this variety was like in its finest detail, it will not be surprising if your findings are different too!

Projects

278 Find a study from, say, 40 years ago. The Survey of English Dialects, carried out between 1948 and 1961, is one place to look. Replicate the procedures of the original study as closely as you can. Concentrate your discussion on whether any differences in your findings are a function of the 40-year gap or not. You should, in this case, consider some of the other factors that might make a difference, such as the procedures used, how comparable the informants were, the precise

geographical area they came from, and how the population of an area may have altered in nature.

279 Using the maps in Upton and Widdowson (1996) or a similar publication (see earlier in this chapter), identify, for your geographical area of interest, a boundary between two pronunciations, dialect words, morphological forms or structures. For example, the map for terms meaning 'silly' shows the boundaries for the use of *silly*, *daft*, *barmy*, *gormless*, *fond*, *addle-headed*, *cakey* and *soft*. Conduct your own survey in the area around your chosen boundary, to see whether it is still in the same place as it was when the survey was carried out.

Comparison of two varieties

In one sense, any study of a single variety entails this anyway, because there will be implicit or explicit comparisons with Standard English. However, there is no intrinsic reason why Standard English (British or otherwise) should represent the point of comparison. If you choose to compare two non-standard varieties, the rationale for your choice should be made obvious: a historical or geographical link or else one relating to cultural or educational influence.

Projects

280 Compare a Scots variety with Geordie or with Northern Irish (in both cases there are historical links that make them sensible to compare).

281 Find out the national and regional origins of settlers in a particular area of a former colony of Britain (e.g. Canada, Australia, New Zealand or the USA) and compare the varieties used today in the two places. For example, are there similarities between London Cockney and the variety used in an Australian settlement originally founded for or by Londoners?

282 Compare the varieties used in two adjacent towns or villages where there is known to be variation.

283 Compare the English of, say, two French informants, one of whom loves British culture and one of whom identifies with American culture.

284 Research the level of similarity between the names for common edible fish in two distant parts of the English-speaking world. For instance, is a *cod* on the fish counter in Australia the same as a *cod* in the UK? Is it even the same thing from fish shop to fish shop? How about *hake* or *mullet*? You may need to contact fish marketing boards and/or interview fishmongers or fishermen. Consider the means by which names might travel with immigrants and the reasons why some names retain their original reference while others do not.

285 Download the 'Stella' passage from one of the examples in the Speech Accent Archive at http://accent.gmu.edu/browse_language.php and record your own informants reading it. Transcribe the readings phonetically, and compare them to each other, and/or to appropriate examples from the Archive.

Things to think about

☐ To explain why a variety is as it is and put it into context, read up on the history of English. Features of regional varieties often shed light on the historical development of the standard language and/or retain features that used to exist in Standard English. In their turn, historical developments can often help explain regional differences.

☐ On the whole, you will get stronger accent and dialect features if: (a) you can understand your informants when they use their variety – if you have to keep asking them what they meant, then they are likely to modify towards the standard to help you; and (b) the informant speaks about particular subjects such as family or home life. Children talking about playground games and elderly people talking about their childhood may also be fruitful.

☐ Beware of a tendency for informants to make value judgements about the language variety that they speak and perhaps to understate what they know and/or use.

☐ Be aware that an informant may tell you that they use a form which they don't actually use. This is clearly problematic if you are trying to get an accurate picture of the variety as it is today, especially if you are comparing different ages of speaker. But it can be turned to your advantage in a couple of ways. If you focus on identifying the features of the variety *in general*, it may not matter that your informant's perception of it is rather old-fashioned. Simply mention this somewhere in your study, as a feature of the way people can sometimes identify with defunct forms. Alternatively, if you have enough data, you could compare *what* your informants say with *how* they say it, looking for examples in their speech of the things they have described. Thus, you can take the interesting angle, for all or part of your study, of how speakers may have limited ability to recognize the form of their own language.

10
History of English

There are innumerable questions to be asked about a language at every point of its history, about every aspect of its form and function, and about the relationship between the language forms at different times. Whatever may be asked about one language can be asked about every other, though languages vary considerably in the amount of research already done on them and, indeed, in the amount of primary documentation that is available for researching them. For convenience, most of the ideas put forward below will make reference to English. This is undoubtedly one of the best-documented and most-researched languages, as well as being one that is unusually rich in its mixture of vocabulary. It also has a striking **diachronic** ('across-time') profile, largely because of its political and economic history. In many cases the suggestions made for English can be transferred to the study of other languages, but it will be important to establish that the information you need, be it historical documents or commentaries upon them, is available.

There are two basic ways of finding out what a language used to be like. Where possible, evidence comes directly from written records. However, writing is not only a recent phenomenon in man's cultural development: it is also highly selective, and much of the information that would most interest the linguist is therefore simply not available that way. Where there are no written records, it is possible, to some extent, to reconstruct features of a language using either other linguistic information from that time or information that we have about one or more languages from a subsequent period that have descended from it. In this way, it has been possible for scholars to reconstruct aspects of the vocabulary and grammar of the prehistoric language Proto-Indo-European, using information from its many descendants today. The same method could be used, however, to reconstruct the dialect of the 'criminal' class in London in the eighteenth and nineteenth centuries by using the modern London dialects and the variety of Australian English that developed in the penal colonies.

Because we cannot time-travel, care must be taken, when working on the history of a language, to ask only questions that it is possible to answer from where we are today. This immediately excludes, for example, questions such as how much aspiration Shakespeare's wife used on a word-initial /t/ or whether the English nobility at the time of the Norman Conquest spoke French as fluently as they wrote it. Unless these specific things happen to have been written about at the time, there is obviously no way of finding them out.

It may seem, then, that the only questions we can ask are the ones that are, by definition, already answered. But this is far from being the case. Nor is it true that we cannot know anything about the spoken, as opposed to the written, language. Linguistic information documented at the time, combined with the many superb surveys and investigations done since, can provide you with both the materials and the theoretical background for exploring a wide range of questions.

Textbooks, reference sources and major journals

We can mention here only a few of the many excellent books that your university or college library is likely to hold. Studies of the history of language do not go out of date as quickly as those in other areas, and you may find books that are 30 or more years old that still can offer you useful information. Your local public library is also likely to hold some books on the history of English.

For readable overviews of how language changes, try Aitchison (2001), Crystal (1997: 50–4), and Trask (1994). The last has many practical exercises that might inspire projects, as does Culpeper (2005). Graddol, Leith, and Swann's (1996) thematic approach to the historical origins of diversity in English may inspire project ideas. For a first overview of the history of English, go to Crystal (2003b). Excellent accounts of the history of English include Barber (2000), Baugh and Cable (2002), Burchfield (2002), and McCrum, MacNeil, and Cran (2003). Williams (1986) takes a particularly imaginative approach to the social history of English that may give you ideas for projects. It includes excellent chronologies of political and linguistic events. Scholarly descriptions can be found in the edited collection by Mugglestone (2006), and in Strang's (1970) classic account, which works backwards from the present. Singh (2005) brings in literary and sociolinguistic perspectives and, like other recent studies, includes material on English outside Britain and America. Watts and Trudgill (2001) provide histories of an impressive collection of non-standard varieties. For data, use Freeborn (1998), for which there exists an audiotape with examples of the texts being spoken, and where there are also plentiful activities that may prompt new project ideas. For information about Early Modern English (c.1400–1650) specifically, try Barber (1997) and Görlach (1991). There is an excellent electronic resource, Early English Books Online (EEBO), which will enable you to view scanned images of thousands of books published between 1473 and 1700. Check whether your university/college library subscribes and if not, ask the librarian to help you find out the location of the closest library that does. If you want to check out the origins of words, go to the complete *Oxford English Dictionary*, Onions (1966) or the very readable Partridge (1977). For the origin of proper names, use Room (1992) and for the origin of slang words, Partridge (2002) and Green (1998).

When it comes to journals, it must be said that much of the research on historical linguistics is highly technical and takes for granted a firm understanding of linguistic theory. However, you may get some ideas from flicking through journals such as these:

JOURNALS

Diachronica
English Language and Linguistics
English Studies
Folia Linguistica Historica
Language
Language and Communication
Studies in Philology
Transactions of the Philological Society

Central themes and project ideas

Researching words and names

Many people find the history of English words very interesting. The ordinary vocabulary of English is particularly rich and derives from a great many different sources. However, a project on words must be very carefully managed. It is excessively tedious to look up word after word in dictionaries, particularly as you really need to check each one in more than one place. Furthermore, it isn't always very obvious what to do with a set of word definitions – just putting them down in a list, even organized under *words from French*, *words from Arabic* and so on, will not convince your assessor that you have done much thinking! It is, therefore, important for your sanity and that of your assessor to provide yourself with a solid theme that allows you to *interpret* your data.

Names can be particularly interesting to research (for inspiration, try Redmonds 2004). Much less is genuinely known about the history of surnames than you will be led to believe by any given book on the subject. Look a name up in one book and you may feel confident of knowing its origin. But look the same name up again elsewhere and it will probably seem less certain that any of them have got it right! So be very sceptical about what you read. Look for interesting questions to ask. For example, while it is true that many surnames derive from place names or geographical features, occupations, physical characteristics or personal names, some apparently straightforward cases are more obscure. At first glance, 'Pope', 'Monk', and 'King' might seem to have derived from occupations, with the surname passed from father to son in the normal way, but a moment's thought indicates that this is fairly unlikely. For an excellent overview of personal names, see Hanks (2006).

Place names can be easier to research than surnames, because while people move from place to place, taking their name with them, places tend to stay put, so you can trace at least the spellings of a place name as far back as there are maps or local records. Again, different books may give different meanings to the same name. The best single source for place-name meanings is the 69 volumes of the English Place Name Society, such as *The Place-Names of Dorset* (Mills 1987) and *The Place-Names of Rutland* (Cox 1994). To avoid just ending up with a list, find a way of *using* place-name research to address a slightly different question than 'what is the origin of these place names?'

Projects

286 Choose a small number of surnames, look them up in every book you can find, and make a critical comparison of what the different sources say. Then try to account for the variation and discuss the significance of it.

287 Choose two very different areas of the country and, using the telephone directory, find out what the most popular local surnames are. Use this as a way of discussing possible differences in the communities today and in the past. For example, London has been a target for waves of immigrants: French Huguenots, Eastern European Jews, Indians and so on, whereas a rural area may have had a very settled local community for many generations.

288 Draw up a list of specific queries to investigate, such as: why *are* there so many people with the surnames 'Pope', 'Monk' and 'King'? Why is the name 'Smith' spelled in so many different ways? What surnames *don't* exist that could, and why (e.g. Mrs Computer-programmer; Mr Obese; Ms Tea-drinker; Mrs Pylon and so on)?

289 Take a wider, more comparative, approach, asking why surnames arose in the first place and how different communities (local and worldwide) have dealt differently with the same problem that surnames were intended to solve. Ask whether they are appropriate and/or sufficient in our modern world and if they are not, how naming practices could be reformed.

290 Track the changes in the spelling of surnames within particular families over many centuries: what sorts of more general linguistic and social change do these changes reflect? Focus on families whose history is well documented.

291 Research the reasons why immigrants have changed their surname on arrival in their new adoptive country. Your study might include work on nineteenth-century immigrants to America registering on Ellis Island, Jewish immigrants to Britain before and after the Second World War, and into the state of Israel from 1948, and subsequent waves of settlers from Vietnam, Somalia, Afghanistan and Iraq. Remember to consider the widest possible range of reasons, such as: transcription errors, deliberate alterations to hide identity or origin, direct translation, making the name easier to spell, attempts to transfer from one cultural naming tradition to another and so on.

292 According to a report in *The Observer* in October 2004, people in Mongolia did not have surnames until modern practicalities made it necessary: being listed in the phone book and the introduction of identity cards. Research the issues that have arisen in Mongolia as a result (one was that most of the population chose the same surname) and use books on the social history of English to compare these modern issues to the pressures that led to the introduction of surnames in Britain many centuries ago.

293 Focusing on a local area of interest to you, find out how the place names have changed their spelling (and pronunciation, if you can manage it) over the years and why. Who would have determined how the name was spelled, and what would the status of any given spelling have been?

294 Are there patterns to the place names in an area that indicate the history of settlements of different peoples? Yorkshire is particularly good for this. Look for indications of who lived on the hills and who lived in the valleys. You don't need to live in the area to do this sort of work: get a good map and read up about it. You may find Cameron (1965) a useful model. He looks at how place names in the five boroughs of Derby, Nottingham, Lincoln, Leicester, and Stamford reflect Viking settlement patterns.

295 What do street names tell us about the history of an area? Consider how the basic vocabulary for thoroughfares must have changed its meaning over the years: what was the difference between a *road*, a *street*, and a *lane* 300 years ago? What do they mean today? Focus on a suburb and use modern and old maps to trace its development as a residential area. Extend your study to look at new towns and/or street names in new estates. Find out who decides what to call them, and look for patterns in the choices from place to place.

296 Look at a particular recurrent word or syllable in place names. What pattern is there to its occurrence within an area and across a region or beyond? Among the useful sources are Zachrisson (1909) on Anglo-Norman influences, Ekwall (1923, 1925, 1928) on place names with *-ing* and on river names, and Sandred (1963) on *-stead*.

297 Make a critical analysis of pub names. Rather than simply recounting the history of a few interesting ones, interview publicans and brewers to find out their preferences and policy on keeping or replacing long-standing names and choosing new names (do they tend to make a new pub *sound* traditional, or might they call one *The Website* or *The Heliport*?). Do they feel that the name of a pub has an influence on its image, so that different names would be used for different clientele? By examining the names that pubs have been given in past centuries, attempt to ascertain whether the influences then (such as market forces) were the same as they are now.

298 Compare local street maps for two different towns in the English-speaking world, one that has been settled only in the past couple of centuries (e.g. in New Zealand or Australia) and one that dates back to very ancient times (e.g. in England). Look for indications of the same natural processes of naming in the streets and local areas, which should still be fairly transparent in the new settlement, but will only be revealed by dictionary research for the more ancient settlement, because of historical changes to the name. For instance, look for roads named after the people who lived there (in many places they still will do – why not email the local librarian or a school or college and ask?). Also look for places that have evidently been named after the town or village from which the settlers came – all of the ex-British colonies are full of such names (small towns called London, Halifax, Brentwood and so on) but can you track down equivalents that indicate Viking or Saxon naming? Using overviews of how place-naming traditionally happened, draw up a comparison: have some naming practices fallen out of use and/or others been introduced? Use the Internet to make contact with people who may be able to tell you about the origins of local names. Before making your final selection of places

to study, sample several to be sure you have interesting ones. Steer away from cities that were obviously designed all at one time, because the naming of streets and local areas may have been a corporate decision (for which see Project 299).

299 When a new housing estate or town is built, who decides on what the street names will be and how are the decisions reached? Interview local town planners about this and see if you can find records of the choices that were considered and the processes undertaken in deciding. Compare these processes with the natural development of place names, choosing, where possible, either geographically adjacent places that contrast the two extremes or paired examples where one street has an ancient name and another has, by quite different modern processes, ended up with the same name.

300 Choose a theme and look up the words that relate to it. This could be equestrianism, things you eat for breakfast, words for modern machinery and gadgets (many of which are much older than the things they describe), plant names, names for zoo animals or words relating to warfare (see Partridge 1948). Then *use* what you find out to account for the ways in which words come about in languages, and how technological advances, or changes in a culture or society, will require new words. Read up on language change so that you can back up your claims. Useful reading, especially for ideas and serendipity, includes Groom (1934), Ayers (1965), and Barfield (1953). A wide-ranging source well worth using is Serjeantson (1935). To look up specific words, use Onions (1966) and Partridge (1977). The latter usefully indicates the links between rather unlikely words, such as *turban* and *tulip*, *asterisk* and *disaster*, *shrub* and *sorbet*, *wench* and *lapwing*, and so on.

Pronunciation and spelling

English has a fascinating history as far as pronunciation is concerned and our modern spelling system bears witness to much of it. Almost all the introductory books will give you an overview both of the sound changes and the spelling system and there are specialized works by Bradley (1916), Brook (1957), Barber (1997), Burchfield (2002), Kökeritz (1953), Zachrisson (1913), Vallins (1954) and many more. For spelling, Baugh and Cable (2002) is useful and includes, on pages 422–8, examples of contemporary writings to illustrate the spelling changes that English has undergone. For a recent study of the nature of English spelling, see Mitton (1996).

Projects

301 English is renowned for having many different spellings of the same pronunciation. Find out which spellings are the most 'characteristic' by reading out made-up words to subjects. Tell them to write down the non-words in whatever spelling will enable them to read them back to you correctly. (Do *not* use linguistics students for this, as they will probably use phonetic script!) Do the subjects all tend to spell a

sound in the same way when being impressionistic? (For example, is /u:/ always written *oo*, or are *ue* and *ough* also used? Does it depend on what consonant precedes?) Are the preferred spellings of each sound today the most long-standing ones (e.g. has *oo* represented the sound /u:/ for longer than the other spellings?). Vallins (1954: 46–9) gives lists of the different spellings for each sound, but you will find other lists quite easily, or you can construct your own.

302 Take a piece of verse (by Shakespeare, for example) and identify which rhymes still work and which don't. What about puns? What pronunciation changes are reflected by them? Argue in a balanced way for and against performing works of literature in their original pronunciation. What wider implications are there for the performing arts?

303 Borrow from your local library some CD recordings of vocal music written in the 1500s, in which the English is performed using historically informed pronunciation. Play selected items to some informants and ask them to write down as many of the words as they can recognize. Then play the pieces again, but this time let them read the texts in advance – does that help their recognition? Finally, interview them about their views of whether the pronunciation enhances the performance or not, and why.

304 What have been the motivations of the spelling reformers in England (and France, perhaps) during the past few centuries? For some ideas to get you started, look up the *inkhorns*, the *Academie* and *George Bernard Shaw*.

305 What would we lose by modernizing our spelling system to match modern pronunciation? Why has no such reform been achieved before now? When did spelling start diverging from pronunciation, why, and what was people's reaction?

306 Go to one of the books issued in facsimile by the Scolar Press, for a contemporary view of issues in the history of English. For example, read the introductory note to Mulcaster's *The First Part of the Elementary* (1582) for an idea of his attitudes towards spelling, before embarking on the description of the alphabet that he presents. Alternatively, use John Hart's *An Orthographie* (1569), one of the most linguistically informed and accurate descriptions of English pronunciation of its time, and incorporating his own phonetic spelling system. Which issues of that time still apply today and why? What role do you think that such writers played in the way that English has turned out? (Both Mulcaster's and Hart's books are in the Early English Books Online collection, described earlier.)

307 Write a critical evaluation of a nineteenth-century or early twentieth-century essay on the 'decay' of language, such as Bridges (1913). Use the modern descriptive linguistic approach to put the other side of the arguments.

308 Interview actors and musicians about the validity of performing works from the sixteenth century and earlier in original pronunciation. For insight into the issues, see Wray (1992a and b, 1995, 1999).

309 Using Mitton (1996) as a basis, evaluate the influence on English spelling that computers and also texting have had since he wrote that book. Collect data from friends, and interview teachers, lecturers, journalists and/or publishers about what changes they are aware of.

History of English dialects

Be careful what you choose here, because some dialects are better documented than others. Read Skeat (1911) to gain a clear idea of how the four major dialects of Old English fit together, and work forward from there. Try to avoid giving just a straightforward chronicle of developments.

Projects

310 Investigate why it was that the variety of English spoken in the East Midlands became the standard English. By careful reading about Northumbrian and about the nature of standardization, speculate about what English would be like now if Northumbrian had continued to be the high-prestige variety that it was in Bede's day.

311 Draw on a range of reading to ask to what extent a topography of the British Isles can account for the development of Standard English.

The profile of a feature of English across time

Aspects of English grammar, meaning, and style have all changed across time, and there are plenty of documents that provide evidence of this. Use what you know about syntactic, semantic or discourse theory to inform your analysis.

Project

312 Focus on a feature such as the passive, the subjunctive, the negative or how speech is quoted, and compare its occurrence in a couple of sample texts for each of, say, three periods between Chaucer and the late eighteenth century or even up to modern times. You can keep the variability down by choosing a text that has been rewritten many times, such as a Bible passage. Examples of such passages can be found in many textbooks, including Fisher and Bornstein (1974), Burnley (2000) and Freeborn (1998).

Sociopolitical trends and influences on English

One much-described aspect of the history of our language is the way in which the Norman Conquest affected, among other things, the vocabulary of English. There has also been some interesting work done on the later 'social' history of English, including the way in which dialects were used to support the trade union movement (Joyce 1994). See Burke and Porter (1987, 1994) for ideas, and Leith (1997) for a more general but socially oriented view of the history of English.

Projects

313 Using the chronologies in Williams (1986), write an account of what linguistic life would have been like in Norman England for, say, three or four individuals from different social classes. What language would they have used when, and with whom? How does this relate to the changes in the vocabulary of English between 1066 and 1400?

314 Draw up a list of the proverbs mentioned in Obelkevich (1987). Interview a small group of elderly people and ask them which ones they know, what they mean, and in what circumstances (for example, in conversation with whom) they might use them. Do the same with a group of young adults or children. Comment on the following possibilities: the use of proverbs is dying out; proverbs vary from generation to generation; you only really learn (or learn to use) proverbs later on in your life.

315 Make a study of euphemisms and when they are used. Read the introductory pages of dictionaries of euphemisms for an impression of their range. Make a list of euphemisms for the same thing (e.g. words for having sex, for excrement, or for parts of the body) and interview a group of informants about when they would use each one. Which do they consider shocking, which 'cute', and which old-fashioned? What words do they consider to be non-euphemistic (i.e. the direct term) for each concept? Look these words up to establish whether they too are, or have been, euphemisms. Consider the 'shelf life' of euphemisms and when they need replacing. For an outline of the scope of taboo words, including their use as swearwords, see Crystal (2003b: 172–4).

English as a world language

Read Crystal (2003b, Ch. 7 or 2003a) to gain a clear impression of the current status of English as a world language, and Phillipson (2003) for an in-depth consideration of the role of English in Europe. Issues arising from the worldwide dominance of English Language Teaching are explored in Block and Cameron (2002).

There are many interesting questions that we can ask, including how English came to be such a widespread and influential language, what mark it has left on other languages, and what mark they have left on it.

Projects

316 Assuming an unaltered basic political history for Europe and America, how would foreign policy and/or social structures have had to be different for the English language *not* to have become so important? You can get ideas by looking at other nations that have had plenty of political, but less linguistic, influence. This sort of project is based on speculation and, for it to be successful as a piece of research, you *must* draw upon a range of established theories to support the points you make. You will need to research the processes by which English became so important, and draw on sociolinguistic research to demonstrate how social and political influences filter through to the individuals in a speech community, leading them to decisions about their own needs and priorities.

317 Make a comparison between World English today and Arabic in the Middle East or Latin during the Roman occupation of Europe.

318 Interview a range of different types of people, both native and non-native speakers of English, about the future of English in the world. How likely do they think it is that English will become even more dominant in the political and commercial spheres? Does it matter if it does? What about the domestic use of English around the world, where presently other languages are used in the home? How do your informants' views compare with those expressed in the recent literature?

The influence of literacy on language

By researching the history of basic literacy education in Britain over the last thousand years, and linking that to who had influence over whom as far as language was concerned, one can develop a picture of the effect that being able to read and write has on the development of a language. Remember to consider the people at both edges of literacy: those who maybe had to write letters from time to time but who had almost no schooling and those who were highly educated in not only English but also French, Greek and Latin. There is plenty of information about the latter in introductory books like Baugh and Cable (2002) and Crystal (2003b).

Project

319 Find out who was teaching the basic literacy skills to the less privileged in a period of history of your choosing. How good were *their* skills? Link this debate into literacy practice in the modern world, both locally and internationally, but remember to consider to what extent the demands of our society today require different levels of literacy and education from those of the past.

Things to think about

❑ It is possible to download from Early English Books Online (see earlier) or the Internet lengthy texts that may not be easily available any other way, by doing a search on a name such as *Paston* (a family whose letters through the fifteenth century have been much studied), or the name of an event or monarch.

❑ Studies of pronunciation require a working knowledge of phonetic script; phonemic script will not be sufficient for anything other than the most general kinds of observations. For the difference between these two transcription systems, see Chapter 16.

❐   The more research you do into the history of a language, the more you will realize how much of what is presented as *fact* is actually an *interpretation* of often rather ambiguous and confusing original data. Don't be content with reading just one account; expect another one to be different, and take note of where the disagreements occur. The art of writing a good project is to use the disagreement as a pivot for developing your own views (see Chapter 21).

PART II

TECHNIQUES FOR COLLECTING DATA

11

Audio- and video-recorded data

Many kinds of researcher use audio- or video-recording in order to avoid having to make frantic notes at the time and risk missing important information. But in linguistics, the speech itself is often the subject of analysis, and it is especially important to have a good-quality recording.

Places to get data

Provided you take note of possible problems with background noise and interruptions (see below), you can record in many places: the home, a pub, a train, a café, a school, a retirement home, a student room, a club or meeting, a consultation room and so on. You can also get material from the radio, TV and archives, and from the Internet, subject to copyright.

Audio or video?

In most circumstances, audio data is sufficient, but it is certainly worth considering using video equipment. With modern digital technology, either audio or video should provide you with excellent sound quality provided you have a good microphone but if you have several informants, especially children, it may be difficult to tell their voices apart if there is no visual corroboration.

Naturalistic data

Researchers need to be aware of how the act of recording might make the data less naturalistic. However, the inhibitions associated with informants knowing that they are being recorded are usually fairly short-lived. Therefore, although you may be inclined to conceal your microphone or camera, do not assume that this is the only way of getting the data you need. Most people will soon forget about the recording as they become involved in the activities.

Ethics and legality

There are important ethical considerations when it comes to recording people. Either ask their permission first or, if you feel that your data will be less 'genuine' if they know you are recording, ask them afterwards. You should be prepared to let them hear what you have recorded and you must give them the option of asking for part, or all, of it to be erased (see Chapter 15).

Recording from the radio or television and downloading from the Internet does not entail such ethical problems, because the material is in the public domain. However, some broadcast and Internet material is copyright and if you intend to use it in a publication or other public presentation, you should ask the permission of the copyright owner. Increasingly, digital-radio broadcasts are offered for download from official websites (e.g. the BBC, www.bbc.co.uk) and, there, copyright is unlikely to be an issue for researchers.

Quality

Golden rule number one in collecting recorded data is to remember that you will have to listen to it over and over again till you're sick of it. You will need to listen for detail, so it must be well recorded, otherwise background noise will increasingly become a problem. When you are deciding where to record, think about the noise implications. Pubs, trains, cafés, schools and retirement homes can offer wonderful opportunities for natural conversation or interviews, but they can also be excessively noisy, so do a trial recording before you commit yourself to collecting the data there.

How much data do you need?

The amount of data you need depends on two key things. One is what questions you are asking of your data, and how thick and fast the answers will come. If you want to know how the word *the* is pronounced in continuous speech, you won't need more than a few minutes' worth, because *the* is such a common word. But, if you are interested in how topics are linked together in debates, you will need enough material for sufficient topic changes to occur. As you collect the data, listen to it to gauge how many examples you have accumulated so far.

The second thing that determines how much data to collect is the detail of your analysis. A narrow phonetic transcription of speech will take a great deal of time, and it may be sufficient to analyse no more than short stretches of a few seconds each. A detailed conversation transcription will also take a lot of time to complete and four to five minutes in total may well be plenty. You should be discerning about what you choose to transcribe – not just everything you recorded!

❐ The first five minutes of a conversation might not be the most interesting part. Go for interesting features such as story-telling or argument.

❐ If you are studying accent, you will want to find at least a few examples of each phoneme. Some of the sounds may be quite rare and it will be frustrating if you find you have too little data to provide everything you need. So record more, so you have more to select your examples from.

❐ For dialect studies you may need a longer recording, because certain forms and structures may not appear in a five-minute stretch.

❑ If you need specific forms or examples to occur, don't leave it to chance. Design interview questions or a task that is likely to elicit them.

❑ If you plan to record on more than one occasion, transcribe or do a preliminary analysis of the data you already have before you get the next lot, as this may help you to see what you still need.

Practicalities

❑ Record digitally if you can, because the quality will be better and there is software that will help you with transcription.

❑ Use a good machine, and make sure you know how it operates. If it runs on batteries, carry sufficient spares to change the entire set at once.

❑ If using tapes or disks, buy new ones and ensure you have plenty. If you think you will use several, label them in advance and use them in order. In any case, make sure all your recordings are labelled by the end of the day, or you will forget which is which.

❑ If your machine has limited capacity (tape length or digital memory), consider having a second machine set up and ready to record, to switch on just before the other one stops. The overlap will help with continuity later and it avoids interrupting proceedings to change tape or memory stick, reminding interviewees that they are being recorded, just when they had forgotten. Another obvious advantage is that you can still continue with the collection even if one machine breaks down.

❑ Avoid recording on a mini-cassette Dictaphone, as the quality is poor even before the data is transferred onto normal-sized cassettes.

❑ If possible, use an external microphone. In particular, try to avoid using a machine with a built-in condenser mike that is right next to the motor, as the background hum will be a problem.

❑ If using video, consider whether you want to hand-hold the camera (more flexible but quite intrusive) or put it on a tripod (leaving you free, but risking the action falling outside the frame).

❑ If you decide to conceal a camera or tape recorder, plan carefully how you will achieve this. If there is any danger of it being discovered midway through the recording, or if you will have trouble secretly retrieving it afterwards, you might be better off making it visible in the first place.

❑ Where possible, get informants to identify themselves on the recording, so that you have a reference to link their voice and their name later. When a new speaker contributes, make a note of their name and the counter number/time elapsed.

❑ You may want to plan to collect data from more subjects than you need, in case anything goes wrong with the recording.

❑ Make an edited copy of your original data, containing just the extracts you are focusing on; this reduces the endless fast-forwarding and reversing. With digital data, insert bookmarks at the important locations.

❒ With video data, ask at your institution if there are studio facilities for editing your material.

What to submit

When you submit your project, you may need to provide a copy of your audio/video data for the assessors.

❒ It does *not* need to be a complete recording of everything. Create a short, edited version that contains just the parts that you report on. Provide a menu list of what you have supplied and where it can be found.

❒ Check what media your assessors have and provide the data in that format. For instance, they may not have minidisk or MP3 players or mini-cassette Dictaphone players. Standard audio and video cassettes are increasingly obsolete too. Saving to CD or DVD is probably safe. Data saved to DVD may not be playable on all machines, so check what format to save to.

❒ Listen to the start of the recording, the end, and any transitions between tracks, to make sure you have presented what you intended. If you have recorded over something else, record some silence at the end of the data so that you do not confuse the assessor with unrelated material or deafen him/her with your favourite band.

❒ If the data are not at the beginning of the tape, wind it to the right place or, with digital recording, indicate where it can be found.

❒ Label the tape or disk and its sleeve with your name (or student ID number if your institution operates anonymous marking), module number and tape contents.

❒ Keep a copy of all data and of the project itself, in case it gets mislaid.

Things to think about

❒ How well do you know your informants? It can save a lot of time if you already know them, and many friends and family members will be pleased to help you with your research. On the other hand, a small child who knows you well may mess around, whereas one who knows you less well might be more co-operative.

❒ If recording in a public place, remember that not everyone will necessarily take kindly to being on your recording!

❒ Particularly if there is a high risk of extraneous noise or interruption, request a quiet room if possible.

❒ Plan carefully whom you will record, how long for, and what the agenda will be. If you are interviewing, write a plan of your questions (see Chapter 13).

❒ TV and radio programmes provide good-quality sound. But remember that the sound from a TV doesn't come out of the screen where the mouths are, but from a speaker, often round the side or back.

❒ Scripted speech may not be appropriate to your study, so if you are recording from the radio or TV, look through the schedules to find the most appropriate material to record.

❒ If you want accent features or natural conversation from TV or radio, target 'passer-by' interviews on news broadcasts, schools programmes that use interviews with children, and 'fly-on-the-wall' documentaries.

12
Experiments

Language is a complicated phenomenon and sometimes its occurrence in natural settings does not enable you to see what is going on. Certain kinds of research questions are best answered by creating an artificial situation, where you compare what happens when one specific detail ('variable') is changed, while everything else remains constant. If you find a contrast in what happens in the two conditions, you can reasonably claim that it must be due to that variable.

However, no single individual can be guaranteed to produce behaviour that is consistent or representative of the population as a whole. Therefore, experiments are normally conducted on groups of similar subjects, rather than on single individuals, in the hope that the pooled results will be representative of the wider population.

Conducting experiments can be very rewarding, but it can be a nightmare if the procedures are not carefully planned and executed at every stage. Think twice before embarking on experimental research unless you have a good supervisor who is experienced in it himself or herself.

It is vital to design your experiment round a clearly-thought-through research question, with your focus firmly on what you will do with the results, and what all the different possible outcomes will mean. The skill in running experiments lies in making sure that everything except the variable being investigated remains as similar as possible. For instance, two groups of subjects should be compatible and treated the same way. If you compared women with men on some language-based task and the women performed better, but it turned out that the women were all university graduates in their twenties, while the men were all in their sixties and had left school at 14, it would not be possible to determine which variable (gender, age or education) accounted for the difference in performance.

What does experimentation involve?

Subjects

Normally, you will want to use ordinary people, representative of the general population or some subset of it. However, gathering a sample of practical size that genuinely represents the whole population is virtually impossible, so if it is easiest to only use, say, female undergraduates, do so. In your write-up, just acknowledge the limitations of your subject pool in representing only one subgroup of society.

Since you are likely to need to run statistical tests on your results, you need a statistically viable number of subjects. As a general rule, the problems arise when you have too few subjects, because just one odd result can skew the outcome for the whole group – the more subjects you have, the more that result will be watered down. However, different group sizes can attract different statistical tests. See Chapter 19 for more information.

Conceptual structure

It's absolutely essential to have a clear-cut, well-planned experiment from the outset. Keep it simple and don't be tempted to complicate it while you're running it. It will become complicated of its own accord once you take some basic procedures into account! You should be able to explain in one sentence what you intend to find out and in another one, how you intend to do it.

How do you keep it simple? By generating your design on the basis of a claim in the research literature, and *only* testing that claim. For example, if you read that women tend to use a wider vocabulary of colour terms than men, you might design an experiment to test this claim, by getting comparable groups of men and women to name unlabelled colours on a paint chart, and counting how many different names they came up with.

The **theory** that women use a wider vocabulary of colour terms forms the basis for a specific **hypothesis** about the outcome of your experiment: *Experimental hypothesis: women will produce more different names for colours.* You can then also identify the **null hypothesis**, which states what will happen if the theory you are relying on is incorrect: *Null hypothesis: women and men will not produce a significantly different number of names for colours.*

At this point in your planning, you will need to think through all the possible outcomes of your experiment. List them and consider what they will mean. This is a good way to check that your experiment will work, and it will greatly speed things up later. In our example, there are three possible outcomes:

1   The women produce *significantly* more names, supporting the experimental hypothesis and confirming the theory it is based on. *Significant* is a technical term (see Chapter 19).
2   There is no significant difference between the number of names produced by men and women, supporting the null hypothesis, though there is more than one reason why one might get this result: there really is no difference between men and women; there is a difference, but not a large enough one to show up as statistically significant; there is a difference, but the experiment did not manage to capture it.
3   The men produce more names than women. This would be something of a surprise! Since your experimental hypothesis was not based on a hunch but on apparently reliable claims in published sources, you can ask whether, perhaps, the claims were wrong. By examining the evidence that led to the original claim, you may find an explanation for your finding (e.g. the difference had only ever been observed in natural conversation, not in controlled experiments, so could be a matter of choice rather than vocabulary knowledge).

Procedure

An experimental task should be carefully chosen to be appropriate to the abilities of the subjects. Plan meticulously and run through the steps in a rehearsal and/or pilot study (see Chapter 1). Locate a suitable environment: this must be available when you need it and be within your control. If you use a language lab, make sure you can operate the machinery; if you use a quiet room, make sure the porter, caretaker or secretary will not come and turn you out midway. If you use your own room, negotiate with your flatmates and unplug/turn off phones. If you are testing subjects in sequence, think ahead about the problems of an appointment system – what if someone is late or doesn't show up? If they're early, will they interrupt proceedings and/or overhear something they shouldn't? Perhaps you need an assistant to keep subjects out of the room till the appropriate time, help present stimuli or take notes.

Equipment

You may need equipment for the presentation of stimuli and/or for the collection of data (e.g. recording equipment, a computer, flashcards, a timer). Some procedures used in the published research rely on complex equipment. Computers can display words or pictures for timed periods and can accurately record reactions to them. Fairly simple programs can achieve this. Be practical about what you can achieve and if necessary, use the old pre-technology methods of, say, flashcards and (if it will give sufficient accuracy) a stopwatch. As always, take advice on what is expected of you and how best to achieve your objectives.

Designing an experiment

If possible, base your experimental design on one that has been run before. You can try to match it exactly (replication) or alter one dimension. Published experimental reports vary in how much information they give you about exactly what was done and what stimuli were used, so you may only be able to approximate to previous work. If so, aim to identify what they felt was central to the experimental design.

Experimental comparisons can be made in different ways and may require different statistical treatments (see Chapter 19). The major comparisons are as follows.

Two identical groups . . .

The assumption is that the two groups would perform the same way given the same conditions and input, so that if you vary the conditions or input, that is why their performance varies. Assigning people to groups can be done randomly if the numbers are large enough. Alternatively, share the genders and ages equally between the groups. Do the same for any other factor that you feel could be relevant (such as ethnic origin, past experience, educational background or handedness). Don't go mad, though: hair colour and favourite ice-cream flavour are unlikely to have a bearing on most experiments.

. . . Doing different things

Here, the experiment is based on the assumption that Group A would perform like Group B if it was given Group B's task and vice versa. The reason for not giving both groups both tasks (which is certainly permissible in the right circumstances) is that doing one task spoils you for doing the other. Example: memorizing household items on a tray, compared with memorizing the names of those objects on a list (see Project 2).

... Doing the same thing in different conditions

There are several variations on this, including the following:

- ❐ Both groups perform the same task, but Group A is prepared one way, Group B another: do different things happen? (Look at Project 28.)
- ❐ Group A undergoes a process (such as training), Group B doesn't: do different things happen? Here, B is acting as 'control' group, against which the effect of a process can be measured: in medical trials, one group receives the new drug and another receives a dummy (placebo) drug, to see whether any recovery is due to the drug itself or due to the patient's reaction to being treated (as in Project 3).
- ❐ Both groups complete the same task, but the conditions under which they complete it are different (see Project 1).

Two groups that are different in some specific way doing the same thing

Here, you want to keep the stimuli, training and procedures the same and just compare the effect of being a Group A person as opposed to a Group B person. You need to be able to explain why you think the two groups might perform differently: are you assuming that their brains are wired up differently; that different lifetime experiences will influence their behaviour; that one group will have more confidence than the other? Examples: a comparison of children of different ages; a comparison of males with females; a comparison of native speakers with non-native speakers.

One group doing two different tasks, or one task in two different conditions

This is appropriate where doing the first task (or in the first condition) will not invalidate the results of the second. It is best to take precautions, however, against possible order and practice effects (see below). For example: subjects recite familiar nursery rhymes (or days of the week) and a poem they've only just memorized while bouncing a table-tennis ball on a bat: is their physical accuracy different when they have to think more about what to say next?

Using published results as your control

If you are replicating a published experiment, you can compare your results with those in the original, instead of building a comparison into your own experiment. However, this really does require you to have matched your stimuli, subjects, and conditions very closely with those of the work you are replicating.

More than two groups?

You can compare more than two groups or conditions, but this complicates the results because each group and condition needs to be compared with each other one. Keep to two if you can: to find an age difference, you can compare 18–24-year-olds with 50–55-year-olds: you don't need the ages in between. Don't split groups after the event: if you didn't plan to compare males and females, then don't try to after you have the results.

Things to think about

❒ Will you tell your subjects what you're looking for before they do the experiment? What effect would it have? If you don't tell them, are they likely to try to guess (thereby adjusting their behaviour in uncontrollable ways)?

❒ Will your subjects be intimidated by the experimental set-up (see Chapter 15)? How can you alleviate this without compromising the rigour of the experiment?

❒ Are your stimuli unambiguous? For example, young children may have difficulty interpreting line drawings. Do the stimuli reflect any cultural and social stereotypes that may be inappropriate for some of your subjects?

❒ What exactly are you testing? How will you know if you have found an effect? Does your experiment really measure what you intended? How will you score or assess the data?

❒ Where are you going to get enough subjects and will they be homogeneous enough?

❒ How will subjects, parents, teachers and so on feel about the 'testing' dimension? Can you explain clearly your plans and how the data will be used?

❒ Where can you run it? Do you intend to bring the subjects to one unfamiliar place, so that none of them have the advantage of feeling at home? Can you avoid external interruptions?

❒ Will you have to run the experiment lots of times (on individuals or small groups)? If so, how will you ensure that all the conditions are identical each time?

❒ Do you need special skills or techniques for presenting the stimuli (with child subjects, in operating puppets convincingly, for example)?

❒ Look after your data: summarize your data into clear tables and remember to label them fully. Refer to the content of the tables explicitly, pointing out the important information. Do calculations carefully and check them. Make sure that totals tally.

Order effects

If one group is doing more than one task, or in more than one condition, or with a series of stimuli, how are you to be sure that any differences you find are not simply to do with the order in which the tasks or stimuli were presented? The most straightforward way to cancel out order effects is to split the group in two and present the tasks or conditions in one order to one group and the other order to the other. Then add the results together. If subjects always scored better on, say, the first task or condition, then the differences will cancel out, because half the subjects will have done one task or condition first and half the other.

Floor and ceiling effects

If you make a task too difficult, then everyone will score zero and you'll have nothing to compare! This is called a 'floor' effect. If the task is too easy, everyone will score the maximum and the same problem will occur. This is called a 'ceiling' effect. Your task should be pitched so that everyone performs well inside the range of possible performances (so that, say, if the score potential is 0–20, then the lowest score is about 3 and the highest about 17). Don't expect to know intuitively how to achieve this: that's what a pilot study is for (see Chapter 1).

Practice and fatigue effects

If you were to draw a graph of an individual's performance in a task, you wouldn't be surprised to find that they performed better as they got more accustomed to the task (the 'practice' effect) and worse as they got tired and/or bored (the 'fatigue' effect). Provided that everyone's scores went up and down symmetrically for practice and fatigue and that everyone became accustomed and got tired at the same rate, you could find a way of making allowances for this. But people aren't like that. However, there are ways of reducing the potential of these two effects to skew the results:

❐ Give everyone some practice sessions, so that they don't use the experiment itself to build up to speed.

❐ Design the experiment so that the activities don't go on too long. Obviously, you can't pre-empt at what stage people will become tired, but you can use a pilot study to ensure that you don't seriously overstep the mark.

❐ If some important types of stimuli are positioned at the beginning of the test and there is a general tendency for the scores to be lower than on later ones, you will not be able to tell whether this is due to the nature of the stimuli or the practice effect. Counter this by dividing the different types of stimuli randomly across the test and having different random orders for two randomly split groups. The idea is that a practice or fatigue effect will show on the first or last stimuli irrespective of what those stimuli are, while a genuine stimulus-specific effect should show up on those specific stimuli irrespective of when they are presented. Do not aim to run statistical comparisons on the two groups who get the stimuli in different orders. The results should be pooled, to minimize the effect of those orders.

Emergencies

It can be very distressing if, after all your hard work, your experiment 'goes wrong', whether that simply means that you can't support your hypothesis or that the procedure is actually unworkable, though the latter can be avoided in most cases by running a pilot study. Unforeseen circumstances such as a fire in the building or a breakdown of the equipment are just bad luck. However, many apparent 'disasters' are salvageable:

❐ If the results are inconclusive, that is a result in itself – maybe the claim from the literature upon which you built your hypothesis is not correct or the phenomenon is not measurable in the way you thought. Try to find some possible reasons why you got what you did, especially identifying whether there was any problem with the experimental design. This is how real research actually works: you use each experiment as a way of understanding the bigger picture and working out what to do next time.

❐ If the procedure has gone completely awry, you may have time (or be able to negotiate time) to rerun the experiment, in which case you can treat the original as a(nother) pilot. Alternatively, you may be able to salvage some of the results and report just those.

❐ If there really is nothing to show for it, obviously you need to negotiate with your tutor, but do so in the confidence that anyone who has run experiments has experienced bad luck or bad judgement and so you should get a sympathetic hearing. Offer to write up the experimental design critically and discuss what the various possible results would have meant. Add a section on ways in which problems of the kind you experienced could be avoided in the future.

❐ Occasionally, an experiment turns out to have been a poor way of finding out the thing it was designed for, but incidentally to have ended up measuring something else. So consider whether it is possible to find other patterns in it: you may find that you have another experiment embedded within the one you actually ran. Obviously, however, be careful with this strategy and take advice, because most investigations are only suitable for answering the question they were designed to answer.

Advantages of experimental research

❐ The history of science in the western world clearly demonstrates how important experimental investigation is seen to be. Indeed, there are many who find it hard to conceive of valid research that is not experimental.

❐ A well-planned experiment gives you results that can be processed easily, to provide clear evidence for or against a pre-specified hypothesis.

❐ There are (in theory) no loose ends or awkward corners, and results are easy to relate to each other and to other experiments done in the same way.

❐ A clearly-described experiment can be improved upon in future work or replicated by others.

❐ Experimental data is much more focused than, say, a recording of spontaneous speech or informal interview/activity data, so it is easier to make sense of, to process and evaluate.

Disadvantages of experimental research

❐ Experiments pare the situation down to its bare minimum. Some situations can be treated in this way, but others can't. There is a danger that in the process of controlling the experimental design you lose the very essence of what you are trying to examine.

☐ It is easy to measure the behaviour of people operating in experimental conditions but how could you compare it to their behaviour in non-experimental conditions? (You couldn't do it by experiment, so what would be your basis for comparison?)

☐ Experiments usually end up being harder than they look, and it is easy to bite off more than you can chew.

☐ The more subjects you have, the less likely you are to know a lot about them; there may be hidden variables contributing to your pattern of results. Experiments on people are always subject to much more 'unexplained' variation than those on white rats or vials of potassium permanganate, and they are liable to give ambiguous results. There is a good chance that when you have made your calculations, there will be no statistically significant differences at all. However, this does not mean that your experiment has been a failure. You can write it up with every bit as much confidence as you would if you had made a major new discovery.

☐ Some people (children, for example) do not make good experimental subjects. They may have too short an attention span, feel uneasy about being tested, or be inhibited with a researcher.

☐ You may discover only when you analyse the results, that a subject has not really understood what he/she is supposed to do.

☐ Avoiding design faults, such as potential ambiguities in the stimuli or instructions, can be difficult.

For guidance on writing up your experimental work, see Chapter 1.

13
Questionnaires, interviews and focus groups

If you want to find something out about people's knowledge or beliefs, one very obvious way is to ask them. There is a range of techniques for doing so, from formal tick-box questionnaires sent by email to open face-to-face discussions. Although you are quite likely to choose only to use questionnaires *or* interviews, rather than both, we discuss them together in one chapter, because they share a lot of features.

For present purposes, when we refer to the 'questionnaire' we mean a document that is filled out in writing (or electronically) by the informant. An 'interview' entails the researcher presenting the questions to the informant orally and recording the responses either in written notes or on an audio recording for later transcription and analysis. Thus, we include under 'interview' what is sometimes referred to as the 'spoken questionnaire'. Mixed formats are also possible, however. You could administer the questions in writing and ask the respondents to record spoken responses on audio or video. Conversely, you could administer questions orally (say, to a group of respondents) and ask them to write their responses down. A 'focus group' involves interviewing a group of people together about a particular topic, in order not only to discover their individual views but to observe how the group's interaction develops those views towards patterns of consensus and/or disagreement. You can find useful guidance on all three of these techniques in Bryman (2004). For guidance on using questionnaires in second-language research, see Dornyei (2002).

Focus groups, interviews and questionnaires can help you find out about people's linguistic and social behaviour, attitudes, beliefs and perceptions. They can also be used to elicit comments on a recording, text or picture.

Deciding if you need a questionnaire, interview or focus group

What exactly is it that you want to know? Is asking your informants the best way to find it out? If you want to know how good people are at something, then asking them to tell you how good they are may not be as effective as testing them. But, if you want to know what they think or believe about something, or what they do in situations that you cannot observe, asking them may be the obvious approach. Whether a questionnaire or an individual or group interview will work best may depend on the potential impact for *your* investigation of the key advantages and disadvantages of each approach (see later). It is worth considering all your options at first, until you are certain you have what is best for your needs. As a general guide, remember that certain consequences arise from each method. Questionnaires administered without your being present are capable of providing a large quantity of data that you cannot easily control the detail of, while interviews tend to give you detailed information from a few people. Focus groups enable you to 'interview' more people, but you will not end up with a totally clear impression of each individual's views – the strength of the focus group lies in the construction of a group view. Which approach is most appropriate for answering your research questions?

Common uses of interviews, focus groups and questionnaires

❑   Traditional dialectology, to help produce linguistic maps and atlases.

❑   Urban dialectology, to elicit information on how speakers' accents and dialects change between informal and formal situations, vary according to sex, age and social background, and change over time.

❑   Sociolinguistic work on attitudes towards language, including such matters as non-standard accents and dialects, slang, new vocabulary or pronunciations, female vs male speech features, dying or minority languages, and multilingualism.

❑   Second- or foreign-language teaching and learning, including motivation, learning style, aspirations and needs analysis.

❑   Language surveys, investigating, for example, which languages are spoken in a specific area, when these languages are used, and proficiency levels in the different generations of speakers.

❑   Ethnographic ('whole-culture') research (see Chapter 7), to gather a wide range of information about aspects of specific cultures and societies, including linguistic data.

❑   Data-gathering about perceptions and memories of a linguistic experience, such as asking jury members about their reaction to technical explanations provided in the course of a trial.

❑   Focus groups are particularly useful when investigating topical issues, on which people may not yet have formulated a clear individual opinion, so that discussion with others helps them think through aspects of the issues for the first time.

Subjects

Any subjects can be used, provided they are able to understand the questions and can provide responses (that is, that they can write and/or speak intelligibly in at least one language or dialect shared with the researcher). See Saville-Troike (2003: 99–103) for considerations relating to the selection of subjects, including child respondents.

The number of subjects you use often depends on entirely practical matters. Focus groups need a critical mass to work well (between six and ten participants seems to be effective), and you will normally need more than one group in order to establish the range of views that can emerge. Although questionnaires work with any number of subjects, their true usefulness is with large numbers of subjects. A large sample will be more representative and can lend greater weight to your claims. Interviews cannot be administered to as many people and care needs to be taken that the few whom you select for interview are truly representative of the population you are interested in.

Indeed, for all three approaches, the subjects have to be selected carefully to ensure that as reliable and representative a sample as possible has been obtained. You may work either with a 'random' sample, where 'everyone in the population to be sampled has an equal chance of being selected' (Wardhaugh 2006: 155) or with a 'judgement' sample, where you select your participants according to your preferred criteria, or else a range of representative criteria such as social class, age, gender or education.

If you use a judgement sample, you need to consider two major things: compatibility and representativeness. To ensure compatibility, you need, where feasible, to obtain at least minimal reliable background information on your subjects/respondents. To compare responses from a group, there need to be some baseline features in common, so that it is clear why a comparison is valid. For example, if you were comparing attitudes to mother-tongue teaching in a Polish immigrant community and a Somali immigrant community, it would make sense to ensure that all your interviewees had children, that all used the mother tongue to a similar extent at home, and perhaps, even, that all of them were of the same sex, as differences in any of these variables could otherwise confound your results.

Representativeness is not always easy to achieve. Saville-Troike comments that 'often the people who make themselves most readily available to an outsider are those who are marginal to the community, and may thus convey inaccurate or incomplete information' (2003: 102). She also notes that such 'marginal' group members may 'interfere with the acceptance of the researcher by other members of the group' (ibid.).

Personal information, confidentiality and anonymity

In seeking personal information, a balance needs to be found between getting what you need and being intrusive, or costing people time and extra work. With child subjects, be aware that they may not even know their own name and address, and that school records may not be up to date. If you promise anonymity or confidentiality to subjects, you must keep your word (see Chapter 15).

Limitations of self-report

The 'self-report' element of an interview or questionnaire means that you gain a direct window onto the informants' own views and beliefs. However, there are some limitations:

❏   Respondents cannot always tell you what they actually do, only what they *believe* they do – self-reporting is not necessarily very accurate because we often don't know ourselves very well. This limitation is difficult to overcome but it is important to report your findings appropriately: rather than saying 'All the teachers prioritized content over accuracy', say 'All the teachers said that they prioritized content over accuracy', for you only know the latter, not the former.

❏ The information you get will heavily depend on the way that the questions are formulated and what choices, if any, you offer as possible responses. Thus, care must be taken not to unintentionally influence the findings by building assumptions into the formulation of the questions, or omitting potentially important details.

Ways of getting information

The best way to get information is not always the most obvious. Your aim is to help the informant give you the information you need, and you must think about whether the questions you have formulated will do that successfully. There is a lot to be said for the **direct** (or **explicit**) **approach**, where you are straight and truthful about your interests. It minimizes the risk of being misunderstood and can help your informants to trust you and your questions. However, there can be disadvantages too. Saville-Troike (2003: 102) notes that respondents will sometimes try to provide the answer that they think will please you (courtesy bias) or, conversely, may deliberately try to mislead you (sucker bias). In addition, if your topic includes stigmatized or distasteful issues, they may feel negatively about participating if you tell them directly what you are aiming to research. Direct questioning takes quite a lot of preparation. Investigating a dialect, you would need to go armed with wordlists to elicit pronunciation, and objects, pictures and/or carefully worded probing questions to elicit vocabulary.

In an **indirect** (**inexplicit**) **approach**, the questions you ask are a distracter, and provide the information you want indirectly. For instance, if you wanted to gather data on an elderly person's pronunciation, you might get better data by asking them about their childhood than by asking them about pronunciation itself. You might find out more about a teenager's use of swearwords by asking about emotive issues than by quizzing him/her about the words. Thus, for some kinds of investigation, an indirect approach will make the informants' responses more reliable: there is less motivation to hide or distort anything. On the other hand, your informants may well develop their own opinion about what you are really looking for and perhaps, in trying to be helpful, go off at an irrelevant tangent.

The form of a question matters too. An **open question** offers the respondent a chance to talk or write at length, and that is often just what you want. The classic open question begins with *Why*, or *Can you tell me about …* In an interview, open questions are the gateway to following up interesting issues. In a questionnaire, they provide you with qualitative detail. On the other hand, they can lead to digressions, leaving you with irrelevant material. Open questions are particularly effective in focus groups, where the intention is to generate discussion.

A **closed question** requires only a short answer, with no direct opportunity to expand. Examples include: *What other languages do you speak?* and *Do you like the sound of this voice?* One advantage of closed questions is that they allow you to gather a great many pieces of precise information. However, they have drawbacks too. One is that they can appear rather patronizing. Informants do not want to feel that they are being treated like idiots and you run the risk of receiving flippant, unhelpful answers. Another disadvantage is that closed questions may tend to prejudge the issues and possible responses. Open questions might reveal things you did not know were even there to ask about.

The reason why closed questions nevertheless remain a popular and valued means of gathering data is because they provide answers that are easier to process and score for. Closed questions make possible a range of formats for tallying and comparing responses, and often lead to quantitative analyses. Two of the most familiar types of closed question are **true/false questions** and **yes/no questions**. However, these are rarely useful in linguistic research because, on their own, they give so little information. Fortunately, several other more useful closed-question designs also exist.

A **semantic differential** scale provides respondents with pairs of adjectives with opposite meanings, at either end of a scale. Respondents indicate the approximate position on the continuum between the two that best represent their attitude to, or impression of, a stimulus (Fig. 13.1). It is a means of eliciting subjective reactions to words, speakers' voices on tape, and so on. In order to avoid the respondent construing one end of the scale to be 'worth more' than the other, it is a good idea not to use numbers for the points on the scale, though they can, of course, be added later by the researcher in order to make the data processing easier. One objection to using the semantic differential scale is that it relies on respondents having the same understanding of the adjectives you use. So avoid using adjectives for which this problem might be particularly acute – those, for instance, that are likely to be interpreted on the basis of personal experience, such as *motherly*, *educated*, or *stressed*. For examples in second-language research, see Larsen-Freeman and Long (1991: 35–6).

Your impressions of voice A on the tape:								
friendly	—	—	—	—	—	—	—	unfriendly
unintelligent	—	—	—	—	—	—	—	intelligent
inactive	—	—	—	—	—	—	—	active
reliable	—	—	—	—	—	—	—	unreliable

Figure 13.1 Semantic differential

Another scale that elicits informants' subjective responses is the **Likert scale**, also known as the **attitude scale**. A statement expressing an attitude is presented and the respondents indicate how strongly they agree or disagree with it (Fig. 13.2).

One disadvantage of using the semantic differential and Likert scales is that you force people to choose from a range of responses, of which, perhaps, none might really fit their ideas. You may find that interview respondents sometimes offer an explanation along with, or instead of, a straight response, and questionnaire respondents alter the categories by hand or do not indicate any response on the scale. In both cases, you will then have problems when you come to analyse the data, which you will have expected to be clear-cut and complete. Another problem can arise if all the scales are oriented in the same direction. In written presentation, the positive adjective (semantic differential) or the

Figure 13.2 Likert Scale

'strongly agree' category (Likert scale) might always be to the right, say. Some researchers like to swap the direction between questions, to ensure that respondents have to read each one carefully. However, if you do reverse the scale, and respondents do not notice, they may mark the wrong location on the scale, giving a different answer from the one they intended. Since you may have no way of knowing if this is the case or not, you could have some data that you suspect, but cannot prove, is invalid.

Another way to elicit closed-question judgements from respondents is using a **ranking scheme**. This approach will be familiar to you if you have ever entered a product-promotion competition where you had to put a set of desirable features into their order of importance. In the linguistic domain, Dorian (1981) asked English/Gaelic speakers to order a set of 13 reasons for being a Gaelic speaker into their order of importance (see Dorian 1981: 166; Romaine 1995: 313–14). For general information, see Fasold (1984: 152).

A technique most people are familiar with, though it is by no means the easiest to design well, is **multiple choice**. The respondent is presented with a question (or an incomplete statement, or stem), and must select the appropriate answer (or completion) from a list of several possible alternatives (Fig. 13.3). Whereas in a multiple-choice test of knowledge each question has one correct answer and a set of three or four distracters, in an exploration of attitude or motivation, all the answers might equally be valid, with the choice indicating a range of potential views. Multiple-choice questions benefit from a written format, because it is difficult to keep several choices in your memory at once if you only hear them spoken.

The **matched guise technique** is a specific technique that is often used in association with a questionnaire investigation of language attitudes. Though the precise format may vary, the basic technique usually involves respondents being played recordings of voices and then being asked to evaluate them, using semantic differential scales (see above), on a range of criteria including intelligence, friendliness, co-operativeness, reliability, honesty

I have known her ____ three years now.

(a) whilst   (b) for   (c) since   (d) besides   (e) at

Figure 13.3 Multiple choice

and so on. The technique can reveal which languages or linguistic varieties (accents, dialects) the respondents unconsciously associate with the most positive and most negative personality attributes. On the basis of such tests, several large companies have located their telephone sales or services departments in regions where the local accent is associated with high ratings for intelligence, friendliness and trustworthiness. The recordings typically involve a single person speaking first in one dialect, accent, or language and then in another (that is, in two 'guises'), giving the same information. The respondents must not realize that both recordings were made by the same person. See Fasold (1984: 149–58) for more information. Hughes *et al.* (2005) and Wardhaugh (2006) also provide summary examples.

Things to think about

❐   There are many potential pitfalls with interview and questionnaire studies and a potentially high price to pay if the main study encounters practical problems. So it is very important to run a pilot study (see Chapter 1).

❐   How will you make your respondents trust you and want to help you with your research? Do they really understand who you are and why you are asking them questions?

❐   Do not make too many assumptions about your respondents, especially if they are much older or younger than you are, differently educated from you, or from a different country. Will they know what a questionnaire is? Might their previous experience of interviews have led them to perceive them as threatening or intrusive? Will they understand your speech? Can they read sufficiently well to cope with written questions?

Having considered some of the general approaches and issues relevant to asking people questions, we now consider separately the details of the two main techniques, the questionnaire and the interview.

Questionnaires

Questionnaires can be used to collect both qualitative and quantitative data, and are suitable for a range of research questions, including ones that require several types of information. At their most tightly controlled, questionnaires allow data to be collected in the same, replicable way from a large number of informants. This makes a comparison of the results easier and the conclusions clearer.

For some research, the questionnaire can act as the sole source of data. For other research, it is best used in association with other methods of data elicitation (e.g. interview, test, observation), to gain the full picture. Because of this, questionnaires often do not operate as a substitute for transcription and analysis, but rather complement them.

Advantages

❐   Useful for surveying a lot of people in many different locations.

❏   The identical format means you can easily find corresponding answers across your cohort of informants.

Disadvantages

❏   If an interesting issue is mentioned, about which you would have liked to ask more, you will not know until afterwards.

❏   If you send the questionnaire to people (by post or electronically), you may have a low response rate (perhaps only 20 to 30 per cent). Low response is not only disappointing, but may skew the sample, since taking the trouble to reply may reflect a personality trait that also colours the answers. Those who do not respond might have given different answers.

❏   Unless you are there when the questionnaire is completed, you will never be certain whether: the right person filled it out and without help; it was done in one sitting; the questions were answered in sequence order; all the respondents took roughly the same amount of time over it and completed it in comparable circumstances.

❏   If you have had to rely on someone else to distribute or administer the questionnaire (e.g. in another country), there are inevitable risks. No one will understand the aims as clearly or be as committed to obtaining good data as you are. If you have left it to someone else to identify 'suitable subjects', you have lost control of that aspect.

Formulating your questions

The aim of designing an effective questionnaire is to make it as easy as possible for your informants to provide you with good-quality reliable information. Think through the stages carefully and try things out before committing yourself. With limited space, every question must be there for a good reason. Aim not to collect any information that you have not already planned a specific use for. The test is: point to a question on your questionnaire and ask yourself 'Why do I need this information?' If you can't think of a good reason, consider dropping the question.

Questions must be **simple and unambiguous**. Be careful not to combine several questions into one big one, because you may not get a complete answer or know what exactly the answer refers to. For instance, a question like 'If you have visited a Spanish-speaking country, where did you go, or if you have not, where would you like to go, and why?' is far too complex. Also avoid **loaded questions**, where an underlying assumption is built in. For instance, in 'Why do people think that the Birmingham accent is unpleasant?', you do not allow for the possibility that people *do not* think that the accent is unpleasant. Similarly, don't use **leading questions**, where the wording suggests the 'right' answer, e.g. 'If someone has a strong regional accent and dialect, don't you expect them to be from a lower social class?'

Begin the questionnaire with some easy questions, so that the respondents feel they are getting on well. If there are several harder or more time-consuming ones, space them out, or, alternatively, preface them with a statement such as: 'The following three questions require slightly more detailed answers.' This indicates to the respondent the nature of the new task and how much of it there is.

If you provide a choice of answers, make sure that you cover all the possibilities. Try to imagine a range of different people trying to find an answer to match their precise circumstances.

Include one or two cross-referencing questions, in which you ask, in different words, for the same information as in a previous question. This gives you a check on the reliability of the responses. It is often possible to 'turn the question round' so that a positive response in one version corresponds to a negative one in the other. Be particularly careful, however, that, in doing this, you do not alter the emphasis. For the answers to be comparable, you must have asked for exactly the same information.

Presentation

The single most common response to questionnaires is to throw them in the bin, whether that is immediately they arrive, when completing them gets too difficult, or six months after the deadline, when they turn up in a pile of 'things to do some time'. How can you minimize the risk of non-return?

❑   Provide a covering letter or other form of explanation of who you are, what you are doing and why, and why the respondents' help will be so valuable to you. Also explain your intentions regarding confidentiality or anonymity (see earlier, and Chapter 15).

❑   If your informants are geographically dispersed, will you post them a hard copy, or could you perhaps email one? The latter is quicker and cheaper, and although people ignore or forget electronic documents as much as they do paper ones, at least they don't have to buy a stamp and find a postbox.

❑   Postal questionnaires are cheaper than telephone interviews but the costs are not negligible, especially if you need to pay for the photocopying and both directions of the postal charges.

❑   If your informants are all in one place but too far away for you to go to, how about asking someone else to administer the questionnaire for you, at a set time and place, such as at a meeting or in a class? There are potential disadvantages (see above) but it might be the best solution all the same.

❑   If you can be present, would it be better to ask people to complete the questionnaire while you wait than to let them take it away with them? (It may depend on how long the completion will take and how detailed you want the answers to be.)

❑   Electronic questionnaires give you data that are already transcribed for quick searching and analysis.

❑   Even more analysis-friendly might be a web-based questionnaire, where the responses are automatically catalogued in the format you need, and stored in an archive – if you cannot set this up yourself, see if anyone in your university's computing service can.

You can learn a great deal about the design of questionnaires by considering your own response to the ones that you have had to complete in the past. For example, have you ever:

❒ not felt that any of the answers on offer actually reflected your view?

❒ not really understood what the question was getting at?

❒ not wanted to answer a particular question because it was too personal, painful or difficult?

❒ not really cared whether you gave accurate or truthful answers, because the whole thing seemed rather silly, or ill-thought-out?

❒ been reluctant to give certain details because the questioner wanted your name and address and you were worried about where the information would end up?

These common reactions, and many others, can seriously compromise the success of a questionnaire survey. Do a careful pilot study (see Chapter 1) to ensure that you have not made it in any way difficult for your respondents to provide accurate and honest information.

❒ Make sure that the instructions make the task look easy. If there are different routes through the questionnaire, mark them clearly and ensure they look logical (e.g. If you answered 'No', please move to question 13).

❒ Give it a clear and roomy presentation, including adequate space for answers, but . . .

❒ . . . don't let the questionnaire get too long.

Here are some key points to bear in mind:

❒ How clear are your instructions and the questions themselves? If something turns out not to be clear, will circumstances make it possible for you to clarify it to everyone, or just to the person who queries it? Is there any risk that different understandings of a question will make your results difficult to interpret? How can clarifications be provided that do not suggest particular answers?

❒ Even one question that respondents consider to be too difficult or too intrusive could jeopardize the number of returns you get, if the questionnaires are completed out of your sight.

❒ Have you experimented with different formats for different questions? You might combine various of the closed-question formats described above, with requests for more open-ended answers.

❒ If you are using closed questions, give opportunities for 'comments', if you think they might help you interpret the responses you get. However, only do this if you plan to write about your data in a qualitative way: if you only need to count up how many of each response you have got, then you won't want to engage with discussion based on voluntary comments.

❒ At the bottom of each page (paper or electronic), give an instruction to go to the next page. It may seem obvious, but it is not worth risking even one respondent missing a whole page or more of questions by not realizing they were there.

❒   What will happen if pages get separated on your paper questionnaire? See if you can think of a way to make sure you will be able to reunite loose pages with the right document.

❒   At the end of the questionnaire, leave a space for and invite final comments, thank the respondents for their trouble, and provide clear instructions about who it is to be returned to, how, and by when.

❒   Have your respondents ever seen a questionnaire before? They are relatively unfamiliar in some communities and respondents may not be sure how to deal with them. Children may never have filled one in before.

❒   Some people may be suspicious of what looks like an official form.

❒   People with low levels of literacy, or whose native language is not that in which the questionnaire is written, may find the whole exercise intimidating.

❒   People can suffer from 'questionnaire fatigue', if they have been confronted with too many other questionnaires before yours. This may make them less willing to take part or they may tend to give irresponsible answers.

Interviews

Interviews are stressful to administer and must be carefully planned. You will need a list of questions that you know will work – if you modify your questions too much during the course of a set of interviews, then you may find that the answers from the earlier ones and the later ones cannot be pooled or compared. You need to find a balance between simply barking out questions in a preordained order, and letting the interviewee take over and tell you things you don't want to know.

Open questions (see earlier) are highly desirable in order to get detail and depth, but they can create difficulties if the informant digresses in one question into the territory of a later question. You need to be able to quickly assess the risks and benefits of curtailing an account now and returning to it later, versus letting the interviewee continue, and perhaps losing the logical flow you had planned for your questions later on. Because they don't fully understand the 'routine' of questionnaires, children are particularly prone to digress and to think it strange if information which has already been given is asked for again.

One solution is to plan out a series of potential pathways through your list of questions, according to how the interview is developing. Doing this can also enable you to include questions that become relevant only if a particular previous question has been answered in the affirmative, say, or others if it has been answered in the negative. While it is impossible to anticipate every possible answer, the more you are ready for, the less likely you are to be disorientated by what a respondent says.

Conversely, you can deliberately plan to control the order in which topics are covered, so that you gradually develop a particular line of thought in your respondent. It is even possible to pose the same question twice, once near the start of the interview and again near the end, and quite naturally elicit different answers, because of what has happened in between. This sort of sequential control is much easier to achieve in an interview than in a written questionnaire, where the respondent might look ahead, or go back and alter an earlier answer. However, carrying it off requires a lot of confidence.

Be aware of your own personality. How well do you think you will succeed in getting the kind of rapport with your subjects that you need for your particular study? Doing a pilot study can make this easier to judge, and will give you practice in approaching the task in a way that works for you.

Similarly, consider whether your respondents might be influenced in their responses by who you are, or what (they perceive that) you represent. If your racial, social or gender identity might influence what they say, is there anything that you can do about it? Perhaps someone else could do the interviewing? In all events, remember to mention any such concerns in your write-up, and to comment on what effect they might have had. Respondents might also be affected by the very fact of sitting face to face with someone, particularly if the information being provided is sensitive or embarrassing. Remember that your primary aim is to get answers to your research questions. If your respondents would be more comfortable with the anonymity of a questionnaire that does not bear their name, then this might better meet your research needs in the end.

General procedures

Where possible, you should expect to audio- or video-record interviews. Although this means that you must allow time for transcribing the key points later, it is well worth it. You can concentrate all of your attention on the interviewee(s), rather than continually having to break eye contact by looking away while you write things down. You can also avoid having to make snap judgements about what to note down and what to omit. A third advantage is that you are not a victim of your own handwriting, which may be less than legible during hurried note-taking.

You can interview people individually or in a group. Group interviewing enables you to collect data from a lot of people very quickly and individuals can spark off ideas in each other. On the other hand, you may find that one person influences others by inhibiting them from saying what they really think or by leading the group into apparent agreement. People may speak at the same time, so it is hard to hear all the different points being made and might possibly be difficult later on to tell who is who on the tape. One type of group interview is the focus group, which we consider separately below.

Interviewing makes possible the collection of certain types of information that would be less easily gathered by questionnaire or in a focus group. In **data elicitation**, you deliberately set up situations, or ask specific questions, that will give you the data you want. This gives you a considerable level of control. For obvious reasons, an interview is particularly suitable for collecting oral data, and is often used for dialect studies.

Questions can be asked either directly (e.g. 'What is your word for this?', 'Do you like the local accent here?'), or by tightly controlling the conversation so that relevant information naturally emerges. Although direct questioning about language or attitudes towards it is a well-tested technique (as in, for example, the Survey of English Dialects – see Chapter 9), it does have its disadvantages. While it is straightforward to ask someone directly about their memories of the war or what their school years were like, asking them questions about language does not always produce useful results, as speakers do not always know much about how their variety works and/or may be self-conscious about it.

In conversation, the different forms of a verb can be explored by asking questions like: 'So, did you do that often?' and 'What did you do exactly?' This might provide replies like: 'Oh, we were always X-ing' and 'We only X-ed when it was a games lesson.' For more guidance on investigating accents and dialects, see Chapter 9.

Asking for intuitions is rather different from general questioning or eliciting linguistic forms, because you are trying to get a 'view round the back' of the process that has led your informants, or would lead them, to their linguistic responses. As we do not by any means always know what we are doing when we speak or write, this technique has a limited scope but is quite useful within that. It requires the subject to have self-knowledge and the vocabulary to talk about language (metalanguage). Unlike other types of data collection, it is important that you conduct the interviews yourself, rather than delegating the job to someone else. Questions can be concurrent with a task (such as 'Tell me how you're working that out' or 'Why did you choose that one?'), retrospective (such as 'Look at the video/listen to the tape and tell me what you were thinking as you wrote/said that'; 'Why do you think you said it that way?') or even more direct, such as asking a simultaneous interpreter 'Do you think that you plan a whole sentence before you start speaking? Why?'

Subjects' accounts of their own opinions and intuitions, possibly alongside the results of a task they were completing, will appear initially chaotic and may add up to several hours of taped material. When taping or videoing, try out the position of the microphone in advance, as people tend to speak quietly when they are talking about their thought processes.

There are several advantages to intuition data. There is a real sense in which you can get inside the mind of the subject. Whereas in experiments you are trying to interpret the mind of the subject solely from observing his/her behaviour, here you can actually get the subject to help you. Also, subjects know that they are being recorded, so there's no need for clandestine activity. The fact of their knowing is unlikely to compromise the results, unless they are inhibited from being totally honest, for some reason (e.g. if you get them doing word association for sex vocabulary). Disadvantages, however, include the following.

Data based on people's intuition is scientifically imprecise and will never give you more than a rather cloudy view of what is 'really' going on. Not everyone sees intuition studies as valid. It can be argued that intuition is like an iceberg: nine-tenths hidden, so the little bit you can get at is not representative of the whole. There is no way of controlling how much information of a particular type people either have access to or choose to give, nor whether it is accurate or not (they could even lie). Respondents who are not used to talking about language may lack the knowledge and analytic tools to give you anything but brief and vague answers. Finally, the intuition itself is filtered through the interpretation and expression of both the informant and the researcher. This is not insignificant: to what extent are we able to verbalize our intuitions about brain processes at all? And how compatible are the experiences of two people (interviewer and interviewee) or their vocabulary for talking about internal processes?

As with most types of research, what you get out depends on what you put in. In this case, what you put in must be designed to access information that the informant may not even know they have, and also to provide you with something that you can make sense of. If you have a long set of comments from different informants, you need to find some way of presenting them thematically, to tell more of a story than you'll get from just listing them.

Gathering general data for later analysis

In this approach, you are conducting a general interview simply in order to gather a body of language data. You might do this if you wanted to avoid the subjects knowing what you were looking for (because if they did, they might behave differently). Alternatively, you could simply want to use this 'personal' method to obtain data from particular individuals (such as elderly neighbours), as an alternative to, say, taping speech from the radio.

By definition, you will be letting the conversation go where it will, even if you prompt with questions. Certain types of topic may elicit good accent and dialect material, such as reminiscences; others may increase the likelihood of language that is not influenced by the presence of the interviewer, as in the case, say, of emotive issues, such as recalling a bereavement or an emergency situation. You can usually increase the chances of getting speech that is relaxed and that contains informal features (such as strong dialect or accent) if the speakers talk about things they are familiar and comfortable with, and/or things associated with their childhood. If you want to avoid them knowing you are interested in their language, enlist them to help you draw their family tree, or say that you are studying changing fashions in forenames, the history of games played in the street and playground, childhood pranks and punishments, or changes in occupations and work patterns. Alternatively, you could ask about the history of the local area. If possible, have some old photographs and read up on the area beforehand.

With children, you may need props in order to elicit the data. Practise in advance with any pictures, toys, games, flash cards and so on, and have a trial run with subjects like the ones you will use in the data collection. Check with parents or teachers that the activities you have chosen are appropriate for the age of the informants.

A word of warning: the general questioning technique might seem like a good way to collect data before you have developed a clear idea of what you want to study, but it is not. You could well end up with a lengthy tape of data and not know what to do with it. In other words, make a positive decision to gather data in this way, for reasons related to the specific analysis you have planned.

Focus groups

Focus groups have been used for years in commercial settings, to find out how consumers react to products, and they are increasingly used to canvass the political views of 'ordinary people'. They can also be very productive for linguistic research of many kinds but, before you decide to use them, be sure that they are the best way to meet your needs. The word 'focus' is there for a reason and they are most successful where the topic under discussion is very clearly focused. The focus comes from some shared topic, often a video that everyone has just watched, or an experience they have jointly been through. This focus enables the researcher to be confident that everyone is talking about the same thing, since there is no opportunity, as there is in an individual interview, to probe about each person's specific experiences or understanding of key concepts under discussion.

Effective focus groups tend not to be heavy on formal questioning, as you might find in a group interview, but rather facilitate guided discussion. Part of your interest needs to be the way that being in a group affects how the individuals respond – that is, how individuals develop or defend their views in the light of what others say. If, conversely, the group dynamic will be a complication for you, as you try to find out what each individual would have told you on their own, then you should be conducting individual interviews.

The role of the 'interviewer' minimizes in an effective focus group, and becomes closer to that of a 'facilitator', who sets the ball rolling and then tries to stay out of the way as much as possible. Doing this effectively is a skill that may require some practice. A major advantage of the reduced role of the interviewer is that it is left to the participants to determine which of the issues is foregrounded and which backgrounded. Even though you will expect to intervene at certain points to introduce new topics, you will find that each group discusses different things, and indeed not necessarily the things you had expected or hoped – something you need to anticipate and be prepared for. The more different groups go off in different directions, the more you may be tempted to conclude that it is something *about* that group's characteristics (jointly or individually) that determined its focus. However, that may not be so: conversations in groups reach crossroads at regular intervals, and going down one path rather than another can be somewhat arbitrary – the same group on another day might have done something different. So you need to develop a sense of how much it is reasonable to read into the specific outcomes that you got.

Organization

Organizing focus group meetings takes time and thought. Where should you meet? Where will people go if they arrive early or late? Can they park? Do you need to pay their travel expenses? Should you provide them with refreshments? What will you do if some people don't turn up? If someone arrives late, when you have already started the meeting, should you let them in even though they have not received the same briefing? But the biggest question of all is: Whom should you invite? This depends, once more, on what you are trying to achieve. A useful test is to write, at the planning stage, the following extract from your write-up: 'This particular profile of participants was selected because …' and then try to fill in the rest of the sentence with an eye to how it will fit in with your research account. Suitable completions might be 'they were all within an age range that made them likely to have done X/studied Y/confronted Z' or 'they had all identified themselves in a survey as having an interest in X/experience of Y', and so on. Try to avoid putting yourself in a position where you would have to say 'they were the only people I could find in the Student Union bar'.

Since you will expect to have several groups, you can decide whether you are interested in how *similar* the discussions from similarly constituted groups will be, or how *differently* things develop in groups of different types. In the first case, you may be able to assemble a full list of participants and assign them randomly to groups. However, you may have to be pragmatic in accepting that people's availability on certain days or at certain times will play a role in who ends up with whom. In the second case, you will need information in advance about each person, that will allow you to allocate them to the appropriate group. 'Appropriate' groups are determined on the basis of what you are trying to find out. For instance, if you were interested in the question 'Should minority languages be used in nursery schools?', you might choose to have contrasting groups: minority language-speaking mothers of nursery-age children; teenagers whose parents speak minority languages and who did and did not attend nursery schools that used the language; nursery-school teachers from ethnically mixed and unmixed areas and so on. In this way, you would hope to demonstrate that the issues are complex, and differently perceived by different contingencies – something that might not emerge so clearly if you had random groupings.

Reporting

What you can report from a focus group will be different in kind from what you can report from questionnaires and interviews, since you will not necessarily have a clear sense of anyone's full view, nor, if the group has worked well, that any individual has only one unchanging view.

For fairly obvious reasons, it is a particularly good idea to video-record focus groups and, if possible, with more than one camera, so that you can capture everyone visually. Without that visual record, you may struggle to work out who is saying what. For more guidance on recording, see Chapter 11. When it comes to transcription, you may be faced with a great deal of complex conversational data. Don't assume that you must transcribe everything before you start. Wait until you know what you need, and transcribe just that. Remember also that orthographic (conversation) transcription (see Chapter 17) is a device for representing speech so that it can be analysed structurally. If you are interested in the *content* of the conversations and not how the conversations are conducted, then you may in fact not need to transcribe them using the full orthographic conventions at all. Once again, the rule is: ask yourself what you are trying to achieve and then consider the best way to achieve it. With focus groups, in particular, don't make unnecessary work for yourself, for your data will be rich enough to occupy you with relevant analyses.

For more information on focus groups, see Bryman (2004, Ch. 16), Krueger and Casey (2000), and Litosseliti (2003).

14
Observation and case studies

The terms 'observation study' and 'case study' are not mutually exclusive: you may be doing both. Observation studies involve the collection of data without manipulating it. The researcher simply observes ongoing activities without making any attempt to control or determine them. In a case study, some or all of the data may result from observation but it is also possible to collect data in other ways. In this chapter, we first of all consider observation studies and then case studies.

Observation studies

Normally, you would study ordinary people or people with some recognized disability, about which generalizations can be made. You can use any number of subjects. Remember, however, that you may need quite a lot of background information on each subject and that each will produce quite a large quantity of unsorted data, so small numbers are advisable. Data from subjects who are expected to share patterns of behaviour can be pooled. Subjects with contrasting characteristics can be compared. They can be of any age, gender or background but if you are pooling results, the fewer variables there are of this kind, the more compatible the subjects will be. You may gather your data in various ways, including audio- or video-recordings when you are present or absent, recording from the radio or TV, or re-using data previously collected for some other purpose (but in this case you may not have access to all the background material that you need).

Observation data is qualitative in the first instance, consisting of recordings, transcriptions, and notes relating to your subjects' behaviour and language (spoken and/or written). You may subsequently derive quantitative data from it (such as the number of words in each utterance).

Advantages

While many types of research can only measure *elicited* behaviour because specific tasks are presented in a controlled environment, observation enables you to examine non-elicited behaviour as and when it occurs (e.g. slips of the tongue, paralinguistic behaviour, interactional behaviour and pathological phenomena). This allows a much more 'holistic' view of how language is being used in context. For this reason, it is a technique much favoured by ethnographers (see Chapter 7). It is also more flexible than, say, a controlled experiment, where any extraneous or unplanned event could potentially invalidate the results. Another advantage is that observation studies are relatively easy to administer. Indeed, by using pre-recorded or broadcast material, you can avoid many of the practical difficulties of data collection. Observation can be used at the planning stages of other types of project in order to get ideas or to determine the feasibility of the main procedure and can supplement information gathered by other methods.

Disadvantages

Making secret recordings is generally considered unethical, yet sometimes the subjects' awareness of an observer or of recording equipment can affect how they behave (the observer effect or the observer's paradox). Another disadvantage is that some observable phenomena (such as slips of the tongue) are not densely packed in data, so you may need a great deal of material to get even a small set of interesting observations. However, you do not need to transcribe or analyse anything that is irrelevant to your study. Also, it can be difficult to predict what sort of material you will get: topics may shift, the things you were looking for may not occur, and observation studies are difficult to replicate on another occasion because there are so many uncontrolled variables. Finally, it may not be easy to produce well-focused conclusions because the data is so unstructured and multifaceted. It may be hard to decide which parts of the data to submit to the assessor as part of the project, as the points of interest may be spread over a large quantity of material.

Things to think about

☐   Be very sure of precisely what you are looking for. While you may not be able to envisage what specific *examples* of a phenomenon you will gather, you should know before you start what phenomenon you are investigating. In other words, don't just switch on a tape recorder and hope that something of interest will materialize! Try to ensure that you are looking for something that is likely to occur reasonably often.

☐   To remain within ethical guidelines, you should normally aim to get consent in advance of your observation and/or recording. If you do collect the data secretly, you will need the subjects' permission after the event. With child subjects, you will always need the consent of parents and schools.

☐   Different types of phenomena will come from different sources. For example, if you wanted to look at spontaneous slips of the tongue, there would obviously be no point in recording a play from the radio. Nor would you be likely to find many in an interview between an experienced journalist or presenter and a politician. Slips of the tongue tend to occur when the speaker is tired, nervous, flustered or drunk, so you would need to consider how best to record someone in that state. Asking your subject to read out loud some very complicated unfamiliar text would be one way to increase the likelihood of observing speech errors.

☐   Be aware of what role you, as the observer, might be playing in the dynamics of the situation you are observing (see Chapter 1). You might put subjects at their ease by being a full participant in the procedures. You would be counted by them as one of the group and you would join in with what they were doing on an equal basis. However, it is important, as a 'participant observer', not to try to direct or manipulate, nor to test or interview.

☐ Alternatively, you may decide not to be present at all during the recording. In the Bristol Survey of Language Development, begun in 1972, spontaneous speech was recorded by fitting children with radio microphones. Taping was activated at random preset times, so neither subjects nor carers knew when they were being recorded. The researchers then talked through the tapes with the carers to get clarification of any difficult passages and to find out about the concomitant activity. Expensive equipment may well not be available, but you might still consider leaving a tape running while you are out of the room. You can read about the Bristol Survey in, for example, Wells (1981, 1985).

☐ To help summarize your results, devise a checklist for features based on other studies and use this as a framework. For each feature, systematically record whether the subject(s) used it or not. At the end of each section, you can then produce a table or list, bringing out any patterns. If you have a transcript available, remember to note line numbers for occurrences of features, so that these can be stated in the project.

☐ Consider carefully how to draw conclusions from your results. Focus on finding patterns in the data that relate to your original research questions. Are there any differences between individuals for the features you were interested in? If you have not found the differences you expected, explain why this might be. Scrutinize your sampling, data collection and analysis procedures for possible causes. Perhaps previous studies on which your expectations were based were flawed and your results have helped to demonstrate this.

Case studies

A case study is usually most appropriate where a given individual has some behaviour worth observing, but where the circumstances are so individual or rare that there would be no benefit in combining the results of observations of that person with those of others. A case study would also be appropriate if the phenomenon being observed is so complex that a variety of different kinds of data is needed in order to gain a full picture, with the interest lying in how that particular individual manages the different processes. Case studies are particularly suitable for longitudinal research (where you observe the individual change over time and the focus is on comparisons of the individual's performance on a sequence of occasions). They are a vehicle for both qualitative and quantitative research.

Data can be collected using the techniques of observation, interview and/or testing, and will often be supported by additional information, both linguistic and non-linguistic, from parents, carers and official records. Whether you are dealing with language plus a special circumstance or creating a 'profile' of a normal individual's development or progress in one or more aspects of language, you will also need to accumulate background knowledge of what the range of normal development is, so that you have a baseline against which to interpret the patterns you observe.

You will normally need the consent of the subject and anyone else involved (doctor, speech therapist, teacher, family) and you must be able to demonstrate strict confidentiality. You may have to travel to your subject on several occasions and fit in with others' schedules. Remember to take into account the cost in time and money, and to consider how you will transport any equipment you need. If you are administering tests, you can design your own or ask the therapist, doctor or teacher for access to some of those that are standard as diagnostics.

Advantages

You can study someone you already know, in his/her own home or some other environment familiar to him/her; this increases the likelihood of observing representative behaviour. Often there are good opportunities for observing the language of carers and/or teachers as well. The data is valid in its own right, irrespective of how representative of a population the individual is. If you are conducting a longitudinal study, this gives a more genuine picture than can be gained by comparing individuals at each of the different stages (a cross-sectional study). As you become more familiar with the case, you can develop your investigation in new directions.

Disadvantages

Relying totally on data from one person can be risky. The subject's personality, disabilities (or limitations), prejudices and anxieties may be difficult to deal with. If you are collecting data over a period of time, the subject might move away or the circumstances change so that your visits are no longer welcome. If your ideas about the study change as you proceed, your early data may be less useful than you hoped or you may be stuck with a test design or observation procedure that is not appropriate to what you later want to find out. Working over an extended period it can be difficult to remain objective. Also, a child subject may take things less seriously as the level of familiarity increases. Other disadvantages of case studies include the time they can consume, not only for you but also for the subject and his/her carers, teachers and so on; the small sample size, which means that few generalizations can be made; and the fact that relevant data can be elusive.

How to set up a case study

Accessing a subject can take time, so it's better to know someone already. If you do not, work through a professional such as a teacher or speech therapist. If you are approaching a patient you don't know, take advice about how to do this or get yourself introduced by someone they know. Do what you can to make it clear to the patient and his/her family that you are *not* an expert and that you are there only because they are kindly doing you a favour. If negotiating with a parent about access to their child, explain your intentions in as much detail as possible. Don't insist on the parent being excluded from the room if they would rather stay. Keep the parent on your side by asking for advice and insights.

A foreign- or second-language learner can be contacted through a school or college, or through an agency providing language support. However, you could also set up your own arrangement with a friend who fancies studying a new language; but remember you will be relying on them to see it through, so make sure they are serious about it and are in a position to continue the study for as long as you need.

Before you begin collecting data, do some initial observation to identify likely areas of interest (you can't look at everything). This will help you to design any tests you need to elicit particular phenomena.

Remember that you are dealing with real people (subject and carers) who may be in a delicate state, and/or sensitive about their language performance or their role in supporting and teaching the subject. So be scrupulous in your preparation and sensitive and professional in your approach. Ensure that the subject *really* does not mind being observed or tested, and *really* understands what's involved. Think carefully about what you expect the subject to do, and how you will cope if they don't, can't or won't. Part of this entails finding out as much as you can about how to do your research *before* you get there: read journals, ask the professionals and be guided by them.

Dealing with the results

Avoid accumulating hours of taped material or other observations without any clear idea of what you will do with it all. Try to transcribe and analyse the data as you go along: it reduces the amount to be done in the final stages and it gives you a chance to see if any of your data-collection methods need refinement. By knowing what you are looking for, you can transcribe just the material that is relevant, saving a lot of time. If you have several types of data to analyse (spoken, written, tests, observed, elicited and so on), keep a careful eye on staying within your project word limit.

It is not sufficient simply to list (even in summarized form) what you have seen; you need to pull out patterns and relate them to models and/or theories. It is fine to home in on one or two interesting aspects and leave the rest aside – don't feel you have to describe everything in equal detail and depth. However, it is important to indicate when you *have* left some things aside, so that your assessor doesn't think you have failed to see them.

15
Ethical considerations in research projects

For obvious reasons, there have always been strict rules about trying out new drugs on people in medical research but, in recent years, attention has also been paid to the rights and welfare of those who are used in other types of research, including language studies and linguistics.

Ethics policies and guidelines

Most universities and colleges have their own ethics policies and you should check with your supervisor whether there are any procedures you have to follow in order to have your research plan approved. Ethics policies generally focus on ensuring that data is handled sensitively, that there is no unnecessary deception or distress caused during the data collection, and that subjects have sufficient information to make an informed decision about their participation.

The key points most relevant to linguistic research are:

❏ The welfare of the client/subject/community representative is paramount.

❏ All research procedures should be within the law and in line with the recommendations of the appropriate community, academic or professional bodies.

❏ All participants (and guardians and/or carers) should be told the purpose and nature of the research project with information on potential benefits being put into the context of any potential risks.

❏ All explanations of the project should be in a form that the participants can understand. This means that you need to:

    ❏ think carefully about the participant's language ability or level of understanding;

    ❏ be sensitive about the demands that your research is putting on any informants with special needs;

    ❏ ask for the consent of an appropriate adult (usually parent or guardian) in the case of a child and the consent of the school if you are carrying out your research in the classroom.

❏ Informed consent should be obtained in writing from all participants.

❏ Participants must know that they have the right to withdraw from the project at any stage without any obligation to explain their decision.

❏   Confidentiality or anonymity should be assured for all participants in any reports of the project and if this is not possible, participants should be told so, as part of the consent procedures.

The difference between confidentiality and anonymity

With anonymous data, even *you* do not know who has provided what. For instance, you might issue a survey questionnaire that does not require respondents to give their name, only information about, say, their age and gender. Generally, there is no way for you to trace back a specific response to an individual. Where data is confidential, you *do* know who is who, but you undertake not to let anyone else know. For example, you might interview or observe people and, in your transcription and write-up, give them a different name and (if necessary) alter certain personal details that do not have a bearing on your analysis.

Anonymity precludes you from using any sort of code number that can lead you back to an identity for each respondent. If you feel you will need to know, for example, who has and who has not returned the questionnaire, or if you may need to do follow-up interviews, then do not offer anonymity, but rather confidentiality. You might favour anonymity when, for example, you are investigating delicate issues, such as names for intimate parts of the body or knowledge and use of swearwords. It is often assumed that respondents will be more candid when anonymous. However, they can also be less responsible, and you may be left unsure about the validity of their answers.

Are your data really anonymous?

Handwriting and linguistic style can be distinctive. If you believe that you will recognize certain responses and it might matter to the respondent (e.g. the information is sensitive or embarrassing), consider designing your data collection tool to gather multiple-choice responses rather than lengthy written ones. If you cannot do this, you could suggest to your respondents that they write in capital letters (to make writing less identifiable), or in note form (to minimize the opportunities for language errors). Alternatively, they could respond electronically, if you can arrange for the files to be deposited in a central database that does not store their identity (ask your computer services support team for advice).

Are your data really confidential?

You must remove *all* clues to identity before submitting your work. This includes what you have written on the jacket of your audio cassettes or disks, and the identification data on any sample transcriptions or analyses in your appendix. It also means *not* thanking the participants by name in your acknowledgments section! If you are submitting audio or video data, then clearly there is a potential problem with confidentiality, since someone might recognize participants even if they don't know their names. You should make clear to the participants that the data you are collecting will be seen by your assessors. You could take the precaution of a statement in your write-up such as:

The material provided in this project has been collected on the understanding that confidentiality will be observed in relation to identities of and details about individual participants. The author respectfully requests that those reading this project maintain this confidentiality code. Thank you.

For further guidelines on ethical considerations in linguistic research, see www.baal.org.uk/about_goodpractice_stud.pdf. A useful chapter on ethics in social science research is Bryman (2004, Ch. 25).

Data Protection Laws

Many of the ethical issues that researchers need to bear in mind are legislated for. In the UK, this is done through the Data Protection Act (1998), the Freedom of Information Act (2000) and the Human Rights Act (1998). The Office of Public Sector Information website (www.opsi.gov.uk) allows you to read the legislation online. Most countries have some equivalent laws and you should be able to find out about these via your local or university library. The following information about the situation in the UK should provide pointers as to the issues that you need to consider.

The purpose of the **UK Data Protection Act 1998** (www.opsi.gov.uk/acts/acts1998/80029—l.htm#sch1) is to protect the rights of people about whom personal/sensitive information is stored on computer. This is achieved by two basic means. Anyone who stores data on individuals must *only store what they actually need*, and must *register as a data user*, saying what the information will be used for. The law does not give an individual the right to control what is done with information stored about them, but it is possible to request a copy of what details are being held and/or distributed. This right was established in the UK in the **Freedom of Information Act 2000** (www.opsi.gov.uk/acts/acts2000/00036—a.htm#1). The **Human Rights Act** (1998, effective from 2000 in UK, www.opsi.gov.uk/acts/acts1998/19980042.htm) was incorporated into UK law to 'give further effect to rights and freedoms guaranteed under the European Convention on Human Rights'.

The problems that the Acts are designed to address are mainly as follows:

❑ gathering data for one purpose and then using it for another, without the permission of the individual involved;

❑ storing information that is incorrect.

How does Data Protection legislation affect academic research?

Data Protection legislation is not designed with academic researchers in mind, but it can affect them. For example, under the UK's Data Protection Act (DPA), if you were doing some case studies and you kept computer files that had personal information in them, then you might need to register. The easiest and most sensible procedure would therefore be to keep any personal information about your research subjects on paper. Note that in the UK, if you put the information onto computer solely as part of the word-processing of your work, that is, just for presentational purposes, it is *not* subject to notification. There are some special provisions in the UK's DPA for data that is for 'research, history and statistics'. These permit data to be kept indefinitely (not normally allowed) and also allow researchers to use data for research that was not collected for that purpose. Data can be held for research purposes, provided that it is not used for anything else and the identity of individuals cannot be worked out from the write-up.

Note

The information provided in this chapter is for guidance only. If you are unsure if you are in breach of ethical or legal requirements, you should check with an authoritative source.

PART III

TOOLS FOR DATA ANALYSIS AND PROJECT WRITING

16

Transcribing speech phonetically and phonemically

In most situations, slight differences in the pronunciation of a sound by different people, or by the same person on different occasions or in different linguistic contexts, can be overlooked. It is enough to recognize what the words were, or that a given sound was a kind of 't' or a kind of 's'. But, where pronunciation is the focus of your work, you need finer distinctions. The sorts of studies where this may apply include:

❐ accents
❐ first-language acquisition
❐ second-language acquisition
❐ language impairment
❐ speech errors
❐ conversation
❐ language and gender.

The difference between phonetic and phonemic transcription

If you are focusing on pronunciation, it will soon become clear to you that you need a means of transcribing sounds in some detail. Specifically, you need to be able to demonstrate on paper the often subtle differences between two sounds that do not contribute to any change in the identity of the words but which are, nevertheless, salient within the study you are doing. This is done using **phonetic** script and transcriptions are enclosed in **square brackets**. On the other hand, in order to write about the *relationships* between two pronunciations, you will also need a transcription system that allows you to consider a sound in general terms, independently of its detailed realization on a particular occasion. For this, you need to use **phonemic** script, enclosing transcriptions in **slanted brackets**. This may seem like a mere difference of degree, but it is not.

Phonetic transcription

Phonetic transcription can be likened to an infinite palette of paints. It is possible, in theory, to depict in phonetic script differences as subtle as the most finely attuned ear can hear. To achieve this, there is a large inventory of symbols, including a set of **diacritics**, which act as pointers to exact articulatory positions or ways of making a sound. Thus, to give just two examples, the diacritic [₊] written beneath a symbol indicates *tongue further forward* and [:] written to the right-hand side of a symbol means *of greater duration*. A full set of symbols, including the diacritics, can be found on the IPA chart on page xiv.

Because the detail that can go into a phonetic transcription is potentially infinite, a phonetician needs to make a decision about what to include and what to leave out. In practice, the relatively untrained ear simply does not hear much of the detail, and so the rule of thumb for most students is *if you can hear it, write it down*. However, as detailed transcription is time-consuming, avoid transcribing material or detail that you know you will not need. A detailed phonetic transcription is termed *narrow* and a less detailed one *broad*. A broad transcription may use few more symbols than a phonemic transcription, but it is *not* one, for all the reasons outlined in this chapter.

Phonemic transcription

Phonemic transcription is like having an infinite palette of colours organized into sets called *green*, *blue*, *red*, and so on, with any given shade belonging to one of those sets. Each language – indeed, each variety of each language – has a small set of **phonemes** (such as /t/, /m/) and each actual utterance of a sound can be categorized as being an **allophone (phonetic realization)** of one of the phonemes (see below). Most (but not all) allophones have a phonetic identity that is predictable from the surrounding environment. The kind of /p/ that you get at the beginning of a word like *patch* in English is, characteristically, an aspirated one [pʰ] and the kind of /d/ that you get at the end of a word like *reward* is normally a devoiced one [d̥]. Linguists have worked out the distributions of the different phonetic realizations of the different phonemes by studying how English works. Each language is different. This implies that you cannot transcribe a language, or a language variety, phonemically until you know what phonemic category to put every sound that you hear into. If you do not – and often part of your analysis will be establishing the phonemic categories – you must use phonetic script.

In summary, phonetic script *describes* what you are hearing; phonemic script *interprets* it. Beware of using phonemic script as an easy option: there are hidden implications within it, which, if not accounted for, could seriously compromise the validity of your analysis.

A few notes on phonemes

Phonemes are *notional* sounds: they are *categories* of sound. You can't hear a phoneme, only example phonetic realizations of one. Compare the category 'red': it is not a colour in its own right. Rather, to illustrate 'red', you need to find examples of it. In the same way, the phoneme label /t/ is just a cover term for the complete set of its possible phonetic realizations, i.e. for what you could actually *hear*. So you will be writing that a speaker's realization of the phoneme /. . ./ is [. . .]. This enables you to compare different speakers (or different speech events in one speaker) while being sure that you are comparing like with like.

Two sounds may be superficially rather similar, but belong to different phonemes. We demonstrate these phoneme categories by identifying words that are identical except for the choice of that phoneme. These are called **minimal pairs**. For example, in English, /ɛ/ and /ɪ/ must be phonemes because there are minimal pairs such as *led* and *lid*, in which the difference in the sound of the vowel is the only thing that keeps the words separate. So part of the definition of the phoneme is that, if you swap one phoneme with another, you can make another word. Contrast this with some sound characteristics that are *not* phonemic for English. Suppose, on one occasion, a person said *sitting* as [sɪtɪŋ] and on another said it as [sːɪtɪŋ] (i.e. with a longer, hissy /s/). This would not stop it being a pronunciation of the word *sitting*, because in English the sounds [s] and [sː] do not contrast in a way that could create a new word. They are therefore not separate phonemes of English, but just different examples (allophones) of the phoneme /s/. However, we can imagine a language in which this contrast *was* phonemic, because there was a minimal pair /sɑrɪt/ (meaning, say, *blossom*) and /sːɑrɪt/ (meaning, say, *big toe*). In this language, you would have to be very careful how hissy you made your 's', otherwise you could end up saying that the big toes in the garden smell very beautiful this year. Native speakers of Japanese and Korean sometimes struggle to differentiate the English phonemes /l/ and /r/, because in their languages this phonemic distinction does not exist, and [l] and [ɹ] are just allophones of the same phoneme.

Categorizing the sounds we hear into phonemic classes allows us to retain a view of the phonological structure of a language, even when the pronunciation is rather odd. If we aren't sure what we heard, we use our knowledge of the language at all levels to make sense of the message, so that we can work out which phonemic category the rogue sound must belong to. Thus, if a foreign learner of English said *I sailed on a [ʃiːp]*, we could tell from the context that he meant *ship* and not *sheep* and conclude that, for him, either [iː] was an allophone of the phoneme /ɪ/, rather than of /iː/, as it would be for native speakers, or else he had not, so far, succeeded in creating two phonemes, /ɪ/ and /iː/, at all (perhaps because his native language did not have that contrast).

You can read more about phonemes in Roach (2000, Chs 5 and 13), Collins and Mees (2003), Davenport and Hannahs (2005, Ch. 7), or virtually any other introduction to phonetics and phonology. To train yourself, you can use Kenworthy's (2000) workbook.

Phonetic and phonemic symbols in word processing

If your lecturer has not pointed you to, or supplied you with, a font, you can download the Summer Institute of Linguistics (SIL) phonetic fonts from http://scripts.sil.org/cms/scripts/page.php?site_id=nrsi&item_id=IPAhome.

Many other phonetic fonts are also available, to match different main fonts (Times Roman, Lucida, Arial, and so on). Search for options on the Internet but remember only to download from a reliable site and ensure you have your antivirus software switched on.

Hints on writing about pronunciation

When you are writing about a real piece of data (or about how a real piece of data would sound if only you had a recording of it), use square brackets and give as much phonetic detail as you can hear, or as much as you need to make your point. When you want to say that the sound in square brackets is an example of, say, a 't' or an 's', use slanted brackets for the latter (/t/, /s/), because you are referring to the categories, that is, the phonemes.

When you explore the pronunciation of an individual speaker, use a phoneme checklist such as the one given below, or the one in Hughes *et al.* (2005) to help you find examples of each phoneme. Next to the phoneme symbols on the list, transcribe your examples with square brackets (because they are real sounds that you have heard) and put in as much information as you can. You are then in a position to compare the pronunciation you have heard with other possible pronunciations of that phoneme.

Despite what most of the books imply, there is *not* simply one inventory of phonemes for English. In other words, it is not simply the case that different varieties of English have different pronunciations for a given phoneme. In some varieties, the actual set of phonemes is slightly different. So look out for examples of a phoneme on the checklist dividing in two parts, or of two phonemes on the checklist collapsing together. The best example of collapse for British English is the phonemes /ʌ/ and /ʊ/. Both phonemes exist in most parts of the south of Britain, giving minimal pairs such as *could* /kʊd/ and *cud* /kʌd/, and *put* /pʊt/, and *putt* /pʌt/. But, in many parts of the north of Britain, these words all contain the same vowel: /kʊd/, /kʊd/, /pʊt/ and /pʊt/. A second example derives from the fact that some varieties of English are **rhotic** (i.e. pronounce the *r* in *car* and *card*) whilst others are non-rhotic. Non-rhotic varieties may not differentiate between words like *law* and *lore*, *spa* and *spar*, which, provided the vowels do not differ, will form minimal pairs in a rhotic variety. Kreidler (2004, Ch. 4) provides a useful set of phoneme inventories for English, into one of which most, if not all, national and international varieties should fall.

You can find some examples of the phoneme inventories for different varieties of British English in Hughes *et al.* (2005). A good impression of the way in which phonemic and phonetic transcriptions will differ for the same data can be found in Brown (1990, Ch. 4). Note that textbooks on pronunciation have to reflect a particular variety. Thus, it is a good idea to use a book written in your own country or in the country that uses your target pronunciation.

Checklist of phonemes

SYMBOL	EXAMPLE BASED ON BRITISH RP	NOTES
/iː/	b*eat*	
/ɪ/	b*i*t	
/ɛ/	b*e*t	
/a/	b*a*t	also often written /æ/; /a/ is arguably the better choice because the phonetic realization in modern RP is closer to [a] than [æ] which tends to sound old-fashioned
/ɑː/	b*a*rd*	
/ɒ/	b*o*dy	
/ɔː/	b*o*red, b*oa*rd*	
/ʊ/	w*oo*d	these two phonemes collapse into one in some parts of Britain. That is, *wood* and *mud* rhyme, whether
/ʌ/	m*u*d	they both have [ʊ], [u], [ə] or (even) [ʌ]
/ɜː/	w*o*rd*	
/ə/	winn*er**	
/eɪ/	b*ai*t	also to be seen as /ɛɪ/, /ei/ and /ɛi/
/əʊ/	b*oa*t	
/aɪ/	b*i*te	also to be seen as /ɑɪ/, /ai/ and /ɑi/
/aʊ/	br*ow*n	also to be seen as /ɑʊ/, /au/ and /ɑu/
/ɔɪ/	b*oy*	also to be seen as /ɒɪ/, /ɔi/ and /ɒi/
/ɪə/	b*eer**	one increasingly common phonetic realization of this in RP is [ɪː]
/ɛə/	b*are**	one increasingly common phonetic realization of this in RP is [ɛː]
(/ʊə/	p*oor**)	this is a prime example of how the phonemic inventory has got out of date. In RP today (except among older and particularly 'posh' speakers) there is no separate phoneme /ʊə/ because it has collapsed with /ɔː/. Wells and Colson (1971) have resorted to using a German place-name to illustrate this pronunciation. When examining data, it is useful to check the pronunciation of the following: *poor, pore, pour, paw* and *pause*. Many regional varieties retain two or more distinct pronunciations for these, though modern RP has only one vowel for them all, approximately [ɔː]
(/aə/	f*ire**)	also written as /aɪə/, and pronounced in a variety of ways, including, by some British southerners, [aː]

SYMBOL	EXAMPLE BASED ON BRITISH RP	NOTES
/p/	ro*p*e	
/b/	ro*b*e	
/t/	wro*t*e	
/d/	ro*d*e	
/k/	spo*k*e	
/g/	ro*g*ue	
/tʃ/	broo*ch*	
/dʒ/	*h*uge	
/f/	loa*f*	
/v/	dro*v*e	
/θ/	brea*th*	
/ð/	brea*the*	
/s/	gro*ss*	
/z/	grow*s*	
/ʃ/	fa*sh*ion	
/ʒ/	vi*s*ion	
/h/	*h*eart	
/m/	roa*m*	
/n/	loa*n*	
/ŋ/	wro*ng*	watch out for varieties in which the 'ng' in spelling is pronounced [ŋg]. In these cases there is no phoneme /ŋ/ at all, because [ŋ] only ever occurs before /g/ and /k/ and never on its own; so there are no minimal pairs like the RP ones *win* /wɪn/ and *wing* /wɪŋ/.
/l/	ro*ll*	
/r/	*r*oll	
/j/	*y*ear	
/w/	*w*ear	

* In **non-rhotic** varieties like RP, the *r* after a vowel and before a consonant or word-end is not pronounced and should not appear in the transcription. It is important not to be influenced by *r* in the spelling of words, and to *listen* in order to decide whether there is a /r/ present or not. In **rhotic** varieties you will be able to hear the *r* and should transcribe it.

17
Transcribing speech orthographically

Fundamental points to bear in mind whenever you are planning to transcribe a stretch of speech include:

- ❏ For any analysis to be valid, the transcription of the data must be accurate. This is a time-consuming activity, as you may have to listen to the same stretch of tape many times, especially where several people are speaking at the same time. Therefore, don't be over-ambitious about the quantity of data you transcribe. Only transcribe what you need, and do not put in detail that is not relevant, such as phonetic details of the speaker's accent, unless you have a reason for doing so.

- ❏ For taped material, see if you can borrow a transcribing machine, which offers the facility to slow the speech down, so that the duration of the pauses can be measured more accurately. For digital data, software is available so that you can listen on your computer, with click-on options for starting, stopping, repeating and slowing down the speech.

- ❏ Never transcribe from the original tape. If an accident can happen, it probably will. Always make a copy of the original and then lock the original away somewhere safe. Work from the copy. Some pessimists work from a copy of a copy.

How to organize the presentation of a transcription

Vertical alignment

The biggest challenge with this kind of transcription is in aligning different material vertically. In order to avoid problems with tabs and spaces, which look ugly and often don't transfer from machine to machine, create a table for your example, using different rows for each line, and columns to match up the vertical alignment. Set the column dividers where they need to be for that particular example. Finally, select the option that makes some or all of the table's lines invisible. In example (1a) the lines are still visible. In (1b) you can see the effect of removing the lines (other than between the transcription and comment). You can dispense with the headings line once your reader can see what you are doing.

(1a)

Line	Speaker			Comment
18	L:	could you br-	[bring that with you	
19	F:		[I can bring this along yeah	*laughs*

(1b)

Line	Speaker			Comment
18	L:	could you br-	[bring that with you	
19	F:		[I can bring this along yeah	*laughs*

If you prefer not to use tables, you can use a non-proportional font such as Courier. In a non-proportional font, each of the letters takes up the same amount of space, so it is much easier to align your material. Compare the phrases in Table 17.1. On the left, the fact that some letters are wider than others means that the phrases take different amounts of space. But on the right, all the letters are the same width, so words and phrases can be easily aligned.

Table 17.1 Proportional and non-proportional fonts

Goudy Old Style font	Courier font
Illicit illusions	`Illicit illusions`
Ambulatory aspect	`Ambulatory aspect`

The key

Always provide a key to your symbols. This is because (a) not everyone uses the same conventions, (b) there are choices regarding how to transcribe some features, and (c) the assessor wants to be reassured that you know what you're doing. Quite deliberately, we are providing only one convention for each feature here. Be particularly careful to include in the key any symbols that might be mistaken for punctuation symbols (they usually mark intonation – see later). Otherwise, you might get penalized for apparently not knowing that punctuation itself is not used!

What to include

❐   Number every line. This makes it possible for you to refer to specific lines and for the reader to find your examples easily and check the wider context if required. Try to ensure that the numbers are not so far into the left margin that they are obscured by the binding or file grip. There is a convention for highlighting a particular line in a transcription (see example 38 p. 194).

❏   Many researchers like to use a column on the right-hand side of the transcription for comments, so that they don't need to be incorporated into the main transcription (see examples 1a and 1b above, and various other examples below).

Long turns

A short turn in the conversation on a single line does not lead to any difficulties for the transcriber. But suppose a speaker talks for a long time. If no one interrupts, you can simply run the speech on like normal text. But if someone says something during that speaker's turn, there will be an intervening line for the second speaker. To show that there is no break in the first speaker's utterance, use the latching symbol =.

(2)   W: tha- was [it? (.)] yeah we ha- we had eighteen of=
       R: [yeah]
       W: =them here a- all at once

Transcription conventions

The information below is organized in terms of what usually happens in conversation, and addresses the procedures of orthographic transcription from the inexperienced user's point of view. The conventions are based on those of Gail Jefferson, as described in Psathas (1995: 70–8) and Jefferson (1989: 193–6). Bloomer *et al.* (2005) provides a similar list linked to examples from some well-known data.

Turn taking

As in a play script, name the speaker in the left-hand margin. Use a short form, such as an initial, to save space, giving a key at the beginning or end (each speaker should have a different initial or short form). If you wish to protect the identity of the speakers, use letters such as A, B, and C. A line of transcription should have one, and only one, letter or name in the margin. If the same speaker has several lines of speech, it is sufficient to label only the first. If several people speak at once, each should have a separate line. The only exception to this would be if two or more people deliberately co-ordinated an utterance in unison (like singing 'Happy Birthday'); in this case, it is acceptable (but not obligatory) to list them on one line:

(3)   J: C-come on then
       R: Yeah (.) ri-
       J: (sung) Happy birth =
       J,R,K,S: (sung) =day to you: happy birthday to you . . .

If two people start at the same time, give them separate lines, beginning with a double opening square bracket:

(4)   W: [[Take it if y-
       E: [[I mean (.) no I

Where one person begins when someone else is already speaking, use a single opening square bracket before the new speaker's words, aligned vertically with another at the appropriate point in the established speaker's line (example 5). If two people interrupt in close succession, do the same again with a third line (example 6).

> (5)   R: so we didn't have to [wait long
>   T: [no we didn't

> (6)   S: would you [li-(.) like o-orange or ap[ple
>   M: [we've got
>   E: [yes please

Where one person finishes while the other continues speaking, use a closing square bracket in both lines:

> (7)   T: till it cam- (0.5) we [weren't all that] all that s-sure
>   G: [but did you]

If someone starts speaking immediately another has finished, this is called **latching**. Use an *equals* sign at the end of the first component and the beginning of the second (example 8). If two people latch at the same time, mark them both (example 9). Latching can also be marked within the turn of a single speaker, if one idea immediately follows another (example 10).

> (8)   A: before Sunday if you can=
>   K: =I'm really busy at the weekend

> (9)   R: so why didn't you after all that=
>   F: =[[yeah
>   G: =[[I was going to

> (10)   E: after y-you turned him down=why did you anyway

Silence and non-verbal communication in conversation

Pauses

A pause too short to measure is indicated by a dot in brackets: (.). Pauses of measurable length are indicated in seconds and tenths of seconds. Give the duration numerically in brackets, e.g. eight-tenths of a second (0.8); one-and-two-tenths seconds: (1.2). Where the silence is in the middle of the speaker's turn, simply put the brackets on the same line as the speaker's words. If the silence comes between one speaker's turn and the next, give the brackets their own line. If there is a very long pause, this can be marked as ((pause)) but it is perhaps more consistent simply to time the pause and insert the time length in brackets.

In-breaths and out-breaths

Most of the time you don't need to indicate breathing, because it is a background activity. But an audible breath, in or out, should be marked. An in-breath might indicate that someone is trying to get into the conversation, for example, or an out-breath might be interpreted as a sigh. Breath is indicated by one or more 'h's, as follows:

❐ breathing out: followed by a dash

   (11) K: He was (0.6) hhh- no I s'pose not

❐ breathing in: preceded by a dot.

   (12) O: Erm (0.4) .hhhh try the other (1.1) way roun-

❐ breath sounds associated with sobbing, laughing, being out of breath: in brackets.

   (13) E: Then (hhh) he said wha(h)t ti(h)me d'you ca(hh)ll this (hhh)

Head movements

To indicate that someone nods (without saying anything), simply write *nods* in double brackets (14a) or in your comments column (14b). The same goes for other gestures, such as pointing, smiling, or head-shaking.

   (14a) S: Who told you=don't tell me=Karen
         E: Mmm ((nods))
         S: ((smiles)) Okay

   (14b) S: Who told you=don't tell me=Karen
         E: Mmm   *nodding*
         S: Okay   *smiling*

Dealing with unusual pronunciations

How to show that a word has been started but not finished

Use a hyphen at the point where the word ends (example 15). Note that because of English spelling it will not always be clear what the sound was that was uttered. If it matters, use phonetic script (see below). This notation works for slips of the tongue too (example 16).

   (15) P: hurt him an- and hit his head on the ste- on the top of the steering wheel

(16)   F: there'll be pi- mist patches and some drizzle in the east

How to show an unusual pronunciation of a word

Because orthographic transcription was invented by sociologists, not linguists, it lacks some of the features that linguists are accustomed to employing for the close transcription of speech. Although phonetic script would be by far the best way to depict any pronunciation that could not be adequately indicated by conventional spelling, it is not often used. There are several ways of coping with the need to show a pronunciation more exactly. You can use conventional spelling and indicate, in double brackets or in the comments column, the relevant feature (example 17). Alternatively, use conventional spelling to approximate the pronunciation (example 18).

(17)   D: he's a real bastard ((northern pronunciation))
(18)   R: you need to move in really sloooooly

Alternatively, skirt the issue in the main transcription and use phonetic transcription in the comments column and when discussing the item in the analysis (example 19). Remember to indicate in your key what an entry in square brackets in the comments column means.

(19)   P: an. then (.) y. you just got to go | [gɔrə]

How to show a word that has been stretched out

Use a colon immediately after the lengthened sound. The more colons you use, the longer the sound:

(20)   S: we- well it was (.) eno: : : : : rmous

Coughs and sneezes

Write *cough* or *sneeze* in double brackets (21a) or use a comments column (21b).

(21a) T: oh God ((cough)) tha- ((cough)) Go- could I h-have ((cough)) that
            wa- wa((cough))ter

(21b) T: oh God ((hhh)) tha- ((hhh)) Go- could I | *coughing*
            h-have ((hhh))that wa- wa((hhh))ter

Transcribing unclear utterances

Sometimes a speaker mumbles. Sometimes there are several people talking at once and one or more of them is virtually drowned out by the rest. Listen to it again. Listen to it yet again. Sit back and try to hear it as if for the first time. Imagine you are there: what is the speaker *likely* to say? Play it to someone else and see if they can decipher it. Do whatever you can to minimize the quantity of indecipherable speech. If it really is impossible to understand, indicate that the utterance is there by putting empty single brackets for the appropriate duration (example 22). Alternatively, put 'indecipherable' in double brackets (example 23) or in your comments column if you have one. It is also quite common to use an asterisk for each indecipherable syllable (example 24). (In these examples, speaker W's turn is long enough to run onto a second line – see example 2, p. 187.)

(22)   W: and just as he's (0.2) he's about to [run off the guy c-come=
       T: [oh God (   )]
       W: = comes o]ver and

(23)   W: and just as he's (0.2) he's about to [run off the guy c-come=
       T: [oh God (indecipherable)]
       W: = comes o]ver and

(24)   W: and just as he's (0.2) he's about to [run off the guy c-come=
       T: [oh God (* * *)]
       W: = comes o]ver and

It may be that you know what was said but not who said it. In this case, put empty single brackets in the margin:

(25)   R: for a few minutes till=
       ( ): =huh you'll be luc-

If you are able to have a guess about what has been said, put your guess inside single brackets – this indicates that you have some doubt about it:

(26)   R: taken [it over again
       E: [(likely to be)

If you can hear the sounds but cannot work out what the words are, the convention is to make an orthographic representation of them inside single brackets. It is not standard to use phonetic script (but see example 19):

(27)   D: (mekka bunit cor)

Marking pitch, emphasis, volume and speed

How to show standard intonation patterns

The intonation of speech is not represented in orthographic transcription with anything like the accuracy that a phonologist would expect. If you want to give greater detail, do a separate transcription of the relevant extract, using one of the standard systems of intonation transcription for phonology (see, for example, Clark and Yallop 1995: 358–62,

Kreidler 2004, Ch. 10, Roach 2000, Chs 15–19). As indicated above, punctuation symbols are used for transcribing some of the specific intonation patterns of English. Although each represents the sort of pattern that we associate with it when it is punctuating written text, the application of the symbols is much more rigid, and they must be reserved for their defined purpose, as follows:

❑   a **falling tone** is marked with a full stop (period). To indicate a particularly noticeable fall, put a downward arrow immediately before it begins:

    (28)   R: There was ↓ nothing there.

❑   a **fall–rise** pattern, as when listing, or continuing at the end of a clause, is marked with a comma:

    (29)   K: I had (.) um (0.7) a ball, (.) a cricket bat, an (.) tha. (0.4) um a ball
              and a cricket bat

❑   a **rise** is marked with a question mark (but beware of using the symbol as punctuation by mistake – not all questions rise at the end, and not all rises are questions!). For a particularly noticeable rise, use an upward arrow immediately before it begins:

    (30)   F: Well would you ↑ like to be left behind?

❑   **animated tone** is indicated by an exclamation mark:

    (31)   B: You've got (.) to be joking!

For changes in pitch not associated with these familiar intonation patterns, see below.

Pitch features

Pitch movement is closely tied up with intrinsic (word-, phrase-) and emphatic stress. In addition, it often requires the stretching of the syllable so that there is time to achieve the effect. Because of this interrelationship, it is possible to mark pitch features by underlining parts of the stretched syllable. Basically, the underlined item is higher in pitch than what surrounds it, as illustrated below.

❑   a **drop in pitch** in a stretched syllable is marked by underlining the vowel immediately before the colon that indicates the stretch. To indicate a prolonged drop, extend the line backwards, i.e. towards the beginning of the word.

    (32)   G: It wasn't pounds it was d<u>o</u>: llars
         R: What d'you mean <u>do</u>: : llars.

❑   a **rise in pitch** is indicated by underlining the colon following the vowel. A lengthened version is achieved by extending the underlining forward, towards the end of the word:

(33)   L: a sto: : : rage container?

❏   a **rise and fall** can be shown by underlining the point of the highest pitch, implying that what comes before and afterwards is lower:

(34)   T: ((sarcastically)) Oh yeah it was rea: : : : : : : : lly good

❏   a **fall and rise** cannot be shown using these tools, so use an arrow to indicate the fall (see example 28).

Emphasis

Underline the relevant words and combine this, as appropriate, with indicators of how the emphasis has been achieved, e.g. a falling tone (see example 28) or a change in volume (see below). If it is associated with a marked change in pitch, you cannot show emphasis independently of that, because underlining is intrinsic to it already. In all events, you can add comments in a right-hand column to describe what is happening.

How to show a change of volume

Use capital letters to show loudness, and a degree sign (superscript circle) either side of a quiet passage. Indicate whispering by writing *whispered* in double brackets or in the comments column:

(35)   H: Mummy look there's FIVE!
       R: °don- (.) make so much   [noise°
       H: [((whispered)) Mum[my there's=
       R: [°yes I know°
       H: = ↓ five!

How to show a change of speed

A faster passage is enclosed in inverted angle brackets, or, to put it another way, in 'arrow heads' with their points inwards (example 36). There is not normally any need for specific symbols to indicate a slower speed of delivery. If someone speaks slowly, they must either be extending the words (in which case, use colons to show the 'stretch') or leaving gaps between the words (shown by the symbols for pauses).

(36)   K: yes (0.5) if you like (0.1) cooking = > if you do like cooking it's <
             (0.3) well it's no problem then

External events

The purpose of the transcription is to record everything that is part of the conversation. This means that an extraneous noise (a fire engine going past or the telephone ringing) does not need transcribing if it is ignored by the participants. But anything that provokes a reaction (e.g. a slight hesitation or a comment) should be transcribed. If in doubt, put it in. Notate it with a description in double brackets, e.g. ((telephone rings)) or a comment in the right-hand column. You should follow this up with a later entry ((telephone stops ringing)) unless it is clear from the context that this is the case. There is a special convention for notating applause, using upper- and lower-case Xs for loud and soft respectively, as in example 37 (Atkinson and Heritage 1984: xv):

(37)   Audience: xxXXXXXXXXXXXXxxx

Presenting the transcription

To draw the reader's attention to something

Put a horizontal arrow in the margin, to the left of the speaker's name/initial (example 38). Alternatively, use a large dot. Only mark things that are central to your discussion, and remember to refer to them in your discussion.

(38)   E: Leave that will you?
    →   K: Wh- ↓ what!

To show that you have omitted something

You are more likely to need to do this when you are quoting from your transcription in the discussion than when doing the transcription itself because, by omitting things, you are expressing an opinion about the relative importance of different parts of the whole. Show that you have missed out bits of a speaker's turn by using a horizontal sequence of dots:

(39)   L: and I said . . . don't just don't try it

Use a vertical line of dots to indicate that turns have been missed out. Give the line numbers to make it clear what quantity of material is missing.

(40)   123   F: so he go- .hhh goes um what's that! and she
          .
          .
          .
          .
       131   F: so an he goes what's that an she says (0.3) it's your
                    birthday pre(hh)sent

When all else fails

To show something for which you have not found, or cannot use, the conventional symbol, invent your own symbol that is not going to be confused with anything else, and indicate clearly in the key what it stands for.

Presenting the audio data

To assess your work properly, the marker will need to listen to a sample of the original material, to satisfy him-/herself that it has been adequately transcribed. Doing this for everyone in the class is a time-consuming affair and you can help the assessor to look favourably upon you by making the job as easy as possible. For guidance on how, see Chapter 11.

For further transcription conventions, see Atkinson and Heritage (1984: ix–xvii), who cover gaze-direction, for example. You can also model your work on research papers themselves, many of which contain a key at the end (for example, Jefferson 1989: 193–6). For guidance on the transcription of spoken data for computer analysis, see Leech *et al.* (1995).

18
Using computers to study texts

The study of language has been hugely influenced by advances in computer technology. Previously, the only way to discover patterns of words in texts was to read the texts and find the examples by eye. Now, it is possible to conduct electronic searches that are sophisticated, reliable, fast and much more extensive than would be possible by other means. Computers have not only provided linguists with new ways of answering old questions, but also helped identify new questions and new ways of thinking about what language is and how it works.

What is a corpus?

A corpus (the plural is **corpora**) is a set of texts in computer-readable form. Many of the largest corpora worldwide have been constructed as part of dictionary projects funded by publishers. A corpus may consist of written texts, transcriptions of spoken material, or both. Corpora are assembled for various reasons, and these reasons will determine both what is included and how the text is **tagged**. Tagging is the process by which the material in the corpus is marked (or coded) to make it searchable. Linguists often like to use corpora that have been tagged for word class (so that it is possible to search for all the examples of, say, *record* as a noun, without also accessing the examples of *record* as a verb). **Lemmatized** tagging makes it possible to find the different forms of the same root, such as *swim, swimming, swam, swum*, without searching for them all separately. Other useful tags might enable one to find examples from speech only, or from different genres of text; to identify recent rather than less recent material; or to select examples from only one gender or age of speaker/writer. Tagging for semantic and discourse features is also occasionally found. For more detail about tags, see 'Making sense of corpus annotation' below.

Why is a corpus useful?

Often, to make a meaningful comment about some aspect of the language in your own data set, it is necessary to refer to a wider tendency in the language. Imagine, for instance, that in a study of the English of a non-native speaker, you find the phrase *a sympathetic friend*, meaning *a good friend*. You want to propose that this expression is not nativelike, but you would like to back up your claim more robustly than just by stating that it seems non-nativelike to you. One solution would be to look up the phrase in, say, the British

National Corpus, and see how often it occurred relative to other expressions with the same meaning, such as *a good friend*, *a kind friend*. You might go further too, and access a corpus of English by non-native speakers with the same first language as your informant, to see if the expression is prevalent there. To take another example, opinion seems to be divided about the current balance of use of the forms *–er* and *–est* (as in *bigger*, *biggest*) and the forms *more _* and *most _* (see the exercise in Chapter 21). A corpus search on selected examples could provide you with evidence for your own contribution to the debate.

How do corpus searches operate?

The corpus is just the raw material. Even if it is tagged, it is still just a set of data. In order to discover what it contains, search tools are needed. All of the main corpora come with certain tools for doing searches, but different tools look for different things. Both because of the tagging and because of the search tools, different corpora may be needed for answering different questions. Some search tools can be applied to a corpus that you have assembled yourself. The main sorts of searches that the tools make possible are:

❐ **Word frequency:** If you are interested in knowing which words occur most frequently in the text(s), you will be using a text-analysis program that tells the computer to count up the occurrences of each word form and list them in descending or ascending order of frequency, or alphabetically, say. Figure 18.1 shows the first 25 words in an alphabetical word-list and in a list of the most frequently occurring words for Thomas Hardy's novel *Far from the Madding Crowd*, produced by means of the WordSmith Tools program (see 'Text analysis tools' below).

❐ **Co-occurrences of words:** You might want to know what sorts of words tend to occur in the immediate environment of a given word. This requires a concordancing program. You choose your key word and the program searches for all the occurrences of it and displays and/or prints them with your preferred amount of context (for example, one line or one sentence). Different orderings are also possible. Figure 18.2 shows a concordance of the word *red* from Hardy's *Far from the Madding Crowd*, again produced using WordSmith Tools. The concordance has been sorted according to the alphabetical order of the word to the right of the search word. The actual appearance of this concordance on the screen would be slightly different: the search word (*red*) would be picked out in one colour and the word to the right in a different colour. Further investigation of the occurrences of this word, using a larger context, reveals interesting connections with the characters in the novel. For guidance on understanding concordances, see Sinclair (2003).

❐ **Distributions of words:** It may be of interest to you to discover how certain words or sets of words are distributed through the various parts of a text. Figure 18.3 shows the distribution of the name of the character *Troy* in *Far from the Madding Crowd* (again produced by WordSmith Tools). The horizontal bar represents the book, and each vertical line is an occurrence of the word. We can see from this that there are only two mentions of this character's name in the first third or so of the book. Information of this kind could be useful if you were exploring the stylistics of narrative in one or more pieces of fictional or non-fictional writing.

1.	RED	42	0 0 0 0 0	-	0 0 0 0 0
2.	THE	24	3 3 1 4 3	-	1 1 4 4 0
3.	AND	22	1 1 1 1 2	-	7 5 1 2 1
4.	OF	15	2 2 3 2 1	-	0 3 0 0 2
5.	A	14	2 1 0 2 5	-	0 0 0 2 2
6.	WITH	14	1 0 2 1 3	-	0 3 2 2 0
7.	HIS	9	1 0 0 1 3	-	0 0 2 1 1
8.	HER	8	0 0 1 2 2	-	0 0 1 2 0
9.	WERE	6	1 0 1 1 1	-	0 0 0 0 2
10.	SHONE	5	0 1 1 0 1	-	0 0 0 1 1
11.	TO	5	1 1 1 0 0	-	1 0 1 0 0
12.	BLUE	4	0 0 2 0 0	-	0 0 2 0 0
13.	IN	4	0 0 0 2 0	-	1 0 1 0 0
14.	WAS	4	0 2 0 0 0	-	0 2 0 0 0
15.	WHICH	4	0 0 1 0 1	-	0 0 1 1 0
16.	AS	3	0 0 0 0 0	-	2 0 1 0 0
17.	BLOOD	3	0 0 0 0 1	-	0 0 1 0 1
18.	EYES	3	0 1 0 0 0	-	0 1 0 0 1
19.	FACE	3	1 0 0 0 1	-	0 0 0 0 1
20.	FLOCKS	3	0 0 0 1 0	-	1 0 1 0 0
21.	FROM	3	0 0 0 0 0	-	0 0 2 1 0
22.	JACKET	3	0 0 0 0 0	-	3 0 0 0 0
23.	LIKE	3	1 0 0 1 0	-	0 0 1 0 0
24.	LIPS	3	0 0 0 0 0	-	1 0 1 0 1
25.	OUT	3	1 0 0 1 0	-	0 0 0 0 1
26.	OVER	3	0 0 0 1 0	-	0 0 0 1 1
27.	SEAL	3	0 0 0 0 0	-	3 0 0 0 0
28.	SHE	3	1 1 0 0 0	-	0 0 0 1 0

Figure 18.4 Collocations

How do you find a corpus?

Although some corpora can be accessed free via the Internet, others are only available for purchase or subscription. Therefore, the first thing to check is whether your university or college library has, or subscribes to, any corpus products. For any resources within your university there is likely to be a manual or set of introductory guidelines. If there is a staff member or postgraduate student in your department who uses corpora, you might do well to ask for some help with getting started.

For a general listing of available English-language corpora, try http://nora.hd.uib.no/text.htm, www.devoted.to/corpora, or http://torvald.aksis.uib.no/corpora/sites.html. For languages other than English, see http://lingo.lancs.ac.uk/devotedto/corpora/corpora2.htm. The main corpora for English that you might want to target are:

❏ The **Bank of English**, containing several hundred million words of written and spoken English, collected at the University of Birmingham and used for the well-known COBUILD series of dictionaries and grammars. Access to more than 50 million words of this corpus is available in Wordbanks Online www.collins.co.uk/books.aspx?group=154, via subscription.

❐ The **British National Corpus** www.natcorp.ox.ac.uk/ (100 million words), involving Oxford University Press, Longman, Chambers, the British Library and the Universities of Oxford and Lancaster. The material is from a wide range of styles of written (90 per cent) and spoken (10 per cent) British English, and each word is grammatically tagged. The corpus is accessed using the search tool SARA though other tools can also be used. The full BNC (100 million words) can be accessed on-line by subscription or by purchasing the World Edition CD-ROM. There is also a cheaper CD-ROM called BNC Baby, which includes 4 million words from the BNC, plus several other features and search software. An alternative and effective way of using the BNC is via View, at http://view.byu.edu/.

❐ The **International Corpus of English (ICE)** consists of 1 million words of spoken and written English (500 texts of about 2000 words each) from each of a growing set of countries where English is a first or second language. Each corpus is tagged in the same way, to make comparisons possible. The British and New Zealand corpora must be purchased, but those from East Africa, the Philippines, India and Singapore are available free on CD-ROM or for download. For the latest list of available corpora see: www.ucl.ac.uk/english-usage/ice/avail.htm.

❐ The **International Corpus of Learners' English** is part of ICE, kept at the University of Louvain, Belgium. It contains over two million words of written English produced by learners of English as a foreign language with 19 different native-language backgrounds. All the data is from essays written by advanced students and the data is tagged to make cross-comparisons possible. Although the corpora themselves are not available without special access rights, a number of the partner websites (listed at www.fltr.ucl.ac.be/fltr/germ/etan/cecl/cecl-projects/icle/icle.htm) do provide results of analyses, such as the top 100 words and their concordances in the Brazilian English component (BRICLE): www2.lael.pucsp.br/corpora/bricle/index.htm.

❐ The **World Wide Web** is for many researchers the ultimate corpus. According to Gulli and Signorini (2005), by January 2005 there were 11.5 billion indexable pages on the web. Such a huge resource makes possible searches for rather rare examples (those where a mere 100 million words of text might provide only one or two instances). However, there are some disadvantages too: variation in the reliability of the language – some examples will be non-standard and non-native, and you cannot easily identify which; repetition of material – as any Google search for a wordstring reveals, the same text is sometimes reported many times as separate hits; changeability – the web is changing all the time, and so any figures you get will probably not be replicable even a day later, nor specific examples necessarily retrievable. Having said that, with a resource so huge, minor differences ought not to impact much on your findings. To search the web as a corpus, either use your preferred search engine (e.g. Google, Altavista, Yahoo) or the Webcorp tool described below.

❐ **Literary works:** If your interest lies in the use of words by one or more literary authors and your searches do not need to be sophisticated, you might be able to use the inbuilt search facilities on a commercial 'library' CD ROM such as the World

Library's *Complete Works of Shakespeare* (2001). However, there are also thousands of complete literary works available for download on the Internet, such as from the Gutenberg Project, www.gutenberg.org/.

What are the main text analysis tools?

❒   **WordSmith Tools** is a reasonably user-friendly software package for text analysis. It is available from Oxford University Press, www.oup.co.uk/isbn/0-19-459400-9, but there is a good chance that your university already has a copy. Examples from WordSmith have been used in this chapter.

❒   **Variation in English Words and Phrases (VIEW)** is a powerful search tool that accesses the British National Corpus as quickly as, and often more effectively than, the BNC's own search tool, SARA. VIEW is free to use, and there is a useful three-minute guided tour on the home page, http://view.byu.edu/.

❒   **Webcorp** is a search tool for linguists who want to use the World Wide Web as a corpus. It operates in a slightly different way from a normal search engine, having been designed specifically to access linguistic data. Webcorp is free to use, and details can be found at www.webcorp.org.uk/guide/.

❒   **LexMC** is a commercial company with several excellent programs including the **Word Sketch** engine. It is worth visiting the site to see what demos and limited free-access opportunities are available: www.lexmasterclass.com/.

Making sense of corpus annotation

As noted above, the most useful corpora to linguists have been tagged in various ways. In SGML (Standard Generalized Markup Language) and XML (Extensible Markup Language), a tag is enclosed in angled brackets < >. Programmers can put any information that they wish in these brackets and know that it will be identified as a marker, as specified in their program. Thus, words in a play might be tagged for Act, Scene, and line numbers, while in a general linguistic corpus that is tagged for word class, each word will be labelled with <noun>, <verb>, etc. (or codes meaning the same thing). An example from the Lancaster Oslo Bergen corpus (LOB) of written English is given in Figure 18.5. In Figure 18.5, the tag **NN** indicates a singular count noun, **BEZ** the third person singular of *be*, **AT** the indefinite article, **JJ** an adjective, and so on. Texts can even be tagged with information on the syntactic structure of the phrases and sentences (that is, they can be **parsed**). The abbreviations used for tags and the theoretical rationales for which tag to use where will normally be provided along with the corpus itself, so look there for a list of glosses of the terms.

Hospitality_**NN** is_**BEZ** an_**AT** excellent_**JJ** virtueNN,_**,** but_**CC** not_**XNOT** when_**WRB** the_**ATI** guests_**NNS** have_**HV** to_**TO** sleep_**VB** in_**IN** rows_**NNS** in_**IN** the_**STI** cellar_**NN**!_**!**

Figure 18.5 Part of a corpus with word-class tagging

Using corpora effectively in your work

❐ Why reinvent the wheel? Some very useful analyses have already been done and are available on the web for you to draw on. For instance, Adam Kilgarriff has listed the frequencies with which all the words in the British National Corpus occur: www.kilgarriff.co.uk/bnc-readme.html. There are separate listings for lemmatized and unlemmatized forms (see above). Remember, of course, that if you use information that someone else has produced, it becomes a *resource* for your own work, not a replacement for it. You need to acknowledge it like any other published source, and use it to help you answer your own, different questions.

❐ As with any research, it is a very good idea to think through in advance what you can use any information from a corpus for. It can become rather easy to spend hours at the computer looking up more and more examples, only to find that you have a long list, and nothing much to say about it. Try to formulate a research question that will lead you to a conclusion. For instance, you might ask, as Stubbs (1995) did: *Are the meanings of 'small' and 'little' differently weighted for negativity, when used to refer to 'man', 'boy', 'woman', and 'girl'?* A question like this always gives you an answer, whether it is 'yes' or 'no', and if it is 'yes' (as it was for Stubbs) you can explore exactly what the distributions are by drawing out examples from the corpus. In contrast, a research question like *Is 'horse' a more frequent word than 'cow'?* is only worth asking if you have a good reason: if you find out that it is, what will that enable you to conclude? In short, corpora are simply resources – they will furnish you with good answers, but only if you ask good questions. Since there are still many good questions that cannot be answered using corpora yet, take note of the kind of work that has already been done.

Compiling your own corpus: potential problems

It is possible to create your own corpus, but in the context of a project this is probably not advisable because you need so much text and it takes so much time to assemble and make suitable for use. Here are some key observations:

❐ To create a corpus, you need to convert very large amounts of material to computer-readable form. This can be done using a scanner, but the results are by no means 100 per cent accurate and need careful proofreading.

❐ It is illegal to put copyright material (that is, almost all published works) into a computer corpus without permission.

❐ Spoken data, if that is what you want in your corpus, must first be collected and transcribed before it can go onto the computer. The permission of the speakers will also be needed.

❐ It is difficult to ensure that your corpus is truly representative of the type(s) of language you want to study.

Because of these difficulties, you should consider using an existing corpus, as long as it will provide the data you require in the format you need.

Limitations of corpora

Large general corpora may be presented as representative of the language in use. But remember that:

☐   Most corpora only give a snapshot of the language at a particular time.

☐   They are reliant on what is electronically available and not restricted by copyright, with the result that certain genres of writing, particularly journalism, tend to be over-represented.

☐   Spoken data needs to be transcribed, which is complicated, expensive and time-consuming, so considerably less spoken data is available than written.

☐   Searching any corpus is constrained by what the tool can look for, and by how the text has been tagged. In both cases, there may be major theoretical models and/or practical aims underpinning the decisions that have been made.

Further reading

For general overviews on the nature of corpora and of corpus linguistics, see Tognini-Bonelli and Sinclair (2006) and Hunston (2006). A useful introduction to English corpus linguistics is Meyer (2002), and Sinclair (2003) is a guide to reading concordances. For ideas about what corpora can contribute to linguistic research, look at Stubbs (2001) and Hoey (2005). For practical guidance on using corpora for projects, see McEnery, Xiao and Tono (2006).

19
Statistics and your project

Do you need graphs and calculations in your project?

If your project provides you with results in the form of numbers, there is a good chance that presenting them in graphs and/or analysing them using statistical tests will enhance your work. But how far should you go? How sophisticated is such work expected to be?

It is unreasonable for your assessors to expect you to use any analytical techniques for which you have not been given input/training unless they are part of the compulsory curriculum of a (high-)school education or part of a preparatory curriculum you have followed at university.

As a general rule, it might well be expected that everyone will have previously learned how to draw simple bar charts and pie charts, and how to calculate percentages and averages. So it would be quite fair for your university assessors to expect you to use those skills in your project.

However, anything more complicated than that, such as determining whether one figure is *significantly* larger than another (see 'The point of statistical analyses' below), requires specific training that you will not be assumed to have had elsewhere. If your university department expects you to use statistical analyses in your project, it will have made provision for you to learn how to do so. If no such provision has been made, stick to graphs, percentages and averages. But if you did attend classes on how to do statistical analyses, then even if you didn't enjoy or understand it all, it is likely that you will lose marks for not using such analyses if they are appropriate.

The good news is that your lecturers will understand that not everyone finds this aspect of analysis easy and as part of the requirement that you will do such analysis, they will expect to offer you support. Find out what support is available, and do everything you can to make yourself helpable (see 'How to avoid common problems' below), because even a wizard statistician cannot turn chaotic figures into a reliable finding. Getting help with this sort of thing, whether from a dedicated statistics expert, your supervisor, another student, or a friend or relation, will not normally be viewed as cheating, unless it has been made clear to you that you are being specifically assessed on this aspect of the work (as would be the case in a statistics module, of course). If in doubt, ask. For the sake of honesty and courtesy, if you have had a lot of help, you should acknowledge this, either in an acknowledgments section at the front of your project or in a footnote at the point when you present the relevant material.

Of course, if you have studied mathematics at a high level, you may have command of certain techniques and confidence about learning new ones: if so, go for it (but do still read the books carefully and take advice, just to ensure you are on the right lines).

In this chapter, we aim to help those who are rather intimidated by the idea of statistical presentations and analyses. We hope to bridge the gap between where many students feel they are and the level at which most of the books (and courses) start. The first golden rule for the mathematically insecure is: *don't panic*. This is easily said, of course, and harder to achieve, but panicking will definitely not help. Divide your work into small clear tasks that you will easily manage and that you will know you have completed. Avoid multitasking (e.g. trying to count three different things at once). Keep a record of what you have done and what it is for.

First we shall look at how to present your findings using *descriptive* statistics: graphs, percentages, averages, and so on. Like your assessors, we are assuming that you have done this kind of thing before, though maybe not for a while. If this is not the case, then you need to find a good textbook to take you through the principles or get a friend to show you what to do. Then we move to considering why statistical analyses are worth the effort and how they work. Finally, we identify some useful textbooks and offer some basic information for the 'mathematically insecure'.

Descriptive statistics and basic calculations

Types of data

Numbers have to be handled carefully and with common sense. You need to have a clear sense of what you are counting and, indeed, when you are not really counting at all. For instance, imagine you asked people what they thought would most enhance the effectiveness of warning instructions on pharmaceutical products: (1) non-technical vocabulary; (2) short sentences; or (3) pictures. Although these three categories have been given numbers for convenience, they are just labels.

In the textbooks, you will find reference to three or four types of data: **quantitative data** (subdivided into **ratio data** and **interval data**), **ordinal data** and **nominal data**. Below, we simply indicate what sorts of data fall into each category, and then provide illustrations for comparison. If you want to know why, or have data that you cannot relate to our examples, then look up the terms in a good introductory textbook, such as Hinton (2004: 21–3), Coolican (1995 Ch. 8), or Coolican (2004: 246–55).

The two easiest types to contrast are **quantitative data** and **nominal data**, so we'll begin there. The question to ask is: what am I counting? If the answer is 'actual scores achieved on a test', or 'actual time taken to do something', or 'actual number of words in each utterance in a spoken text', or 'actual number of interruptions in each line of a conversation', etc., then your data is quantitative. At every point when you are scoring, you are saying 'does this score a point or doesn't it?' You are *not* saying 'I have a point to award, so do I add it to this set or that set?' If you are doing that, you are dealing with nominal data.

Nominal data entails categorizing: you might have a list of languages spoken by different non-native speakers of English in a class, and want to categorize the class members according to which language is their mother tongue. Or you might have a list of ways of learning languages, so that you can ask people which they prefer. Or you might have a list of different words in a text and want to know how often each one occurs. 'Nominal' relates to 'naming', and for as long as your categories are named, you should not have any difficult recognizing nominal data. However, be careful if you number your categories for convenience. Just because Arabic is referred to as '1' and Punjabi as '2', they have not stopped being nominal data. Ask yourself: have I, or could I have, named the categories with which I am operating?

Nominal data is used to gather frequency information by distributing a fixed number of people or pieces of information into the categories. That means that your figures (the frequencies) will always add up to the number of pieces of information you had. For instance, if you categorize a class of 30 children according to their mother tongues, you might have 3 native speakers of Arabic, 7 of Punjabi, 4 of Greek, 12 of English, and 1 each of Japanese, Chinese, Spanish, and Italian.

Next, we consider **ordinal data**. Ordinal scores superficially look like quantitative data, but are not the same, because the intervals between the different possible scores cannot be precise. Consider the marking system used in your university, where, perhaps, you are awarded marks out of 100, with a pass mark of, say, 40. Gaining a mark of 65 does not entail any real counting: it is an impression based upon how well you have met the criteria for the work. There is no guarantee that someone with 62 and someone with 68 have performed exactly equal amounts worse and better than you. The issue is even more extreme if you try to imagine what would justify the ten-mark difference between 80 and 90 or between 15 and 25. Because the scores are impressionistic and unequally spaced, we cannot perform the same calculations as we could if they were genuinely out of 100 (as they might be in a test with 100 questions, where each correct answer got one mark). However, we can still use the fact that all the scores are placed in a particular order: if you get 65, it definitely does mean that you did better than the person with 62, who did better than the person with 58.

Another example might be data derived from asking people to rate voices on a scale of 1 to 5 for friendliness in a set of recordings. We could certainly say with confidence that a voice with an average rating of 4.2 had been considered more friendly than a voice with an average of 2.1, but it would not make sense to say that the first voice was considered twice as friendly as the second: ratings are just not that exact.

There are particular calculations that use ordinal data without placing too much importance on the score itself. They focus on the relative *order* of the subjects or categories on a scale of performance, popularity, or whatever. This process of **ranking** is the only option for ordinal data, but it is also possible to convert quantitative data into ordinal data. Doing so can be very useful in bypassing the need to directly relate the worth of, say, 15 out of 20 in a spelling test, with a score of 3.82 on a progressive reading scale.

When you rank, you lose some information. If Bob comes top with 17/20, Carol comes second with 12/20 and Phil comes third with 11/20, you cannot capture the fact that the difference between Bob's and Carol's scores was greater than the difference between Carol's and Phil's scores.

Here are some examples of fictional studies that produce the different types of data.

Quantitative data

The figures in Table 19.1 are quantitative (ratio) data. The researcher has given 16 subjects a memory test, for which the highest possible score is 20. Deciding what score each subject should get has been a question of looking at how he/she responded to each of the 20 items and asking 'Does this response get a point or not?' Getting 12 points makes a person twice as good as someone who got 6 points. The researcher has, in fact, used two groups of eight subjects: the first eight were prepared for the memory test in one way and the second eight in a different way. Therefore it will be possible to calculate the average (mean) score for each group (see 'Reporting your data' below) and use that to work out whether the two groups performed significantly differently from each other.

Table 19.1 Scores on a memory test (out of 20)

	Subject ID number															
	1	2	3	4	5	6	7	8	9	10	11	12	13	14	15	16
Score	7	11	12	9	3	8	18	12	15	10	10	11	6	7	13	17

Nominal data

To generate Table 19.2, the researcher asked Chinese learners of English 'Which English-speaking country would you most like to visit?' Each subject got one 'vote' and it is allocated to a particular category (country). If you add up all the scores, it will equal the number of votes cast (i.e. the number of people in the survey). Such data might be used to explore the effectiveness of the marketing of each country to potential Chinese visitors or to evaluate the influence on Chinese learners' aspirations of the destinations featured in the textbooks they use or of the English native speakers that they meet in China. (Alternatively, it could be converted into ordinal data, as in Table 19.3).

Table 19.2 Country that Chinese learners of English would most like to visit (number of votes)

	USA	South Africa	Canada	Ireland	UK	New Zealand	Australia	Singapore
Popularity as destination for visit	178	9	53	17	92	71	143	2

Ordinal data

Line A of Table 19.3 has taken the same information as in Table 19.2, and converted it into ranks. The ranking tells us that the USA was preferred over Australia as a destination, but since the original figures are no longer presented in the table, we have lost the information about how much more popular it was. On the other hand, by changing to ranks, we are in a position to make a comparison with the quite different 'scores' in Line B. These are also ranks, but they have been derived not from nominal data but from quantitative data (sub-type ratio): the actual number of kilometres distance between Beijing and the capital of the country. By converting the kilometre figures to ranks, we have, again, lost the information about how *much* further away one country is than another. But we have gained something useful too. Using the two sets of ranks, we can find out whether the desire to visit a place is determined by how far away it is. We could not do that with the raw scores, unless we believe that, say, each additional 1000 km of distance justifies an extra vote!

Table 19.3 Rank orders of countries according to: (A) where Chinese learners of English would most like to visit; (B) distance from Beijing to each country's capital

	USA	South Africa	Canada	Ireland	UK	New Zealand	Australia	Singapore
(A) Rank of popularity as destination for visit (1 = most popular)	1	7	5	6	3	4	2	8
(B) Rank of distance from China (1 = closest)	7	8	5	3	2	6	4	1

Making types of data work for you

You need not feel that you are 'victim' to the kind of data that your study produces. You have two kinds of control over what kind of data you deal with. Firstly, you can decide to design your study to produce the sort of data you are comfortable with. You can even model your entire investigation around the data table that you want to end up with. Then you will know you can handle what you get. The second kind of control is in how you choose to formulate your data and what questions you ask of it. While you will not be able to convert nominal or ordinal data into quantitative data, you may well be able to do the reverse, and that may free you up to make choices about the presentation and analysis of your material.

Reporting your data: averages, percentages, and graphs

What you can do with your data depends on what kind of data it is, so don't try to do everything! If you produce a figure or graph that looks like nonsense, it might well be so. Before you calculate anything or prepare any kind of graph, identify a specific question that you want to know the answer to. Usually, that question will help you work out what sort of treatment to give to your data. Here are some examples, using the tables from the previous section.

Table 19.1 reported quantitative data: the scores out of 20 that 16 people got in a memory test. Subjects 1–8 (Group A) had been trained in one way, and subjects 9–16 (Group B) in another. A sensible question to ask would be: *Did the training method affect the scores?* That is, *Did Group A do better than Group B?* Looking at the distribution of scores, it's clear that some did and some didn't. You need to find out what each group did *on average*, by calculating the *mean*. We explain in the notes at the end of this chapter how to calculate the mean. The means for the two groups from Table 1 are: Group A = 10.00, Group B = 9.875.

Do you think that this indicates that the training made a difference? The figures are very close. You could put them onto a graph and see if that helps you judge. You can create a graph from a table in many word-processing programs, so look in the Help guidance of the program to find out how to do it.

The graph in Figure 19.1 shows how careful you have to be with automatically generated graphs. The difference looks enormous and you might easily choose to conclude that the training for Group A was much more effective. But the scale of the graph indicates that only the difference between 9.8 and 10 is shown – yet individual subjects could only score whole numbers on the test, so the range of actual scores would fall outside the range of that graph! We can see a truer picture if we force the graph to show us the entire scale (Figure 19.2). Now the difference looks tiny. You may think 'Well, how am I going to know what to say? Was there a real difference or not?' This is where statistical analyses would come in – see 'Using statistical analysis' below.

Figure 19.1 Mean scores on a memory test

Nominal data, as in Table 19.2, invites a different question such as: 'What was the relative popularity of different destinations?' This information can be shown on a bar chart (Figure 19.3). Since you are dealing with the relative distribution of a set number of bits of information (in this case, the share of votes out of a total of 565), you can also state the results as percentages.

A percentage is the number of instances *per hundred*. The calculation, therefore, amounts to saying: if there are in total 565 votes (as there are in Table 19.3), and 53 of them were for Canada, how many would there have been for Canada if there had been 100 votes? We show you how to calculate a percentage in the notes at the end of this

Figure 19.2 Mean scores on a memory test (rescaled)

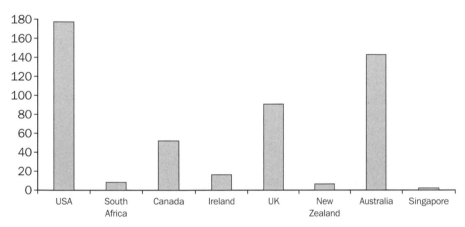

Figure 19.3 Distribution of preferences for visit to English-speaking country (bar chart)

chapter. The answer is just over 9 per cent. To calculate a percentage, you have to know what a score is *out of*. If you cannot provide that *out of* figure easily, then a percentage may not be appropriate. For instance, you cannot provide percentages of reaction times like 817 milliseconds: what are they *out of*?

It is also a good idea not to give percentage values for very small figures. If 7 out of 10 schoolchildren prefer reading French to writing it, does this really mean that if you had asked 100, exactly 70 would have preferred reading? Surely not, because if just one of your 7 had chosen something else, that would change your percentage by 10 – that's ten people out of the hundred. As a result, percentages based on less than 100 in total are not very accurate. If you say that 33.3 per cent of the parrots in your study were capable of reciting an entire nursery rhyme, this sounds pretty impressive. But if you only studied three parrots, that's only one individual! Don't be afraid, therefore, to talk in real figures rather than percentages when you have small samples: it's better to say '17 out of 25' than to use a percentage.

Another way to display nominal data is using a pie chart (Figure 19.4), which divides up the whole 'pie' into slices according to the proportions in your data.

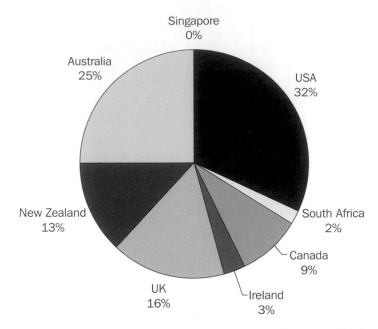

Figure 19.4 Distribution of preferences for visit to English-speaking country

With **ordinal** data, you are asking different questions again, and so a different kind of presentation is likely to help. In Table 19.3 we had two sets of ranks and a good question would be 'Are English-speaking countries that are further from China more attractive as destinations?' How might we use a graph to answer the question? The clearest presentation will result if one of your categories shows a nice rising line. You can then see whether the other ranking follows the same trajectory or not. Thus, you might re-order the information in Table 19.3 so that the 'Visit' ranks are in order – do this by moving the entire columns around, so that the 'Distance' rank and the name of the country also move (Table 19.4). A line graph can then be generated (Figure 19.5). It shows that, in fact, there is not much of an obvious relationship between the popularity of destinations among Chinese learners of English and the distance of the place from Beijing.

Table 19.4 Re-ordered information from Table 19.3

	USA	Australia	UK	New Zealand	Canada	Ireland	South Africa	Singapore
Visit	1	2	3	4	5	6	7	8
Distance	7	4	2	6	5	3	8	1

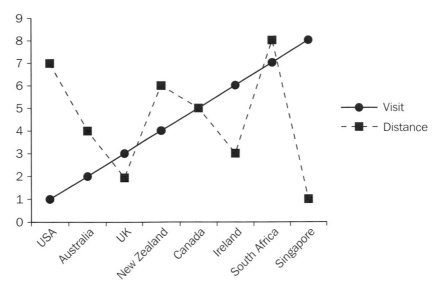

Figure 19.5 Comparison of the ranks for 'Visit' and 'Distance'

Using statistical analyses

Why go any further than graphs and averages?

As we have already indicated, your decision about whether to go any further will depend on what is expected of you and what you are comfortable with. As should have become clear by now, even if you had planned to stick to just noting percentages and drawing graphs, you may find that you are dissatisfied with the limitations of doing so. The telltale sign is when you find yourself asking: 'Yes, but what does all of this mean actually happened?' or 'What is the answer to my original question?' or 'Is that difference big enough to take seriously?'

Statistical analyses assess the degree of confidence we can have that our small set of results is representative of what we would get from a larger **population** of the same type. ('Population' is a technical term, meaning *the entire set of people (or things) from which the sample in the research has been taken*.) In other words, statistical analyses check whether a hypothesis is valid when it proposes a certain relationship between two or more sets of data. And they investigate, in an open-ended way, relationships between different variables. A **variable** is any property whose value may vary (such as gender, age, test score or reaction time).

The point of statistical analyses

The fundamental point of doing a statistical analysis of your data is to find whether the results you got are worth taking seriously. In statistical analyses for the social sciences, a probability value of 0.05, that is 5 per cent, is generally viewed as sufficient to be termed *significant*. The lower the probability value below that 0.05, the *more* significant it is, and if you can attain a probability value of 0.01 or lower (that is 1 per cent), then it is often called *highly significant*. If you read a published research report that contains statistical tests, you will see statements like the following:

$$\chi^2 = 35.95, df = 2, p < 0.01$$
$$t = 2.65, df = 7, p < 0.05 \text{ (one-tailed, related)}$$

The statement of probability is the part that begins $p <$. This means: 'the probability is less than…' Thus, $p < 0.01$ means 'the probability is less than 0.01, or 1 per cent', and $p < 0.05$ means 'the probability is less than 0.05, or 5 per cent'. But what does *that* mean?

What is a statement of probability?

Imagine you toss a normal coin ten times and count how many times it turns up 'heads' and how many times 'tails'. Because the coin is balanced, there is no reason why one side should 'win'. However, experience tells us that there is no guarantee that you will get an exactly equal number of heads and tails. Yes, you might get five heads and five tails, but you might get six and four, or even seven and three – chance can do that, because the coin can't remember what happened last time and so, every time you throw the coin, there is an equal chance of either outcome, irrespective of what has happened up to that point. It's even possible that you could throw the coin ten times and get heads every single time. Having said that, provided the coin *is* balanced, we would consider a score of 10–0 to be very unusual.

Now let's think of a different coin: one that you *believe* (but do not know) to be weighted so that it comes up heads more often than tails. You throw this coin ten times and you get 10–0. What does this mean? It might mean that the coin is indeed weighted. On the other hand, maybe the coin is not weighted and it just happened that you got the unusual outcome of 10–0, which, as we have seen above, can happen just by chance. The obvious thing to do next would be to throw the coin some more and see what happened. If the coin is balanced, you are likely to get a score closer to 5–5 this time, and that will help you interpret your first finding as the result of chance. But if you get another 10–0 or a 9–1, then you may feel more confident that the original 10–0 was down to the coin being weighted. The more you throw the coin, the more of a picture you will develop. But suppose that you only had that one set of ten throws to work from, because the coin is now lost. You are looking at the original 10–0 score and you don't know what it means. You can't throw the coin any more, so how can you find out what the likelihood is that it was weighted?

Mathematically, this can be worked out. The assumption is made that the coin was *not* weighted, that is, that it was equally likely to fall down on either side. It is possible to calculate, using simple principles of probability, how many times in, say, 100 lots of ten throws, a score of 10–0 was likely to come up: not many! In contrast, scores of 5–5, 6–4, and 4–6 would be predicted to occur very often. On the basis of such a calculation, you could state that, were the coin to be balanced, the chances of your getting the outcome 10–0 were very small, though not, of course, impossible. In fact, they are *very very* small: the probability of 10–0 for a balanced coin is 1 in every 1024 sets of ten throws, or 0.0009, less than one-tenth of 1 per cent.

This is the important bit: If the probability of something happening is one in 1024, it means that, assuming the coin is *not* weighted, then you will only get that outcome once in every 1024 times you try the experiment. The other 1023 times you do the experiment you won't get such an extreme result. It follows that since you have a suspicion that the coin *is* weighted, and you predicted that the weighting would indeed lead to more heads than tails, there's a very high chance that the reason you got 10–0 is because it is weighted. It would be very bad luck indeed to be testing the belief that a coin was weighted to favour heads, and to get a 10 heads to 0 tails result when in fact it wasn't weighted at all!

What should be clear from this is that *part* of what gives you confidence in interpreting your outcome is the mathematics. But the other part is that you had made a prediction in advance (a hypothesis) about what the outcome would be, and you did indeed get that outcome. Thus, the hypothesis is a crucial part of your design and should be firmly based on existing theory and findings from research, not just on a hunch (see Chapters 1 and 12).

Let's get away from coins and think about a language-related example. Imagine you are interested in whether words are easier to remember if you see them written down than if you hear them spoken. What do you predict? On the basis of what you have read, you have come to the conclusion that both visual and auditory information helps with memory. But you have also discovered that when people see a word written down, they are likely to silently 'speak' it, giving them both visual and auditory input – a double chance to remember it. On the other hand, when people hear a word, they do not normally imagine it written down. As a result, you are predicting that visual input will be more effective. Your results show that the scores from the visual input group were, indeed, higher, and now you have done a statistical test on the figures. The analysis reveals the probability of getting those results if there was *no* advantage of visual input over auditory input. The probability comes out as less than 0.05, and is therefore termed *significant*. What this means is that if there was no advantage to visual input, you could still get this result, but only five times in every 100 times that you ran the experiment. The other 95 times, you would get a result that showed less difference between visual and auditory. Because of this, it is, as it says, *significant* that you had predicted this particular outcome on the basis of your belief that visual and auditory input were not equally effective. If visual and auditory input *were* equally effective, then running this experiment once and getting the outcome you did would be pretty bad luck, and so it is a reasonable guess that, in fact, you were right all along, and there is indeed an advantage to memory of getting visual input rather than auditory.

How do you arrive at a statement of probability?

It should be evident by now that the statement of probability is the Holy Grail. Probability levels are the result of statistical calculations, not all of which are as straightforward as the coin-throwing example, because people and the things they do tend to be more unpredictable than balanced coins are. We cannot explain the principles of all the different available tests here. Rather, we point you in the direction of the tests likely to be most appropriate for the main kinds of data generated by research into language. You need to find the test in a good statistics textbook (we recommend some later on in this chapter), and check that it does indeed meet your needs.

The principles of five common statistical tests

❑   To see if two sets of real scores (quantitative data) are as different as your hypothesis predicts, use a *t-test*. The scores may be from the same group (*related t-test*) or from two different groups (*unrelated t-test*).

❑   To see if more than two sets of scores (quantitative data) are as different as your hypothesis predicts, you need *analysis of variance* (ANOVA). However, it's a good idea not to use ANOVA until you have got the hang of what the *t-test* does, so try to avoid having more than two sets to compare.

❑   To see if the increasing values in one set of scores (quantitative data) are matched by an *increase* in a second set (*positive correlation*) (e.g. a low reading score is associated with a low spelling score, a high reading score with a high spelling score); or to see if the increasing values in one set of scores are matched by a *decrease* in a second set (*negative correlation*) (e.g. the more often a word occurs in a text, the fewer letters it tends to have), use a *Pearson's product-moment correlation coefficient test*.

❑   To see whether the distribution of frequencies (nominal data) is likely to be due to chance, use a *chi-squared* (χ^2) *test*.

❑   To see whether two ranks are as different as you predicted, use a *Mann Whitney U test* (for two different groups) or a *Wilcoxon signed ranks test* (for the same group doing different things). (Real quantitative data can be converted to ranks for this test, if a *t-test* cannot be used.)

❑   To see whether two ranks are as *similar* as you predicted (positive correlation) or move in opposite directions (negative correlation), use a *Spearman's rho correlation test*. (Quantitative data can be converted to ranks for this test, if a *Pearson's test* cannot be used.)

Remember, if you plan ahead, you can decide *first* what kind of test you can cope with, and then design your research to provide suitable data.

How to avoid common problems with statistical tests

1.   Keep your design *very* simple: compare two groups, or one group doing two different things. Don't add in complications.
2.   Tests that are termed *parametric* (e.g. *t-test*, ANOVA, *Pearson's*) must meet strict criteria for the calculations to be valid. For *all* tests, your results will be more reliable if you minimize unintentional variation:
     a)   In groups of subjects or informants, keep the balance of gender, age, educational level, etc. the same if you know it might have an effect. However, if you have no reason to believe that a variable will affect the outcome (e.g. there is no evidence that gender is likely to make a difference in the data you are examining), then just say so and stop worrying.

b)   If using texts as input for comparison, avoid differences in the length or frequency of words (unless, of course, that is what you are trying to test).

c)   In test conditions, avoid gathering otherwise comparable sets of data in very different circumstances, such as in noisy and quiet environments, early and late in the day, etc.

d)   Check *before* you finalize your design how many subjects you need in each group to make your chosen statistical test valid. If your sample is larger than the recommended maximum or smaller than the minimum, you may need to use a different test, or convert the figures first. Get advice.

3.   Read an account of the statistical analysis you are using. And then read it again, until you can see where your results will fit in, and what they ought to look like. If you can't make it make sense, you may have the wrong test. Get help.

4.   Take care if using computer software, such as SPSS, that will do the statistical analyses for you. It can be difficult to work out what to put in and, if you get that wrong, you will get rubbish out. *First* work out what test you need. *Then* read instructions on how to do that test using the software. If possible, check your first couple of calculations of such tests by also doing them by hand. If the results don't come out the same, then something has gone amiss.

Textbooks

Statistics is an enormous subject and can get very complicated. Textbooks vary tremendously. Some are for advanced mathematicians (leave these alone), others for researchers and students who have a substantial background in statistical work, and others for people who need leading gently by the hand. Most linguists fall into the last category! It is worth using a book written *for* linguists if possible, or at least one that deals with a similar topic area such as psychology or social sciences, because the examples will be relevant, will make sense to you, and may give you ideas for your own research.

Woods *et al.* (1986) and Hatch and Lazaraton (1991), though old, remain key resources for linguistics students. Coolican (2004) is a friendly and practical book for psychology students, which covers the main statistical tests within the context of explaining how to design studies and collect data. The examples are interesting and well illustrated. Coolican's previous book (1995) begins at an even more introductory level. Another introductory book aimed at psychology students is Greene and D'Oliveira (2005). Hinton (2004) is written for social science students and is similarly helpful and clear but does not include the study-design aspect. The most logical guide for getting started with SPSS is Colman and Pulford (2006) but it does not explain the statistical tests themselves. Two books that bridge the gap are Hinton *et al.* (2004) and Brace *et al.* (2006). The latter focuses on the statistics, illustrating it with pictures of the screens that you will see in SPSS, and annotating them with useful explanations. If you need to engage with Analysis of Variance (ANOVA), Reitveld and Van Hout (2005) have dedicated a whole book to it, aimed at linguists, and it is also covered by Greene and D'Oliveira (2005).

Help for the mathematically insecure

Brackets

A sum in brackets should be done first: the brackets indicate that everything inside belongs together. Thus:

$(3 + 2) \times 4 = 5 \times 4 = 20$, whereas $3 + (2 \times 4) = 3 + 8 = 11$

Relationship between adjacent symbols

If you see a figure *next to* a symbol or something in brackets, you need to multiply the two together, e.g.:

4a is the same as: $4 \times \mathbf{a}$

G $(5 - 3)$ is the same as: G times the result when you take three from five, i.e. $G \times 2$

Something on top of something else

One figure or symbol, or an array of them, on top of a line, with something underneath, indicates a division sum. First work out any calculations that are entirely above or below the line. Then divide the bottom value into the top one. Thus:

$\frac{5}{10}$ is the same as: 5 divided by $10 = 0.5$, i.e. ½

$\frac{2\ (6\text{-}1)}{20} = \frac{2 \times 5}{20} = \frac{10}{20} = 0.5$, i.e. ½

Squaring something

When you *square* something, you multiply it by itself. We write this instruction with a superscript 2, so 12 squared is written 12^2 (and comes out as 144). To square something on your calculator, enter the figure, press the multiplication key ($\times$) and then the equals key ($=$). By the way, squaring something gets rid of minus signs (that's one reason why it is used so much). So $12^2 = 144$ and so does -12^2.

Square root

When you find the *square root* of something, you do the opposite to squaring it – you find out which number you would have to multiply by itself to get the figure you have. So, the square root of 16 is 4, because $4 \times 4 = 16$. The square root of 100 is 10 because $10 \times 10 = 100$. Square roots are hard to guess, so you do need your calculator. To work out a square root, enter your figure and press the square root key ($\sqrt{}$).

Which order?

If you see two division sums that have to be added together, do the divisions first, then add the results:

$\frac{5}{10} + \frac{7}{9} = 0.5 + 0.78 = 1.28$

See also the section on 'Brackets'.

How many decimal places?

The majority of calculations will give you figures to many decimal places (i.e. numbers after the decimal point). It is customary to use two or three in most calculations. To operate to two decimal places: look at the *third* figure after the decimal point. If it is 5 or higher, then round *up*, that is, add 1 to the figure to its left. If it is less than 5, round *down*, that is, don't change the figure to the left:

0.7777777777 will round up to 0.78
0.7272727272 will round up to 0.73
0.2727272727 will round down to 0.27

Sometimes you may notice that the third figure is *nearly* 5, and would be if it, itself, was rounded up. 0.314999999 – should it be rounded up to 0.32? Or down to 0.31? Answer: Don't round up – think of it like money: if you owed someone £3.49, how would you feel if they said 'Let's call it £4'?

Calculating a percentage

You start with two figures, one a proportion of the other. For instance, you have counted up how many syllables there are in the words of a text. The text is 4313 words long and 716 of the words have more than one syllable. A percentage calculation can tell you how many words per hundred are polysyllabic. Divide the larger figure into the smaller one, thus 716 divided by 4313, and multiply the answer by 100 (move the decimal point two places to the left). Thus: 716/4313 = 0.1733, or 17.33%. If you convert figures to percentages, you can more easily compare them. Another text might have 893 words with more than one syllable, but the text was longer, at 5148 words, so is the proportion the same or not? The percentage works out at 17.35% – virtually identical, but that would be hard to see without the percentage calculations.

Calculating the mean

The mean is the 'average', and is sometimes written as $\bar{x}$. Add up the scores and divide the total by the number of scores, e.g.:

The mean of: 10, 13, 6, 11, and 5 is:

$$\frac{(10 + 13 + 6 + 11 + 5)}{5} = \frac{45}{5} = 9$$

Key to the most common algebraic symbols used in basic statistics

The symbols used in mathematical expressions can be very intimidating. The secret is to treat symbols as your friends: they tell you unambiguously and succinctly what to do to get a valid answer to your calculations. The point of using symbols is that one statement will cope with lots of different individual calculations. To convert a string of symbols into a calculation, you simply work out what number each symbol stands for in your case, and replace the symbols with the numbers (see Table 19.5). The intimidating thing about them is that they look so strange, but it's just a code.

Table 19.5 The most commonly used algebraic symbols

Symbol	Explanation
x	Any single value or score
y	Another single value or score
N	The number of results or subjects
Σ	This is 'sigma' and it means 'Sum of', so Σx means 'add together all the values of x'
x^2	x squared, i.e. multiplied by itself. Example: if $x = 3$, then $x^2 = 9$
$\bar{x}$	The mean (average)
$\frac{\Sigma x}{N} = \bar{x}$	The sum of all values, divided by the number of values, producing the mean
$\sqrt{x}$	square root of x, i.e. the number which, multiplied by itself, gives x. Example: if $x = 64$, then $\sqrt{x} = 8$ (use a calculator with a square root button)
$\frac{x}{y}$ or x/y	divide x by y, i.e. the same as $x \div y$. Example: ¾ = 3 ÷ 4 = 0.75
f	Frequency: how often something occurs
df	degrees of freedom: a figure used to help you find the 'critical value' you need in your test, to establish the probability level. It reflects the number of columns and rows in your data table, and instructions are given with the relevant test
χ and χ^2	Chi: represents a value used in the Chi-squared (χ^2) test
E	Expected frequency in the Chi-squared test
O	Observed frequency in the Chi-squared test
p	Probability (of getting a result by chance)
ρ	Rho: the Spearman's correlation coefficient
σ	Standard deviation (of a population): a measure of how much variation there is between scores
s or sd	Standard deviation (of a sample)
$<$ $>$	Smaller than, bigger than, e.g. $x < 12$ means *the value of x is less than 12*
$\leq$ $\geq$	Smaller than or equal to, bigger than or equal to
$t, z, U, W,$ etc.	Letters may relate to the value of the *test statistic* for a specific test, e.g. t is used for the test statistic in the *t-test*. You will find the relevant letter to use when you read about the test in a good statistics book.

20
How to reference

Basics

It is crucial to your work that you reference your sources correctly. This chapter aims to answer your questions about why and how to reference.

What is the purpose of referencing?

Referencing has two purposes. First, you must give credit where it is due for the ideas you have used. You do not want to be accused of plagiarism, that is, of passing someone else's ideas off as your own (see Chapter 21), which is a kind of academic theft or cheating.

Second, referencing enables the reader to trace an idea or piece of information right back to its source. The conventions of referencing are such that it should always be possible to do this. The writer is leaving a 'trail', and this trail must be clear all the way back, because:

❐ One of the major ways in which all researchers come across important new information is by reading about it in another source. Without full references, it would be impossible to track the information down.

❐ When your project is marked, your assessors are looking to see that you understand the material you are writing about. If you make reference to, or quote, some work that they do not know (which is not uncommon), or if you back up an apparently wacky idea with a quote or reference, it will be necessary for them to check it. Unless you give the full details, including the page number, it may be impossible – and certainly very time-consuming – for them to find it. As pointed out in Chapter 1, the golden rule of project writing is not to annoy your assessor, and incomplete referencing is a sure-fire way to make yourself extremely unpopular.

General tips

❐ Whatever your precise choice of referencing conventions, be consistent.

❐ If you do alphabetical auto-sorting using your word-processing program, check carefully for date order in each author's works, and the order of second authors.

❐ Alphabetical order is not always obvious. Position names beginning 'Mc' as if they were spelled 'Mac'. List German names with an umlaut over a vowel as if the vowel was followed by an 'e'.

❐   The ordering of authors' names on a paper or book is significant in signalling the importance of each person's contribution, so, to be a correct reference, it must have the names in the order that the authors have designated.

❐   In your text, refer to the authors, not the work. Thus: 'Pearson and De Villiers (2006) argue...', not 'Pearson and De Villiers (2006) argues...'

What does a basic reference look like?

Examples (1) and (2) are from a book by Wardhaugh (1993: 109).

(1)   The 'tip of the tongue' phenomenon (see Brown and McNeill, 1966) is an instance of this last kind of failure to bring an item immediately and completely out of long-term memory.

By referring to Brown and McNeill's paper, Wardhaugh is giving you, the reader, information about where to look for further details. The short reference given in the text (example 1) is backed up by a full reference in the alphabetical list of references at the back of Wardhaugh's book (example 2). This provides you with all you need to locate the original work, and to read for yourself what they did. In this book, as in most of the other books and papers that you will read, referencing according to these conventions is the norm:

(2)   Brown, R., and McNeill, D. (1966). The 'tip of the tongue' phenomenon. *Journal of Verbal Learning and Verbal Behavior* 5, 325–37.

There is more detail later about how to format references like this.

What is the difference between a 'references' list and a 'bibliography'?

These terms do tend to get used interchangeably in some contexts, but there is a difference. Your 'reference list' gives details of the books and articles that have been mentioned in your text. It should contain all of them, and should not contain anything you have read or looked at but not mentioned. A bibliography is a list of books and articles put together for some other purpose, usually to help researchers and/or as recommended reading for study. According to this rule, the list of sources at the end of your project should be headed 'References'.

What happens if I haven't seen the original, just a reference to it or a quote from it somewhere else?

If you have not had access to the original source of an idea or quote, you will have to adopt the convention of citing or giving a secondary quote:

(3)   Noam Chomsky believes that 'The language each person acquires is a rich and complex construction hopelessly undermined by the fragmentary evidence available [to the child]' (Chomsky 1975, quoted in Pinker 1994, p. 23).

You must include in your reference list the source that you used (in the above case, the work by Pinker). Practice varies regarding whether you should also list the original source (in example 3, the work by Chomsky). It is courteous to the reader to do so – it will prevent the need to find Pinker's book in order to track down the details. However, many lecturers dislike seeing secondary sources (works you refer to without having seen) listed in the reference list, because it makes it hard to tell what you have in fact read. Ask each lecturer for whom you write which practice you are to follow. Alternatively, include the secondary sources in your reference list, but indicate (with an asterisk, for instance) that you have not seen them. This practice is not something that you will see in published materials, and it is just a way of covering yourself when your assessors have different views. Remember, of course, to state what the asterisk (or other mark) signifies.

It is a good idea to keep second-hand quoting and citing to a minimum, by finding the original source wherever possible, and drawing from that instead. The only works that you should be quoting or citing second-hand are those that your library does not have, and which you have not had an opportunity to get sight of in any other way.

What is the difference between 'cited in' and 'quoted in'?

Many students muddle these two terms, probably because they have not really understood what they mean. When you *quote* something, you give the words as they appear in the original. Indicate this by putting inverted commas around the quote if it is less than two lines long, or by indenting the quote, with a line space above and below, if it is longer (for an example of this, see p. 92 in this book).

When you *cite* something, you mention it. There is no quotation involved. If you want to mention a source that you have found in another work, then you say 'cited in'. For example, if you read in Wardhaugh (1993) about Brown and McNeill's (1966) experiment (see example 1 above), then you might write:

(4)   The 'tip of the tongue' phenomenon can be investigated experimentally, as Brown and MacNeill (1966, cited in Wardhaugh 1993: 109) have demonstrated.

How do I make sure I have managed to list all and only the sources I have mentioned?

One of your jobs as a writer is to ensure that your reference list is complete and accurate. In order to make sure that you have not omitted a reference, make a print-out of the list and then work through the text, ticking off on the print-out every reference as you come across it. If you find a reference in the text that ought to be on the list and isn't, then add it. If at the end of the process, there is any reference on the list that has not been ticked, then there is no mention of it in the text and it should be removed.

To speed things up, use the search facility in your word-processing program. Type in the first few letters of a name from the reference list and search for it. If the first occurrence that the search comes up with is in the reference list itself, then there is no mention in the text and the entry should be deleted. This procedure cannot be used to find out if a reference in the text is missing from the list. Alternatively, if you are using the Harvard referencing system (see below), every reference in your text should include round brackets, so if you search for an opening bracket, you should find every reference in the text.

What is the best way to keep track of what references I need to put in the list?

There are various methods, two of which are given below.

Method 1

Construct the reference list as you go. The advantage of this approach is that you have one less job to do at the end. There are a couple of disadvantages, though. First, as your work goes through different stages, you are likely to edit out passages containing references. It is not always easy to remember whether there are other mentions of those works in your project, and so you might not be sure whether or not to delete them from the reference list. Second, you may find that it breaks your flow to keep moving to the reference list when you are in the middle of writing. Alternatively, as you write, highlight each reference (on screen, or with highlighter pen, according to your medium). Then they will be easy to find later.

Method 2

When you have finished writing, do a very careful read, identifying all the references at that stage and building up the list. The advantage of this is that, if you are careful enough, you will end up with a list of all and only the references mentioned. The disadvantage is that you have to be quite disciplined to comb the text for only references. It is tempting to combine this job with a final read-through or a proofread for typing errors, and this division of your attention is quite likely to make you less efficient on all of the tasks.

Whichever method you use, remember one golden rule: every time you use a book or article, keep a note of the complete details that you will need for referencing purposes. Don't assume that it will be as easy to get the details later. For a start, without the reference details, how will you know where to look? Also, you cannot rely on a library catalogue to give you all the information you need for a reference list: very often no place of publication is given, and no titles, author details or page numbers will be given for the papers in edited collections. If you assume that you can go back to the library and check the original source later, remember that someone else may have borrowed the book by then.

Is there only one way of referencing correctly?

No. There are two major systems, the Harvard and the Humane, and within each you may spot minor variations. So far in this chapter, and indeed in this book as a whole, we have adopted the Harvard system.

What is the basic difference between the Harvard and the Humane systems?

The distinction between Harvard and the Humane has traditionally been associated with the major division between the sciences (including the social sciences) and the arts, though the Harvard system is now tending to be used in both. As linguistics spans the sciences and the arts, both systems can be found in older publications, but it is rare to find Humane referencing in recent books and journals. If you are studying a subject like English literature as well as linguistics, you may well find that you are required to use both systems. Accept this gracefully, and be careful to use whichever is required in each piece of work. Take particular care not to mix them, otherwise you will be using neither!

As to format, the Harvard system refers to works by their author(s) and date in the text, with full references at the end, alphabetically by author surname. The Humane system uses footnote numbers in the text, and gives the references, in numerical order (that is, in the order of their occurrence) at the foot of each page or at the end. In what follows, the guidelines relate to the Harvard system. A summary of how to reference in the Humane system is provided at the end of the chapter.

The Harvard system

How do I refer to a book?

In the text, give the author's name followed by date of publication (example 5). Where appropriate, give page numbers too (example 6).

(5)   Wardhaugh (1993).
(6)   Wardhaugh (1993: 64–8)

In the reference list, give the author's name, initial(s), date in brackets (although note that, in some versions of this system, the date is not in brackets, and it is followed by a colon; in others, there are neither brackets nor a colon), and title in italics, followed by a full stop, place of publication followed by a colon, publisher, and full stop:

(7)   Wardhaugh, R. (1993) *Investigating language*. Oxford: Blackwell.

As you build up your list of references, apply strict alphabetical order by author surname.

What if the book is an edited collection of papers by other people?

In the text, use the same conventions as for a book (examples 5 and 6). In the reference list, add '(ed.)' for one editor or '(eds)' for two, after the author name(s) and initial(s), but before the date:

(8)   Giglioli, P.P. (ed.) (1972) *Language and social context*. Harmondsworth: Penguin.

However, consider whether it is really the edited collection itself that you should be referencing. If you are pointing to material within that collection, refer to the specific chapter, using the name of its author. Thus, to draw on the paper by Goffman that is included within the collection by Giglioli, refer to Goffman (1972), not Giglioli (1972), and reference the work as outlined below under 'How is a paper in an edited book notated?'

How is a paper in an edited book notated?

In the text, give the author of the paper and the date of the edited book. Do not mention the editor(s) of the book here:

    (9)   Smith (1996)

In the reference list, give the author with the initial(s), date, title of paper (not in italics; in some versions of this system the title of a paper is put in inverted commas), followed by a full stop. Then write 'In', followed by the book details, as described above. Finally, give the page numbers of the paper, preceded by a comma (or, in some versions, a colon, or a comma and 'p.' or 'pp.') and followed by a full stop:

    (10a) Smith, P.K. (1996) Language and the evolution of mind-reading. In Carruthers, P. and Smith, P.K. (eds) (1996) *Theories of theory of mind.* Cambridge: Cambridge University Press, 344–54.

Note that, if you are listing several items from the same collection, one option is to shorten the individual references (example 10b) by cross-referring to a single reference for the collection (example 10c). Doing this is only worthwhile if you have at least two items from the same collection, otherwise it increases the word count and space taken rather than decreasing it. Also, it is imperative that you *do* provide the entry for the collection (example 10c), since entries like example 10b are *not permissible* without it.

    (10b) Smith, P.K. (1996) Language and the evolution of mind-reading. In Carruthers, P. and Smith, P.K. (eds), 344–54.
    (10c) Carruthers, P. and Smith, P.K. (eds) (1996) *Theories of theory of mind.* Cambridge: Cambridge University Press, 344–54.

What are the conventions for a paper in a journal?

In the text, proceed as above (example 9). In the reference list, give the author(s) with initials, date, title of paper (not in italics; in some versions of this system the title is put in inverted commas), full stop. Then give the title of the journal, in italics, volume number, part number in brackets if appropriate, and pages, preceded by a comma (or, in some versions, by a colon, or a comma and 'p.' or 'pp.') and followed by a full stop:

    (11)   Brakke, K.E. and Savage-Rumbaugh, E.S. (1995) The development of language skills in bonobo and chimpanzee – I. Comprehension. *Language and Communication* 15 (2), 121–48.

Note that it is *not* necessary to name the publisher of a journal.

Are there any special conventions for referencing more than one work by the same person?

Practice varies. It is common simply to see the name repeated on line after line where there are a lot of references to one person's work. That is the practice adopted in this book. However, another option is to replace the name by a long dash after its first occurrence:

(12) Trudgill, P. (1974) *The social differentiation of English in Norwich.* Cambridge: Cambridge University Press.
— (1978) *Sociolinguistic patterns in British English.* London: Arnold.
— (1983) *On dialect.* Oxford: Blackwell.

If you choose to adopt this convention, it is a good idea to wait until the last minute before replacing the repeated names by dashes. This is to avoid accidentally inserting another author's work (here, it might be, say, something by Turnbull) under the first entry, so that the later entries are attributed to the wrong person.

What should I do if I have referred to more than one work by the same person, published in the same year?

Since it would be confusing to have two or more works all referred to as, say, Crystal (2003), the convention is to label them a, b, c, and so on. You should use these letters both in the main text and in the reference list, and ensure that you always use the same letter for the same one. Look at the entries in this book for the two works by Crystal that were published in 2003, to see how this operates. Note that the use of letters is local to the piece of writing in question. If you find such a letter in someone else's references, do not simply adopt the letter as if it were a permanent part of the reference – it is not and, if you are only referring to that one work, you don't need it. You should never have in your reference list a date with a letter after it unless there is at least one other work by that author with that date, also with a (different) letter after it. Note also that there is nothing intrinsic in the publication that is referred to as 'a' that means it had to be 'a'. Someone else might list it as the 'b' publication.

What if there is more than one author with the same surname?

In the references, list the authors in alphabetical order of their forenames or initials. In the text, because authors are referred to by surname only, there is the potential for confusion if both authors have published in the same year. If this occurs in your work, add the initial in the text reference, for example G. Cook (2001), so that the reader knows which Cook (2001) reference you mean. In this book we only narrowly missed having this problem with the names Brown, Carroll, Wells and White, and we do indeed have it with Cook.

What if there are two authors?

In the text, give both names, linked by 'and' (example 13) and, in the reference list, give both, with initials (example 14). If they are editors, put '(eds)' before the date (example 15).

(13)   Graddol and Swann (1989)
(14)   Graddol, D. and Swann, J. (1989) *Gender voices*. Oxford: Blackwell.
(15)   Carruthers, P. and Smith, P.K. (eds) (1996) *Theories of theory of mind*.
         Cambridge: Cambridge University Press.

When an author has co-authored with others, which order do the works go in on the reference list?

To illustrate how to do this, we'll use some made-up authors, so that we can imagine various permutations (example 16). We'll call the first author Penelope Wilkinson. First put all the single-authored work by that person, in order of year; then sort the co-authored works alphabetically by the second author's name, and list them in that order. Works by the same two authors are in date order:

(16)   Wilkinson, P. (1986) . . .
         Wilkinson, P. (1989) . . .
         Wilkinson, P. (1994) . . .
         Wilkinson, P. and Armitage, S. (1988) . . .
         Wilkinson, P. and Cooper, M. (1983) . . .
         Wilkinson, P. and Cooper, M. (1991) . . .

If a two-author team has also written with a third person, put the three-author work at the end of the list of works by the first two authors, even if it is of an earlier date than some of them. If there is more than one work by the same three-author team, put them in date order:

(17)   Wilkinson, P. and Armitage, S. (1988) . . .
         Wilkinson, P. and Cooper, M. (1983) . . .
         Wilkinson, P. and Cooper, M. (1991) . . .
         Wilkinson, P., Cooper, M. and Bryant. Q. (1984) . . .
         Wilkinson, P., Cooper, M. and Bryant, Q. (1991) . . .
         Wilkinson, P., Cooper, M. and Caradine, K. (1997) . . .
         Wilkinson, P., Cooper, M., Collins, R. and Bryant, Q. (1989) . . .
         Wilkinson, P. and Davies, K. (1987) . . .

In other words, clear up all the works by the author on his/her own before doing the two-author works. Clear up everything by each two-author team, including works with extra authors, before moving onto the next two-author team. Remember that the order in which the authors' names appear on a book or paper is extremely important and you must not change it. So, in the penultimate line of example 17, Bryant is listed after Collins, and it is Collins's name that determines the position of the reference, below the publication with Caradine.

If there are lots of authors, do they all have to be mentioned each time?

In the text, on the first occurrence of the reference, give all the names and, after that, use 'et al.', which means 'and others' (so don't use it to replace just one co-author!):

(18)   Bates, Bretherton and Snyder (1988) . . . Bates *et al.* (1988) . . .

In the reference list, give all the authors with their initials, linking them with a comma until the last two, which are linked with 'and':

(19)   Bates, E., Bretherton, I. and Snyder, L. (1988) *From first words to grammar.* Cambridge: Cambridge University Press.

What if an author has published more than one work with several other authors in the same year?

If Smith, say, has published two papers with Jones, Brown, and White, both in 2005, then you can refer to them as Smith *et al.* (2005a) and Smith *et al.* (2005b) (see above). If Smith has published with different co-authors in the same year (or with the same co-authors, but listed in a different order), it is more awkward. They will be differentiated in the reference list but, if you refer to them in the text just as 'Smith *et al.* (2005)', the reader will not know which work is being referred to. Yet it would be odd to refer to them as (a) and (b) since the authorship lists are not identical. One solution is to opt out of using 'et al.' for these particular works and list all the authors each time you mention them. This is the best option if there are only three authors. For more than three authors, see how far down the list of authors the differences lie. You may be able to refer to 'Smith, Jones, *et al.* (2005)', 'Smith, Brown, *et al.* (2005)', and so on. You can only do this if at least two names remain captured by 'et al.'.

How do I handle family names with more than one part?

Names like Robert de Beaugrande and Wilhelm von Humboldt can be difficult: should they be listed alphabetically under the second or the third part of the name? Where three names are given, such as Alonso Zamora Vicente, Susan Ervin Tripp or Suzette Haden Elgin, does the middle one count as the first part of the family name, or as part of the given name? Don't give yourself a hard time over this: individuals with such names will have their own preferences, but other forces are at play too, including the practices of individual publishers. Here are some handy hints for what to do:

❐   Go back to the source of your information. If you have read the name in a book or article, find it in the reference list and follow the practice there. If you have something by the author him-/herself, there may well be citations of his/her other works in the reference list, so check there.

❏ Aim for consistency in your own reference list. So if you choose to list De Beaugrande under 'D', do the same for De Saussure, and list Von Humboldt under 'V'. If you list De Beaugrande as 'Beaugrande, R. de' then it will be 'Saussure, F. de' and 'Humboldt, W. von'.

Some names from other countries can be difficult to list too. In China, it is customary for the family name to precede the given name in everyday usage, and this can mean that in a reference, the given name is inadvertently listed as a surname. Additional complications arise because many Chinese scholars adopt western practices when presenting their name, and because it is not always easy even for a Chinese person to tell which name is the family name and which the given name. In order to list the name correctly, check the author's own publications to see how reference is made to his/her previous works. You can also search for the author's web pages for the same purposes.

Where do I find the information I need?

In a book, the details are usually in the first few pages at the front. Be careful to copy the authors' names and the book or paper title correctly. The date of publication will normally be on the same left-hand page as the ISBN number and the British Library or Library of Congress (or other national library) cataloguing data. It is not usually difficult to spot the publisher (but beware of giving the printer or typesetter by mistake). However, it is sometimes difficult to work out the place of publication. If there is an address for the publisher, give the town and, if American, the state as well. If there are several addresses, give the top one, or the one associated with editorial as opposed to marketing concerns. Some large publishing houses publish simultaneously in two countries (such as the UK and the USA): if you can't tell which country the book was probably commissioned in, give both places.

In a journal, the name of the journal and the volume number and part should be printed somewhere on the article as a header or footer. If they are not, and you have the whole journal in your hand, look in the front, or on the back cover. If you have only a photocopy, you obviously needed to write down the details when you made the copy. If you didn't, you have a problem, so remember to do that in future! To find details you forgot to write down, use a web search engine such as Google, to see if anyone has listed it on a website. Alternatively, see what electronic search facilities your library has.

How do I reference a work with no apparent author?

This situation can arise when you cite an official report, a newspaper article, or a large work such as a dictionary or encyclopedia. For an official report (example 20) or newspaper (example 21), treat the commissioner or publisher of the report as the author. For a dictionary, give the name (example 22). Do the same for an encyclopedia, unless the author's name is given at the foot of the article, in which case, treat it like a paper in an edited volume (example 23):

(20) Department for Education and Science (1975) *A language for life* (The Bullock Report). London: Department for Education and Science.
(21) *Times* (2005) Google must win 'keyword' battle. *The Times*. 22 October, p. 66.
(22) *Oxford English Dictionary* (2nd edition). Oxford: Oxford University Press.
(23) Cameron, D. (2006). Gender. In Brown, E.K. (ed.) *Encyclopedia of language and linguistics*. Oxford: Elsevier, vol. 4: 733–9.

If a book has more than one edition, or has been reprinted or revised, which date do I use?

Inside a book all sorts of information is given and only some of it is relevant to academic referencing needs. The basic rule is to give the earliest date for the text in its current form. When a new edition of a book is produced, material is added and the page numbers end up different, so it is important that you indicate which edition you have used, and give the correct date for that edition. Indicate an edition by putting '(nth edition)' after the title, where *n* stands for the edition number (e.g. 3rd, 4th). However, when a book is reprinted or comes out in paperback, the material is not altered, so you should not make any reference to reprint or paperback dates. Sometimes there is a date given for a reprint with revisions. In this case, give the reprint date, and in the reference, put '(revised edition)' after the title.

What if the date of publication is different from the copyright date?

Use the publication date, unless there is evidence to the contrary in the reference lists of others. If there is a large discrepancy it will probably be because the work has been re-issued, in which case the 'copyright' date coincides with the original date of publication. In the case of key papers that end up in a 'reader', it can be useful to indicate the original publication date as well (see the section 'Which date?' on p. 233).

If I am referring repeatedly to the same work, do I have to keep mentioning it?

It certainly is possible to overdo referencing of the same work. If you are drawing heavily on one source for a while, it is acceptable to write something like: 'In the following discussion, much has been drawn from the work of Brown (2005).' However, have a think about why you are so dependent on one work. Could it indicate that you have not read sufficiently widely? See Chapter 21 for guidance on how to work effectively with multiple sources.

If you refer more than once to the same work, it is possible to use the abbreviations *op. cit.* (short for *opere citato* – 'in the work cited') or, if there is no other reference in between, *ibid.* (short for *ibidem* – 'in the same place'). Both indicate that the referencing information is exactly the same as last time, including the page number, if any (example 24). If the page number is different, indicate this (example 25):

(24)   According to Brown (2005: 10) … In addition, …. (*ibid.*)
(25)   According to Brown (2005: 10) … In addition, …. (*ibid.*: 17)

However, these abbreviations are used much less frequently than they used to be. If you do use *ibid.*, only introduce it in the final draft, as it *must* refer to the immediately preceding reference. As text often gets moved around, added or removed in the rewrites, you could end up with an *ibid.* referring back to the wrong work if you put it in too soon.

What are the conventions for punctuation in reference lists?

These do vary considerably; however, as long as you are consistent, it doesn't matter too much which conventions you use, unless you are preparing something for publication, when you should check in the author's notes issued by the publisher. Certain conventions, however, are fairly standard. We recommend the practice adopted for referencing throughout this book (giving you plenty of examples to refer to):

❐   Names: Follow each initial by a full stop; follow names in a list of authors by a comma, except the penultimate (which is linked to the final one with 'and').

❐   Date: Put the date of publication in brackets.

❐   Titles: Use 'sentence case' (only the first initial and proper nouns are capitalized); put book and journal titles in italics, but not the titles of papers within a book or journal.

❐   Publication: Put the place of publication first, followed by a colon, then the publisher's name.

❐   Pages: introduce the page numbers by a colon.

❐   Other: Use a full stop after abbreviations such as 'ed.' (for editor).

As the reference list is organized alphabetically, do not use bullet points to indicate each entry.

What should I do if I can't print italics or I am writing by hand?

Wherever italics would occur (in reference lists and also in the main text), it is acceptable to use underlining.

Is it possible to put into the reference list a work that has not yet been published?

Yes. If you have had sight of a paper or book that is currently being printed but hasn't yet appeared, write *forthcoming* or *in press* where you would otherwise write the date and, if it is a paper and the page numbers are not available, omit them. It is also possible to refer to a work that is at an earlier stage. Do this in the same way as above, but replacing *forthcoming* or *in press* with *in preparation*. Beware of using these labels when you have found the reference in another source. A work that was forthcoming, in press, or in preparation in 2004 is probably published by now, so you need to try and find its publication date.

If, in the text, I refer to more than one work at once, what order do I list them in?

There are two permissible orders: alphabetical (example 26) and chronological (example 27). Whichever you choose, be consistent. If you are mentioning several works by the same author, you will save words by using alphabetical order:

> (26) ... (Brown 1998, 2004; Smith 1999, 2001; White 2000)
> (27) ... (Brown 1998; Smith 1999; White 2000; Smith 2001; Brown 2004).

Suppose I asked an expert about something face to face or by email – how do I acknowledge the source of my information?

You can write 'Brown (personal communication)' or 'John Brown (personal communication)', depending on whether the reader will know from the context who Brown is – often you check a fact with a researcher whose work you are already engaging with. You should not list anything in the reference list at the back. Information from your lecturers, family, or friends will not usually make the grade of a 'personal communication' citation.

How do I reference information from my lecture notes?

Ask your lecturer if it is okay to reference your lecture notes. Usually it is not recommended. Go and find the information in a published source and refer to that instead.

Which date?

Sometimes a work has more than one publication date, because it is a re-issue or a modern edition (prepared by someone else) of a classic work, or a reprint (sometimes edited) in a 'reader'. By referring to the original and the later date, you signal to the reader that you have used the more recent one, and that any page numbers will be from that, not the original. Examples in the reference list of this book include Maltz, D. and Borker, R. (1982/1998) and Carroll, L. (1865/1971).

How do I reference something I found on the Internet?

Internet referencing conventions are not fully standardized yet, and you may see various practices. However, keep in mind the golden rules of *all* referencing:

1   Give due credit to the author.
2   Make it possible for your reader to track the work down.

These two principles, between them, lead to the following recommended good practice for referencing a web source. Use the following:

❐   the author's name or that of the organization that the author represents;
❐   the title of the piece;

❏   the address;

❏   the date on which you last accessed it.

If you cannot tell who wrote or authorized the page, look for a link to a home page, or remove sections of the address from the right, to see if you can find one. Since not all material from the Internet is trustworthy, be suspicious about pages that you cannot associate with a named person or organization with credentials. (See also Chapter 1 for advice on how to avoid ending up with untrustworthy material.)

❏   *Don't* just provide the web address as the reference. This is the equivalent of referencing a book by saying which shelf it is on in the library. (However, if it is indeed the address rather than the information on the page that you are referring to, then it is acceptable to give the web-page address in the main text, as we do, for instance, in Chapter 18, when we are advising you where to go to. In your project, such a reference is likely to be the exception rather than the rule, so think twice before taking this course of action.)

❏   Make sure you give the *full and correct web address* for the material, so that the reader can go straight there. For each web address that you give, try entering the address yourself and see whether it does get you to the right place.

❏   By way of illustration of the above observations, it is *not* good practice to write:

(28) There is no single agreed definition of formulaic language (www.cf.ac.uk/
      encap/clcr/ flarn/formulaiclanguage.html).

Instead, you should find out who wrote the material and name that person (example 29a) and/or his/her affiliation (example 29b) and give the Internet reference in the reference list at the end (examples 30a, 30b):

(29a) There is no single agreed definition of formulaic language (Wray 2005).
(29b) There is no single agreed definition of formulaic language (Formulaic
      Language Research Network, Cardiff University, 2005).
(30a) Wray, A. 2005. What is formulaic language?
      (www.cf.ac.uk/encap/clcr/flarn/formulaiclanguage.html). [Last accessed
      6th January 2006]
(30b) Formulaic Language Research Network, Cardiff University. 2005. What is
      formulaic language? (www.cf.ac.uk/encap/clcr/flarn/formulaiclanguage.html).
      [Last accessed 6th January 2006]

The Humane system

In the Humane referencing system, a superscript number in the text points the reader to a footnote or endnote containing the reference information. Thus, in the text, place a superscript number adjacent to the word that precedes the reference you wish to make:

(31)   Messages in language fall into three situation types: states, events, and actions.[18] These situation types are . . .

In the footnote or endnote, adopt the following procedures (examples 32 and 33).

For a book

Give the initial(s), author(s), title in italics, place of publication, publisher, and date together in brackets, and page(s) relevant to the point you are making, if any:

(32)   [18] D. Graddol and J. Swann, *Gender Voices* (Oxford, Blackwell, 1989), p. 77.

If you have to refer to it again, you use a shortened form, with just the surnames, a shortened title if it isn't short enough already, and the page:

(33)   [20] Graddol and Swann, *Gender Voices*, p. 54.

For an edited book

Proceed as above (examples 32 and 33), but add '(ed.),' after the author name(s).

For a paper in an edited volume

Give the initial(s), author(s), title in inverted commas, 'in', editor's name, '(ed.)', comma, title of book in italics, place of publication, publisher, and date together in brackets, and page(s) relevant to the point you are making, if any (not the page range for the entire paper) (example 34). Use a short reference for later mentions (example 35). There are no rules for what the title gets shortened to, provided a reader will be entirely sure which work you are referring to.

(34)   [41]G.R. Guy, 'Language and Social Class', in F.J. Newmark (ed.), *Linguistics: The Cambridge Survey IV – Language: The Socio-cultural Context* (Cambridge, Cambridge University Press, 1988), pp. 60–61.

(35)   [45]Guy, 'Social Class', p. 63.

For a paper in a journal

Give the initial(s), author(s), title in inverted commas, journal name in italics, volume number, date in brackets, and page(s) relevant to the point you are making, if any (not the page range for the entire paper) (example 36). Use a short reference for later mentions (example 37):

(36)   [3]N. Alm, J.L. Arnott and A.F. Newell, 'Discourse Analysis and Pragmatics in the Design of a Conversation Prosthesis', *Journal of Medical Engineering and Technology*, 13/2 (1989), p. 12.

(37)   [12]Alm *et al.*, 'Prosthesis', p. 11.

The use of punctuation

This varies somewhat between users of the Humane system. The Hodder Arnold guidelines, from which the above information has been taken, require the capitalization of every initial letter in titles, full stops at the end of the entire reference, and commas in the places illustrated in the examples above.

21
Plagiarism and how to avoid it

What is plagiarism?

Plagiarism is the *theft* of other people's words and ideas. Plagiarism happens when you claim (or *appear* to claim) that an idea, or the expression of it, is your own when in fact it is someone else's. Plagiarism falls into two types: deliberate and accidental.

Deliberate plagiarism

Deliberate plagiarism includes getting someone else to write your essay for you and then saying it's yours or copying chunks of text out of a book or from the Internet, with the deliberate intention of deceiving the reader into thinking they are in your own words. Why would people engage in deliberate plagiarism? Perhaps out of laziness and a disregard for the requirements and expectations of university study. Perhaps when it seems pointless to restate less expertly what someone else has said well. Perhaps because the copied material is in better English. Or perhaps because of the mistaken belief that everyone else is doing it and getting away with it. It would be as well to treat this claim with the same scepticism as you would the claim that 'everyone' is shoplifting or that 'everyone' is using hard drugs. It is not everyone, nor does the fact that some people are doing it make it right or safe. And it's your choice. Leaving aside the very serious penalties for plagiarism – failing your module, losing the credits, perhaps even being expelled from your course – think back to your aspirations when you came to university. Did they include cheating your way to a qualification you are supposed to gain through study and skills development? Will you respect yourself if you know you never really earned your degree? Will you be able to cope in your career if you have ducked out of learning key skills by cheating?

Accidental plagiarism

Accidental plagiarism is, as the term implies, unintentional. However, since it looks identical to deliberate plagiarism, many institutions penalize it equally heavily. It comes about through oversight and/or lack of skill in manipulating information. You need to be alert for the dangers of accidental plagiarism and have the techniques for ensuring that you avoid it (see below). The problem is that we all rely heavily on other people's ideas. How else can we learn? And unless we have a photographic memory, how are we to be sure that an idea that occurs to us really is our own and not something that we read somewhere? The dangers of accidental plagiarism can seem to loom like hidden icebergs in the sea – you know they are there, but you can't really see if you are going to hit one.

Here are some examples of how accidental plagiarism can happen:

❑ You make notes from a book or other source, copying out useful passages. Later, you cannot remember what is copied and what is not, and you simply take passages from your notes and use them in the essay.

❑ You find material in a book or other source that covers exactly the area you are dealing with. You are aware that you mustn't copy it out, so you deftly rephrase little bits, replacing 'small' with 'little', 'major differences' by 'main differences' and swapping over the order of two halves of a sentence. *You* think that this is now legitimate but your assessors do not.

❑ You use entirely your own words but you don't acknowledge the source of your information.

❑ You draw from notes you made or were given in some previous course of study (school notes, for example), without realizing that these were copied or adapted from some other source.

Will you get found out?

University lecturers are intelligent people. They have read a lot of essays and they know their subject. If you have plagiarized material in your essay, it may not be all that evident to *you*, but it probably will be to them. With the possibility of electronic searches, it is now very quick to check whether something is plagiarized, and there are a number of dedicated software programs available too. So, yes, there is a good chance that, if you have plagiarized, you will be found out.

How to avoid accidental plagiarism: some strategies

There are four key skills that will enable you to avoid plagiarizing by mistake: thorough referencing, care with note-taking, skilled writing and finding your 'voice'. They are very much interrelated, so mastering all four is important.

Referencing

In an essay or project, you will be presenting three different kinds of material: (1) general knowledge; (2) evidence and ideas from other people; (3) your own evidence and ideas.

1   General knowledge (e.g. *English is a Germanic language*) is not open to dispute, and there are many possible places that you could get that information, so it does not need to be referenced.

2   Evidence and ideas from other people include findings in work they have done and claims about what their findings, or those of others, mean for some wider question. This kind of material must be referenced clearly, both to give credit where it is due,

and as a means of distancing yourself from it. Just because they say something, it doesn't make it true.

3   Your own evidence – from data you have collected, for example – and your own ideas, developed out of that evidence in conjunction with what you have read, cannot, of course, be referenced as such. However, you can certainly help the reader to see where your evidence lies (by presenting your data in tables, for example) and how you have got to your idea (by referring to your evidence, and also to ideas from others that you are drawing on).

Sometimes you will simply not be sure whether something needs referencing or not, because the boundaries between general knowledge, others' ideas, and your own ideas are not always clear. If in doubt, err on the side of *over*-referencing until you get the knack. Having too many references in a text breaks up the flow of your writing but that is the lesser of two evils. One problem can be the need repeatedly to reference the same work. For ideas on how to avoid this, see 'Skilled writing' below. Information on how to reference in the correct format is given in Chapter 20.

Taking notes

Good note-taking involves thinking. It is the time to develop your ideas, so get into the habit of asking more than just 'What does X say?' You need to ask 'What does it mean that X says this?' and 'How can X say this when Y says that?' Rather than just summarizing what you are reading, make notes relevant to the task in hand and identify the major points that relate to your purpose. Make the notes under headings, so that similar ideas from different sources end up together. When you come to write, read through all the notes under that heading and try to work out how they relate. This is a productive and positive way to avoid any danger of plagiarism, because you will never simply transfer material from a source, via your notes, to your own work. You will quite naturally repackage ideas according to your own interpretations and priorities. You will also be keen to reference others' claims, because you will be taking issue with them (see 'Skilled writing' below).

When making notes, *never* copy anything out without putting it in inverted commas and putting a page reference next to it. Also write down the *full* reference details, as you will need them later and you will be frustrated if, a few hours before your deadline, you don't have all you need. *Never* copy and paste material from a website into your notes unless you mark it in some way as a quote: with highlight, perhaps. Always include, with material from the Internet, the full web address (that is, what you will need in your browser in order to get back to exactly that material). Also keep a note of the date that you accessed it, as you will need that for the reference (see Chapter 20).

As you read and take notes, try to think of examples of your own to match the ones provided. This is a good way of ensuring that you understand what you are writing about. However, if you are in doubt about whether your example is valid (e.g. where the examples have been drawn from a particular source that you cannot access), you can quote the ones you have been given provided you acknowledge them appropriately, i.e. as quotes. If there is any terminology you don't understand, look it up, don't just copy it out.

Skilled writing

Sometimes an assessor will incorrectly suspect that a student has plagiarized, because there is insufficient difference between the presentation of ideas from others and the student's own ideas. Clear referencing of others' ideas can be supplemented by the use of discourse markers that indicate where the student is expressing his/her own opinion. Consider the following passage:

> *Ji (2004) describes how Mao's Cultural Revolution affected the Chinese language. A number of politically-charged linguistic formulas introduced during that period made it difficult for speakers to think in counter-revolutionary ways. The result was something similar to the linguistic control described in Orwell's novel 1984. The television-bound culture of modern western life may have a similar effect. Because people are highly vulnerable to cultural influences, governments have a responsibility not to be too directive.*

It is not clear in this passage which ideas are Ji's and which are the writer's. However, a few simple markers can make it clear that the writer has developed two new ideas out of Ji's, leaving the reader confident that there has been no plagiarism:

> *Ji (2004) describes how Mao's Cultural Revolution affected the Chinese language.* **She proposes that** *a number of politically-charged linguistic formulas introduced during that period made it difficult for speakers to think in counter-revolutionary ways.* **She argues that** *the result was something similar to the linguistic control described in Orwell's novel 1984.* **It is interesting to consider whether** *the television-bound culture of modern western life may have a similar effect.* **It could be argued that**, *because people are highly vulnerable to cultural influences, governments have a responsibility not to be too directive.*

What should you do if you are referring for some time to just one work? How often should you mention the reference? The first trick is to avoid that situation. Why are you so reliant on one source? Perhaps you need to read some other works, and see if you can draw them in. We show you how to do this in 'Finding your voice' below. However, if you can't avoid repeated references, you may be able to say at the beginning of a section or paragraph: *The following is a summary of information given in Smith (2005).* Note, however, that it is *not* sufficient to give one vague reference to your source somewhere and then draw directly from it for page after page.

To get the knack of skilled writing and referencing, take note of how it is done in the books and papers you read.

Finding your voice: an exercise in using published sources, creating a sophisticated account, and avoiding plagiarism

Correct referencing, the avoidance of plagiarism, and the use of a variety of sources in your account are inextricably linked. The one most common reason why students end up accidentally plagiarizing is because they find it impossible to express the information they have read in a new way. There are two major causes of this problem. One is using only one source. Reading about something in only one place can beguile you into thinking that this is the only way to see the issue, and that there is nothing else to say and no other way to say it. In fact, it is a mistake to assume that all books will tell you the same thing, so it is always a good idea to look up the same information in more than one place. The second cause is needing the same quantity of information as the source provides you with. You are more likely to avoid plagiarism if the source has 20 pages and you only need five lines, or if you need to write 20 pages and the source only gives five lines.

In this exercise, Part 1 demonstrates the problems with drawing from only one source and suggests some ways of finding a new approach to the material. Part 2 challenges you to use two sources to create a tension, giving you an opportunity to take sides or act as referee. Part 3 shows how to add extra information and references to a text you have already drafted. Although this study will make sense if you just read the commentaries, it will make more impact on your skills if you do the exercises for each section before moving on.

The theme

For the purposes of this exercise, imagine you need to write a section of an essay on the way that English expresses comparatives (e.g. *faster*) and superlatives (*fastest*) and how it used to do this in the past. This is not a very complicated subject, and most books deal with it in a few sentences. So will you, but how do you avoid simply reproducing the sentences in a book word for word?

1 Using one source only

Exercise

Read the extract from Barber (2000: 274) given in Figure 21.1 and then write a paragraph on the subject, in your own words. Try to apply the guidelines on how to avoid plagiarism given in this chapter. When you have finished, read the commentary below.

Commentary

This is actually an extremely difficult task, because using only one source gives you very little room for manoeuvre. The referencing can look rather silly if you are acknowledging the same page of the same work all the time. You may have felt under-confident about inventing your own examples, in case they were not valid ones. You may have found it very difficult to express things in your own words. Remember that it is still plagiarism if you change the odd word but leave the text effectively the same. Example 1 illustrates a 'rewrite' that would constitute plagiarism, because the underlined changes to the original are only superficial ones:

(1)   Once, -er and -est were used much more <u>than they are</u> today, and in Early Modern English <u>forms could be found</u> like ancientest, famousest, patienter, perfecter, and shamefuller.

You need strategies that enable you to break out of the narrow restrictions imposed by the source text. One possibility is to approach the subject from a different direction:

Changes in grammar

In grammar we can see the continuation, in small ways, of the long-term historical trend in English from synthetic to analytic, from a system that relies on inflections to one that relies on word-order and grammatical words. An example is the comparison of adjectives, where *more* and *most* are spreading at the expense of the endings *-er* and *-est*. At one time, *-er* and *-est* were used much more widely than today, and in Early Modern English you meet forms like *ancientest, famousest, patienter, perfecter,* and *shamefuller*. In the first half of the present century, adjectives of more than two syllables always had *more* and *most* ('more notorious, most notorious'), while adjectives of one syllable normally had *-er* and *-est* ('ruder, rudest'). Adjectives of two syllables varied, some being compared one way ('more famous, most famous') and some the other ('commoner, commonest'). In this group of two-syllabled adjectives there has been a tendency in recent years for *-er* and *-est* to be replaced by *more* and *most*, and it is now quite normal to say 'more common, most common', and similarly with *cloudy, cruel, fussy, pleasant, quiet,* and *simple*. Recently, moreover, *more* and *most* have been spreading to adjectives of one syllable, and it is not at all uncommon to hear expressions like 'John is more keen than Robert' and 'It was more crude than I expected'.

Figure 21.1 Barber, C. (2000) *The English language: a historical introduction.* Cambridge: Cambridge University Press, 274.

(2)   Within living memory the expression of some comparatives and superlatives has changed . . .

Another is to present some of the facts in list form, as in example 3, where you can also see how it helps to use phrases like 'according to' and 'X claims', to distance yourself from the author, making it clear that this is only one view and that others might exist:

(3)   According to Barber (2000: 274), a study of the forms used in Early Modern English through to the present day indicates that a change has been in progress. He believes that there has been a decrease in the tolerance for *-er* (comparative) and *-est* (superlative), which were once acceptable endings on even polysyllabic words (e.g. *ancienter, ancientest; famouser, famousest*) but which have gradually been replaced by *more* and *most* (e.g. *more ancient, most ancient; more famous, most famous*). This change happened earliest on the longest words. By the early 20th century, the preferences were:

☐   polysyllabic adjectives (more than two syllables): add *more* (comparative) and *most* (superlative), e.g. *more beautiful, most beautiful; more interesting, most interesting.*

☐   monosyllabic adjectives: add *-er* (comparative) and *-est* (superlative), e.g. *richer, richest; bluer, bluest.*

☐   disyllabic adjectives: either form, e.g. *most famous, commonest.*

Barber claims that the transition is now almost complete, with the *-er* and *-est* endings apparently being edged out of the picture entirely, as even monosyllabic words form their comparative and superlative with *more* and *most* (e.g. *The star is more bright than it was yesterday, but it will be most bright tomorrow*).

2 Using two sources and any arising

Exercise

Read the extracts from Strang (1970: 58 and 138) in Figures 21.2 and 21.3. Write a new account, incorporating the information from both Barber and Strang: note that the relevant extract from Barber (1964) has also been provided for you (Figure 21.4, p. 245). When you have finished, read the commentary below.

---

§ 41   It is very much more difficult to show how synchronic variation in grammar provides a model for variation through time. A recent book on *Linguistic Change in Present-day English* (Barber, 1964) has substantial sections on pronunciation (33–76), and vocabulary and meaning (77–128), but a much shorter one on grammar (129–45). About the developments mentioned in the chapter on *Grammatical Changes* some people might have reservations – for instance, under the heading 'loss of inflections' Barber discusses the distribution of *who* and *whom*, though uncertainties in this area of usage can clearly be traced back to the time of Shakespeare, and sequences like *he gave it to my brother and I*, though many will feel this is non-standard (i.e., not a change in the variety of English under discussion). Barber thinks there is an increasing use of *more, most*, rather than *-er, -est*, in comparison, in keeping with a trend which again goes back at least four hundred years; he may be right, but we lack precise numerical information on the subject.

Figure 21.2 Strang, B. (1970) *A history of English*. London and New York: Routledge, 58.

Commentary

The thing you should have noticed is that Strang (1970) and Barber (2000) do not hold entirely the same position. It is extremely good news for you when writers disagree. First, you can demonstrate that you noticed their doing so. Observe how much reservation Strang (1970) expresses on p.58 about Barber's claims. This can be highlighted by foregrounding the disagreement as a theme.

The roles of adjectives and nouns were perhaps less sharply distin-guished than now; such uses as *better than he* (= better men), *full of poor* (= poor people), and, with a determiner, *in many's eyes*, now require a nominal head. This is related to the growth of the prop-word as a noun-place filler, an aspect of the general sense that there are places that ought to be filled by certain form-classes or certain clause-elements.

Double comparatives and superlatives were perfectly acceptable at the beginning of the period (*more properer, most handsomest*), though they came under corrective treatment in the 18c. In certain cases where the forms of comparison had, for phonological reasons, come to be irregular, such as *late, latter, last*, new analogical forms, *later, latest*, had been developed before II, but they were quite recent, and were alternatives in free variation with the historic forms. It is only more recently that the two sets have been differentiated.

Figure 21.3 Strang, B. (1970) *A history of English*. London and New York: Routledge, 138.

But, first, notice that Strang is referring to an earlier work by Barber, not to Barber (2000). So direct reference to Barber (1964) may be appropriate. In Barber (1964), the tone is very different from that in Barber (2000). In the former, he is much more personal. He lists examples that he has encountered. He refers to 'twenty or thirty years ago' (p. 131): remember that he is counting from *then*, not now, so he means the 1930s and 1940s. (The moral is, always check when a book was written.) But is the *sentiment* the same in the two books? You must not assume that it is without checking. An author is at liberty to change his mind in the course of his career. In fact, it can be seen that Barber *does* still hold the same opinion in 2000 as in 1964. So that too can be incorporated, by giving both dates:

(4)   Barber (1964, 2000) claims that the transition is now almost complete, with the *-er* and *-est* endings apparently being edged out of the picture entirely, as even monosyllabic words form their comparative and superlative with *more* and *most* (e.g. *The star is more bright than it was yesterday, but it will be most bright tomorrow*). Barber (1964) cites examples that he has observed, including *more crude*, *more plain*, and *more keen* (p.132). Strang (1970), however, is more cautious about the final stages of this change: 'Barber thinks there is an increasing use of *more, most*, rather than *-er, -est*, in comparison, in keeping with a trend which . . . goes back at least 400 years; he may be right, but we lack precise numerical information on the subject' (p.58).

Once you have identified a disagreement, you can join in! Who do you think is right? Why? How could the conflict be resolved? Adding your views when you have explained those of others is a very good way to find your voice. You are able to speak with authority

> The continued loss of inflexions, and their replacement by syntactic devices, is also seen in the comparative and superlative of adjectives, where forms with -er and -est are being replaced by forms with *more* and *most*. Here we see the continuation of a trend of long standing: Milton wrote *elegantest*, *famousest*, and *sheepishest*, and Archbishop Laud *notoriousest*, where we should write *most elegant*, and so on. To-day, adjectives with three or more syllables are normally compared with *more* and *most* (*beautiful, more beautiful, most beautiful*); monosyllabic adjectives, on the other hand, are normally compared with -er and -est (*bright, brighter, brightest*). The adjectives with two syllables are divided, some usually being compared one way, the others the other; and it is in this dissyllabic group that the change is most noticeable, adjectives formerly taking -er and -est tending to go over to *more* and *most*. A word where this is especially noticeable is *common*; twenty or thirty years ago, *commoner* and *commonest* were normal, but nowadays nearly everybody says *more common, most common*. Indeed, I recently borrowed from a university library a book written in the nineteen-thirties by a distinguished literary scholar: in one place, the word *commonest* occurred; this had been vigorously crossed out by some borrower (presumably a student), who had written in the margin "most common!!!" Another example is heard in B.B.C. weather-forecasts, which frequently say that it will be *more cloudy*, instead of *cloudier*. Other adjectives that I have heard with *more* or *most* include *fussy, quiet, cruel, subtle, clever, profound, simple*, and *pleasant*; all these, I think, were normally compared with -er and -est before the War. I have also been struck by the frequency of forms like *more well-informed* and *most well-dressed*, where people would formerly have said *better-informed* and *best-dressed*. Recently there have been many cases of *more* and *most* spreading even to monosyllabic adjectives; examples I have noticed in educated speech and writing include *more crude, more plain*, and *more keen*. In Miss Iris Murdoch's well-known novel, *The Bell*, occurs the remarkable phrase *one of the most good people that he knew*.

Figure 21.4 Barber, C. (1964) *Linguistic change in present-day English*. London: Oliver and Boyd, 131–2.

because you have clearly understood both sides of the argument. Here is one example of how you might develop a position:

(5)   It is probably fair to say that there is no one correct solution to this conundrum. In the post-war period, English has diversified, as places other

than Britain, particularly America and Australia, have become influential in setting trends. There is never any guarantee that a change, once begun, will continue in the same direction, as Aitchison (2001: 56ff.) illustrates with the case of postvocalic *r* in New York English, studied by Labov. It is perfectly conceivable that, in a hundred years, the changes in comparative and superlative forms will have reversed, so that *famousest* and *perfecter* (Barber 2000: 274) are as common as they were in Early Modern English.

Note that a reference to Aitchison (2001) has appeared in this example. This illustrates how, as you develop an argument, you may be reminded of something you read elsewhere, which turns out to be relevant to your point. We have not reproduced the text from Aitchison (2001) here, as it is rather long, but in essence she describes how postvocalic *r* disappeared from British and some east-coast American English by the end of the eighteenth century, with the *r*-less pronunciation continuing to spread into other parts of the USA well into the 1930s. But by the 1950s and 1960s the change had reversed, with postvocalic *r* considered higher status, a trend headed by the class-conscious lower middle class in New York, as Labov's research of the 1970s demonstrated.

3 Incorporating other information into what you've already written

Once you have written your draft, that doesn't mean that you can't incorporate other information and references at even quite a late stage.

Exercise

Read the extracts from Crystal (2003b: 199) and Pyles and Algeo (2004: 181–2) in Figures 21.5 and 21.6, and try to add references to them in relevant places. You can add them either to your own version or to one of the examples given above. Then read the commentary.

Commentary

Neither of these extracts provides sufficient new material to justify a complete rewrite. But there are opportunities to indicate that you can see how their standpoint and/or illustrations relate to what you already have. Pyles and Algeo (2004) refer to the preference for avoiding *-er, -est* with polysyllabic words as a 'stylistic objection', which 'had somewhat less force in the early Modern English period' (p. 181). This way of putting things is quite elegant, so a quote might be in order. In the example below, we have underlined the passage that has been added:

(6)   According to Barber (2000: 274), a study of the forms used in Early Modern English through to the present day indicates that a change has been in progress. This <u>has entailed the development of a 'stylistic objection to affixing the endings [-*er* (comparative) and -*est* (superlative)] to polysyllables' (Pyles and Algeo 2004: 181), such that forms that used to be acceptable (e.g. *ancienter, ancientest; famouser, famousest*) have gradually been replaced by forms with *more* and *most* (e.g. *more ancient, most ancient; more famous, most famous*)</u> . . .

ADJECTIVES

Inflections provide one of the ways in which the quality expressed by an adjective (p. 211) can be compared. The comparison can be to the same degree, to a higher degree, or to a lower degree.

• The base form of the adjective is called the *absolute* form: *big, happy.*

The inflections identify two steps in the expression of a higher degree.

• Adding *-er* produces the *comparative* form: *bigger, happier.*
• Adding *-est* produces the *superlative* form: *biggest, happiest.*

There are no inflectional ways of expressing the same or lower degrees in English. These notions are expressed syntactically, using *as... as* (for the same degree: *X is as big as Y*) and *less* or *least* for lower degrees (*X is less interested than Y, Z is the least interested of all*).

There is also a syntactic (often called a *periphrastic*) way of expressing higher degree, through the use of *more* (for the comparative) and *most* (for the superlative): *A is more beautiful than B and C is the most beautiful of all.*

Figure 21.5 Crystal, D. (2003b) *The Cambridge encyclopaedia of the English language* (2nd edition). Cambridge: Cambridge University Press, 199. Reproduced with permission of Cambridge University Press.

Note how a clarification of the forms under discussion has been added within the quote by enclosing it in square brackets. This indicates that it is not part of the original quote, where the immediate context made the focus clear.

Pyles and Algeo also say something else very interesting. They claim that, in Early Modern English, it was not unusual to find monosyllables with *more* and *most*. This is quite contrary to Barber's hypothesis that the trend towards these forms has taken 400 years. And in the light of this new evidence, Strang seems positively *timid* in her non-committal stance. This means you can make even more of a meal of the disagreements and, subsequently, of your own views on the matter. Rather than supporting any one opinion too wholeheartedly, treat everyone with scepticism. Example 7 demonstrates how this can be done, the new text slotting onto the end of that given in example 4.

> Adjectives and adverbs continued to form comparatives with -er and superlatives with -est, but increasingly they used **analytical comparison** with mo(e) (a semantic equivalent of more, though not comparative in form), more, and most, which had occurred as early as Old English times.
>
> … The present stylistic objection to affixing -er and -est to poly-syllables had somewhat less force in the early Modern English period, when forms like eminenter, impudentest, and beautifullest are not particularly hard to find, nor, for that matter, are monosyllables with more and most, like more near, more fast, most poor, and most foul. As was true in earlier times also, a good many instances of **double comparison** like more fitter, more better, more fairer, most worst, most stillest, and (probably the best-known example) most unkindest occur in early Modern English. The general rule was that comparison cold be made with the ending or with the modifying word or, for emphasis, with both.

Figure 21.6 Pyles, T. and Algeo, J. (2004) *The origins and development of the English language* (5th edition). Boston, MA: Heinle and Heinle, 181–2.

(7)   Such prudence on Strang's part is certainly wise, if Pyles and Algeo's (2004: 181–2) claim that monosyllables with *more* and *most* were quite common in Early Modern English is to be believed. If they are right, then Barber may be mistaken when he says that there has been a change since Early Modern English *towards* these forms. On the other hand, such evidence may simply serve to remind us that no language changes either all at once or in only one direction, as Aitchison (2001: 56 ff.) illustrates with the case of postvocalic *r* in New York English, studied by Labov. Perhaps trends are *only* trends, and it is not necessary to believe in a time when a form *never* existed in order to identify a shift towards its increasing popularity.

Now look at Crystal's (2003b: 199) comments. He is not being *prescriptive*, so we have no reason to doubt that he intends to simply describe English as it is today. His account of the rules for today looks very similar to Barber's for the first half of the twentieth century! What does that mean? There is potentially quite a lot of mileage in identifying all the possible interpretations of this correspondence. Does Crystal have an exceedingly old-fashioned view and/or has he not noticed the forms that Barber describes? Did the trend stop in the first half of the twentieth century, with Barber's later examples just 'noise'? Did Barber wrongly understand how things were then, but happen to predict how they would be now? Was Barber's basic idea right, but the speed of change much slower than he assumed? Does Crystal know about the forms that Barber describes but not think they're important? Have the trends that Barber reported in the 1960s reversed since (and he just reproduced his 1960s findings in his later book)? The point is, of course, we don't know which is right. We can't know. That means we are free to argue whichever one we like, provided we can justify our preference:

(8)   A different challenge to Barber's view comes from Crystal (2003: 199), who describes the *current* rules for the formation of comparative and superlative forms in virtually the same way as Barber gives for the first half of the 20th century. There are many possible explanations for this. One of the most plausible is that the speed of change is slower than Barber suggests. Another is that the system for expressing these forms has reached a steady state: perhaps the 'stylistic objections' (Pyles and Algeo 2004: 181) that have powered the change for so long have lost their momentum for some reason.

Crystal says that, in disyllabic words, 'the choice is often made on stylistic grounds' (p. 199), which is reminiscent of what Pyles and Algeo said. That parallel can be highlighted. Example 9 could be added directly to the end of example 8.

(9)   Those very stylistic considerations might even be responsible for maintaining the steady state. Crystal (2003) suggests that it is our preferences in rhythm and lexical context that determine which form we choose in disyllabic words (p.199).

Summary

Having begun with one text which it was difficult to avoid simply copying or paraphrasing, we now have an account that draws together information from several sources, contrasts opposing views, and provides a forum for personal opinions that are not simply plucked out of the air, but are firmly based in the possibilities provided (explicitly or implicitly) in the literature. Here is one possible outcome, based on the examples given above. It ends with a list of references in the format described in Chapter 20. This list is an essential feature of academic writing and must be both complete and accurate.

(10)   According to Barber (2000: 274), study of the forms used in Early Modern English through to the present day indicates that a change has been in progress. This has entailed the development of a 'stylistic objection to affixing the endings [*-er* (comparative) and *-est* (superlative)] to polysyllables' (Pyles and Algeo 2004: 181), such that once-acceptable forms (e.g. *ancienter, ancientest; famouser, famousest*) have gradually been replaced by forms with *more* and *most* (e.g. *more ancient, most ancient; more famous, most famous*). This change happened earliest on the longest words. By the early 20th century the preferences were:

❑   polysyllabic adjectives (more than two syllables): add *more* (comparative) and *most* (superlative), e.g. *more beautiful, most beautiful; more interesting, most interesting.*

❑   monosyllabic adjectives: add *-er* (comparative) and *-est* (superlative), e.g. *richer, richest; bluer, bluest.*

❏   disyllabic adjectives: either form, e.g. *most famous, commonest.*

According to Barber (1964, 2000), the transition is now nearing completion, with the -*er* and -*est* endings apparently being edged out of the picture entirely, as even monosyllabic words form their comparative and superlative forms with *more* and *most.* Barber (1964) cites examples that he has observed, including *more crude, more plain,* and *more keen* (p.132). Strang (1970), however, is more cautious about the final stages of this change:

> *Barber thinks there is an increasing use of* more, most, *rather than* -er, -est, *in comparison, in keeping with a trend which . . . goes back at least 400 years; he may be right, but we lack precise numerical information on the subject. (p.58)*

Such prudence on Strang's part is certainly wise, if Pyles and Algeo's (2004: 181–2) claim that monosyllables with *more* and *most* were quite common in Early Modern English is to be believed. If they are right, then Barber may be mistaken when he says that there has been a change since Early Modern English *towards* these forms. On the other hand, such evidence may simply serve to remind us that no language changes either all at once or in only one direction, as Aitchison (2001: 56 ff.) illustrates with the case of postvocalic *r* in New York English, studied by Labov. Perhaps trends are *only* trends, and it is not necessary to believe in a time when a form *never* existed in order to identify a shift towards its increasing popularity.

A different challenge to Barber's view comes from Crystal (2003: 199), who describes the *current* rules for the formation of comparative and superlative forms in virtually the same way as Barber gives for the first half of the 20th century. There are many possible explanations for this. One of the most plausible is that the speed of change is slower than Barber suggests. Another is that the system for expressing these forms has reached a steady state: perhaps the 'stylistic objections' (Pyles and Algeo 2004: 181) that have powered the change for so long have lost their momentum, for some reason. Those very stylistic considerations might even be responsible for maintaining the steady state. Crystal (2003) suggests that it is our preferences in rhythm and lexical context that determine which form we choose in disyllabic words (p. 199).

References

Aitchison, J. (2001) *Language change: progress or decay?* (3rd edition). Cambridge: Cambridge University Press.

Barber, C. (1964) *Linguistic change in present-day English.* London: Oliver & Boyd.

Barber, C. (2000) *The English language: a historical introduction.* Canto edition. Cambridge: Cambridge University Press.

Crystal, D. (2003) *The Cambridge encyclopaedia of the English language* (2nd edition). Cambridge: Cambridge University Press.

Pyles, T. and Algeo, J. (2004) *The origins and development of the English language* (5th edition). Boston, MA: Heinle & Heinle.

Strang, B. (1970). *A history of English.* London and New York: Routledge.

Of course, everyone's finished product will be different – indeed, that is the whole point. You can be sure, if you approach your work like this, that it will be individual as well as sophisticated and informative. Precisely because your own ideas, interpretations, and conclusions are integrated with the information from your sources – fully acknowledged of course – you can be sure that no one will be able to accuse you of accidental plagiarism.

22
Hints on writing good academic English

Before you start to write

Model your style on what you read

A general awareness of what academic writing looks like will help you to adopt that style yourself. The best models are journal articles and subject-specialist books, but most introductory textbooks also use a suitable style.

Write a plan

A plan will keep your ideas organized. Start off by dividing the work into an introduction, between three and six major sections, and a conclusion. Then plan a breakdown of each section, itemizing what will go in it. If you allot to each section and sub-section an approximate number of words, you will have almost total control over keeping to your word limit. By using a plan you are much less likely to wander off the point or say something twice. For big pieces of work, keep a separate sheet of paper or electronic file for each chapter or section and jot down your ideas, references and any other material on it. Then, when you come to write, all the information is already in the right place.

Know your weaknesses

Take a careful look at your previous marked work and write a list of the problems with structure or presentation that have been highlighted in it. If there are any criticisms that you don't understand, ask the tutor in question. Identify strategies for avoiding these problems in the future, such as keeping a list of words that you tend to spell incorrectly. Most people have only a few words that they always get wrong. Write the correct spelling of each on a sheet of paper and stick it on the wall above your desk. Don't worry about memorizing the correct spelling but do try to remember which words are on the list, so that you look at it when you need to! Although electronic spellcheckers may seem to be a reasonable substitute for spelling with care when you write, they have some major shortcomings, and it will serve you well to develop an eye for spelling errors.

As you are writing

Develop and sustain a sense of audience

Be aware of who it is that you are writing for, and why. Remember that you are writing in order to explain your research, so you need to say *why* you did what you did (why it was an interesting research question, for example) and be explicit about the issues and your procedures. You are writing for assessment purposes, so make sure you demonstrate that you know what you are talking about. If in doubt, err on the side of being too explicit: assessors will tend to assume, if you explain something inadequately, that you do not understand it properly. Your work may be read by a second internal assessor and/or an external examiner, so do not make references to information that they are not party to (such as module names, residence halls and local clubs, or activities or running jokes from within a lecture course) unless you clearly explain and contextualize them.

As your assessors are knowledgeable about the general field, you can make certain assumptions about what they will understand, particularly when it comes to peripheral information. For example, it is acceptable to make a passing reference to Chomsky when writing about something in which his ideas are not central. However, no one, including your assessors, knows about *everything*, so, if you are making reference to work or ideas that you judge not to be commonly known about, give all the details necessary to make your account comprehensible.

Use the technology

Most universities now expect you to word-process your assignments. By word-processing from the start, you can:

- [ ] make alterations and still have a clean copy,
- [ ] keep a back-up copy of earlier versions in an archive folder,
- [ ] keep a copy on a memory stick or CD as well as on the hard drive of your computer, in case the computer crashes,
- [ ] email yourself the latest version so that you can work on it wherever you have access to a computer,
- [ ] run spellchecks and use thesaurus and dictionary facilities at any stage.

Mark problems for later checking

You may feel that stopping to check a spelling or to rephrase an awkward sentence will break your flow when you are writing the first draft. If so, simply mark any problem by underlining or highlighting it. Then, later, you can easily return to the right place and find a better alternative. The same technique can be used if you have a fact or a reference to check: just highlight it and carry on, coming back to it when you have finished.

Use a dictionary and thesaurus

Do not be reticent about using a dictionary. Even the best writers have to do it. There is no shame in not knowing the meaning of, or how to spell, a word, providing you know that you don't know, and look it up. Where terminology is concerned, use a specialist dictionary or a subject textbook with a glossary. Use a thesaurus to widen your vocabulary: it will increase the accuracy with which you express yourself, as well as making your prose more stylish. However, take care not to assume that words are entirely interchangeable. Prefer words that, once you see them in the thesaurus, are immediately familiar and compelling alternatives. If you have not seen the word used by other writers in the way that you plan to use it, then it may be that your planned usage is not quite appropriate. For example, a thesaurus may mislead you into believing that *insinuate* means the same as *suggest*. In fact, *insinuate* is very loaded with negativity. As a result, it is rarely possible to interchange them (*the informants suggested that...* does not mean the same as *the informants insinuated that...*). One advantage of studying language is that you will have access to academic staff who have a good sense of what 'sounds right', so, if in doubt, ask.

Copy correctly

When quoting, citing, or otherwise taking information from another source, pay attention to the form. In a quote, copy the punctuation and spelling correctly. Take particular care with proper names.

Use headings

In keeping with your plan (see above), use headings in your work. These can save words, and make it much easier for both you and your assessor to follow the structure of your work.

Write summaries

In a lengthy piece of work, and especially in data analysis, it is often helpful to provide a one- or two-sentence summary at the end of each section. Doing so helps both the writer and the reader to retain a focus and a sense of the structure of the whole piece of work.

Draft it and craft it

Don't be beguiled into thinking that everyone else gets it right first time. Drafting and rewriting is part and parcel of the process. The best writing is carefully crafted – in itself an absorbing and rewarding aspect of the work. Stand back from your draft and ask yourself whether you could make it flow better, say something more succinctly or draw out the points in a more appropriate way.

After you have written

Proofread

Leave enough time to put your work aside and then come back to it with a fresh eye. Try to read it as someone would who was seeing it for the first time. Check that the argument and ideas are clear and that there are no problems with the grammar or spelling. If it is too late to change typed or word-processed work, make neat legible corrections by hand. Always allow plenty of time for proofreading – it can take far longer than you think it will.

The uses of apostrophes

Apostrophes are important because they contribute to the meaning in a written text. Most people who use apostrophes incorrectly do so because no one has ever explained the rules to them. So here they are. The apostrophe has *two* major functions. One is to indicate that one or more letters are missing. The other is to indicate possession.

Omission of one or more letters

The use of the apostrophe to indicate an omission accounts for *can't*, *don't*, *won't*, for *ha'penny*, *o'clock*, and for abbreviations like *S'hampton*. It can also be used when depicting non-standard speech in dialogue as in *I s'pose so*. Importantly, it also accounts for the word *it's*, which in this form means *it is* or *it has* (**not** the possessive form of *it*).

Possession

There are several parts to the pattern:

- ☐ **Singular nouns that do not end in s already** take an apostrophe + s to form the possessive form. Examples include: *the dog's bone* and *Michael's concern*.
- ☐ **Singular nouns that end in s** either take an apostrophe at the end of the word, or apostrophe + s. Examples include: *the class' assignment* or *the class's assignment*, *Her Royal Highness' schedule* or *Her Royal Highness's schedule*, *Mr. Jones' complaint* or *Mr. Jones's complaint*.
- ☐ **Plural nouns that already have an s** (i.e. most of them) take an apostrophe at the end. Examples include: *three horses' heads* and *20 boys' results*.
- ☐ **Plural nouns that do not end in an s** take apostrophe + s. Examples include: *the children's games* and *the women's semi-finals*.
- ☐ **Pronouns**: The possessives of pronouns do *not* take apostrophes. *His*, *hers* and *its* are all examples of possessives. Remember that *it's* means 'it is', while *its* means 'belonging to it'.

Using punctuation

Using punctuation correctly is important, not only on stylistic grounds, but because you may end up saying something you didn't mean otherwise. Truss (2003) is full of examples. Common problems include the following.

Commas where full stops should be

In speech, we tend to chain sentences together without stopping for breath, but in academic writing, sentences must be separated by full stops. For example, *The subjects sat at separate tables, they read the text for ten minutes*. It would be better to use a full stop: *The subjects sat at separate tables. They read the text for ten minutes*. Alternatively, the two parts could be linked with *and*, particularly if the writer is implying a logical connection and sequence between the two facts.

Full stops where commas should be

In this case, only half a sentence has been written before the full stop comes. It tends to occur where a dependent clause (a clause that needs another one) has been stranded. An example is: *Although the subjects had several minutes to prepare themselves*. Here, *although* has been treated as if it means *however*, whereas it actually needs an answering clause: *although this . . . (nevertheless) that*. Example: *Although the subjects had several minutes to prepare themselves, they seemed flustered when the stimulus presentation began.*

Another common cause of the incomplete sentence is using a verb in non-finite form, as in: *The reason being clear*. In academic writing, there needs to be a finite verb in the main clause of every sentence, as in: *The reason is clear.*

Semi-colons for colons

The **colon** (:) is little used these days, but it still has one important function: it introduces items (as in this sentence). When you write a list, a colon indicates that the list is about to begin. A list may define (e.g. *There are three primary colours: red, blue, and green*) or it may illustrate (e.g. *The stationery shop sold various things: pens, paper, diaries, etc.*). Avoid using the semi-colon for these purposes.

The **semi-colon** (;) is rarer in standard written English than it is in students' essays, where it is rather overused. Its purpose is to act as a weaker version of the full stop and the clause that follows it may contain a finite verb (e.g. *Eight subjects failed to complete the task; four others left early*), but need not (e.g. *He glanced round the room; what to do now?*). Pay particular attention to not using the semi-colon to introduce information (use the colon) or speech (use inverted commas around the speech).

Other common problems

Subjectivity

It is not customary in academic writing to use the first person or to make personal comments (e.g. *After interviewing my subjects, I transcribed the tapes*, or *I found this book very interesting*). In particular, avoid undermining your case by self-deprecating comments such as *This was all I could find out about the subject* or *Here is one explanation for the phenomenon but, knowing me, it's probably wrong*.

Referencing

There are clear conventions for referencing, which are laid out in Chapter 20. Poor referencing will be interpreted as indicative of carelessness or ignorance, and can lead to charges of plagiarism (see Chapter 21).

Troublesome pairs

Use of 'i.e.' and 'e.g.'

The abbreviation **i.e.** means *that is*, as in: *I filled him in on the situation, i.e. I explained what had happened.* The abbreviation **e.g.** means *for example*, as in: *If you have anything for the* *sale, e.g. old clothes or toys, please bring them.* Some people feel that *i.e.* and *e.g.* should not be used in prose writing at all, and your tutors may prefer that you avoid them. The important thing is that if you do use them, you know which is which.

Use of 'imply' and 'infer'

The words *imply* and *infer* are easily confused because they express two sides of the same coin. When you *imply* something, you attempt to place an idea of yours into the mind of your reader or hearer by indicating it indirectly. When you *infer* something, you figure out an idea that a writer or speaker has *implied* by providing indirect information about it. In our experience, students tend to use the word *infer* when they mean *imply*. If you find the distinction difficult, ask yourself the question: is the idea coming *into* my head (*infer*) or going *out of* my head (*imply*)?

Use of 'amount' and 'number' and of 'less' and 'fewer'

If you can sensibly put a figure in front of a noun, and if you can make it plural, then it is a count noun and needs to be paired with *number* (or *quantity*) and *fewer*. For example, *A small number (quantity) of responses had to be discarded, but fewer than anticipated.* Avoid writing: **A small amount of responses had to be discarded but less than anticipated.*

   If the noun cannot be counted or pluralized, it is a mass noun, and needs to be paired with *amount* and *less*. For example, *A small amount of information was gathered, but less than anticipated.* Avoid writing: **A small number of information(s) was (were) gathered, but fewer than anticipated.*

   For more detailed guidance on how to improve your writing skills, see the excellent *Student's Guide to Writing* (Peck and Coyle 2005a) and *Write it Right* (Peck and Coyle 2005b).

REFERENCES

21st Century China Daily (ed.) (2005) *Speaking for success*. Shanghai: Shanghai Foreign Languages Education Press.

Aitchison, J. (1998) *The articulate mammal* (4th edition). London: Routledge.

Aitchison, J. (2001) *Language change: progress or decay?* (3rd edition). Cambridge: Cambridge University Press.

Aitchison, J. (2002) *Words in the mind: an introduction to the mental lexicon* (3rd edition). Oxford: Blackwell.

Alderson, C. (1997) Models of language. Whose? What for? What use? In Ryan, A. and Wray, A. (eds) *Evolving models of language: papers from the annual meeting of the British Association for Applied Linguistics 1996*. Clevedon: Multilingual Matters, 1–22.

Anderson, S. (1988) Morphological theory. In Newmeyer, F. (ed.) *Linguistic theory: foundations. Linguistics: the Cambridge survey*, vol. 1. Cambridge: Cambridge University Press, 146–91.

Appel, R. and Muysken, P. (1987) *Language contact and bilingualism*. London: Arnold.

Aronoff, M. and Rees-Miller, J. (eds) (2001) *The handbook of linguistics*. Oxford: Blackwell.

Atkinson, J.M. and Heritage, J. (eds) (1984) *Structures of social action*. Cambridge: Cambridge University Press.

Austin, J.L. (1961) Performative utterances. In Austin, J.L. *Philosophical papers* (ed. by Urmson, J.O. and Warnock, G.J., 3rd edition, 1979). Oxford: Oxford University Press. Reprinted in Martinich, A.P. (ed.) (1996) *The philosophy of language* (3rd edition). New York: Oxford University Press, 120–9.

Austin, J.L. (1962) *How to do things with words*. Oxford: Oxford University Press.

Ayers, D.M. (1965) *English words from Latin and Greek elements*. Tucson, AZ: University of Arizona Press.

Bailey, K.M. and Nunan, D. (eds) (1996) *Voices from the language classroom*. Cambridge: Cambridge University Press.

Baker, P. (2002) *Polari, the lost language of gay men*. London: Routledge.

Baker, P. (2005) *Public discourses of gay men: that's so gay*. London: Routledge.

Barber, C. (1964) *Linguistic change in present-day English*. London: Oliver and Boyd.

Barber, C. (1997) *Early modern English* (2nd edition). Edinburgh: Edinburgh University Press.

Barber, C. (2000) *The English language: a historical introduction*. Canto edition. Cambridge: Cambridge University Press.

Barfield, O. (1953) *History of English words*. London: Faber and Faber.

Baron, J. (1973) Phonemic stage not necessary for reading. *Quarterly Journal of Experimental Psychology* 25, 241–6.

Bauer, L. (2002) *An introduction to international varieties of English*. Edinburgh: Edinburgh University Press.

Baugh, T. and Cable, A.C. (2002) *A history of the English language* (5th edition). London: Routledge.

Bavin, E.L. (2006) Syntactic development. In Brown, K. (ed.) (2006) vol. 12: 383–90.

Beal, J. (2006) Dialect representations in texts. In Brown, K. (ed.) (2006) vol. 3: 531–7.

Bell, A. (2006) Speech accommodation. In Brown, K. (ed.) (2006) vol. 11: 648–51.

Berko-Gleason, J. (1975) Fathers and other strangers: men's speech to young children. In Dato, D. (ed.) *Developmental psycholinguistics: theory and applications*. Washington: Georgetown University Press.

Berlin, B. and Kay, P. (1969) *Basic color terms: their universality and evolution*. Berkeley and Los Angeles: University of California Press.

Bhatia, T. (2006) Bilingualism and second language learning. In Brown, K. (ed.) (2006) vol. 2, 16–22.

Bhatia, T. and Ritchie W.C. (eds) (2003) *The handbook of bilingualism*. Oxford: Blackwell.

Block, D. and Cameron, D. (eds) (2002) *Globalization and language teaching*. London: Routledge.

Bloomer, A., Griffiths, P. and Merrison, A. (2005) *Introducing language in use: a coursebook*. London: Routledge.

Bloor, T. and Bloor, M. (2004) *The functional analysis of English: a Hallidayan approach* (2nd edition). London: Arnold.

Booij, G. (2005) *The grammar of words*. New York: Oxford University Press.

Brace, N., Kemp, R. and Snelgar, R. (2006) *SPSS for Psychologists: a guide to data analysis using SPSS for Windows* (3rd edition). Basingstoke: Palgrave Macmillan.

Bradley, H. (1916) Shakespeare's English. In Bradley, H. *Shakespeare's England*. Oxford: Oxford University Press.

Bridges, R. (1913) *A tract on the present state of English pronunciation*. Oxford: Clarendon Press.

Brook, G.L. (1957) *English sound changes*. Manchester: Manchester University Press.

Brook, G.L. (1978) *English dialects* (3rd edition). London: André Deutsch.

Brouwer, D., Gerritsen, M. and de Haan, D. (1979) Speech differences between men and women: on the wrong track? *Language and Society* 8, 33–50.

Brown, G. (1990) *Listening to spoken English* (2nd edition). London and New York: Longman.

Brown, J.D. and Rodgers, T. (2002) *Doing second language research*. Oxford: Oxford University Press.

Brown, K. (ed.) (2006) *Encyclopedia of language and linguistics* (2nd edition). Oxford: Elsevier.

Brown, R. (1973) *A first language: the early stages*. Cambridge, MA: Harvard University Press.

Brown, R. and McNeill, D. (1966) The 'tip of the tongue' phenomenon. *Journal of Verbal Learning and Verbal Behavior* 5, 325–37.

Bryman, A. (2004) *Social research methods*. Oxford: Oxford University Press.

Burchfield, R. (2002) *The English language*. Oxford: Oxford University Press.

Burke, P. and Porter, R. (eds) (1987) *The social history of language*. Cambridge: Cambridge University Press.

Burke, P. and Porter, R. (eds) (1994) *Language, self and society*. Cambridge: Polity Press.

Burnley, D. (2000) *The history of the English language: a source book* (2nd edition). London: Longman.

Burstall, C., Jamieson, M., Cohen, S. and Hargreaves, M. (1974) *Primary French in the balance*. Windsor: NFER.

Burton-Roberts, N. (1997) *Analysing sentences* (2nd edition). London: Longman.

Caldas-Coulthard, C.M. and Coulthard, M. (1996) *Texts and practices: readings in critical discourse*. London: Routledge.

Cameron, D. (1995) *Verbal hygiene*. London: Routledge.

Cameron, D. (2001) *Working with spoken discourse*. London: Sage Publications.

Cameron, D. (2006) Gender. In Brown, K. (ed.) (2006) vol. 4: 733–9.

Cameron, D. and Kulick, D. (2003) *Language and sexuality*. Cambridge: Cambridge University Press.

Cameron, K. (1965) *Scandinavian settlement in the territory of the five boroughs: the place-name evidence*. University of Nottingham, Inaugural Lecture, 4/3/65.

Cameron, K. (1996) *English place names*. London: Batsford.

Cameron, L. and Low, G. (eds) (1999) *Researching and applying metaphor*. Cambridge: Cambridge University Press.

Caplan, D. (1987) *Neurolinguistics and linguistic aphasiology: an introduction*. Cambridge: Cambridge University Press.

Carey, J. (1997) *Eyewitness to history*. New York: Avon Books.

Carroll, D.W. (2004) *Psychology of language* (4th edition). Belmont, CA: Thomson Wadsworth.

Carroll, J.B. (ed.) (1956) *Language, thought and reality: selected writings of Benjamin Lee Whorf*. Cambridge, MA: MIT Press.

Carroll, J.B., Davies, P. and Richman, B. (1971) *Word frequency book*. Boston: Houghton Mifflin; New York: American Heritage.

Carroll, L. (1865/1971) *Alice through the looking glass*. London: Macmillan.

Carstairs-McCarthy, A. (2002) *An introduction to English morphology*. Edinburgh: Edinburgh University Press.

Carter, R. (ed.) (1982) *Language and literature*. London: Allen and Unwin.

Carter, R. (1998) *Vocabulary* (2nd edition). London: Routledge.

Carter, R. (2004) *Language and creativity: the art of common talk*. London: Routledge.

Carter, R., Goddard, A., Reah, D., Sanger, K. and Bowring, M. (2001) *Working with texts* (2nd edition). London: Routledge.

Carter, R. and Nash, W. (1990) *Seeing through language*. Oxford: Blackwell.

Carter, R. and Nunan, D. (eds) (2001) *The Cambridge guide to teaching English to speakers of other languages*. Cambridge: Cambridge University Press.

Chambers, A. and Trudgill, P. (1998) *Dialectology* (2nd edition). Cambridge: Cambridge University Press.

Chaski, C. (2001) Empirical evaluations of language-based author identification techniques. *Forensic Linguistics: The International Journal of Speech Language and the Law* 8 (1): 1–65.

Cheshire, J. (1978) Present tense verbs in Reading English. In Trudgill, P. (ed.), *Sociolinguistic patterns in British English*. London: Edward Arnold, 52–68.

Cheshire, J. (1982) *Variation in an English dialect*. Cambridge: Cambridge University Press.

Chiaro, D. (1992) *The language of jokes: analysing verbal play*. London: Routledge.

Chilton, P. (ed.) (1985) *Language and the nuclear arms debate: nukespeak today*. London: Pinter/Cassell Academic.

Chomsky, C. (1969) *The acquisition of syntax in children from 5 to 10*. Cambridge, MA: MIT Press.

Clark, H.H. and Clark, E.V. (1977) *Psychology and language: an introduction to psycholinguistics*. New York: Harcourt Brace Jovanovitch.

Clark, J. and Yallop, C. (1995) *An introduction to phonetics and phonology* (2nd edition). Oxford: Blackwell.

Clark, J.L. (1987) *Curriculum renewal in school foreign language learning*. Oxford: Oxford University Press.

Clifton, C. Jr. and Ferreira, F. (1989) Ambiguity in context. *Language and Cognitive Processes* 4 (3/4), Special Issue (SI), 77–103.

Coates, J. (1996) *Women talk: conversation between women friends*. Oxford: Blackwell.

Coates, J. (ed.) (1998a) *Language and gender: a reader*. London: Routledge.

Coates, J. (1998b) Gossip revisited: language in all-female groups. In Coates, J. (ed.) (1998a) *Language and gender: a reader*. London: Routledge, 226–33.

Coates, J. (2003) *Men talk: stories in the making of masculinities*. Oxford: Blackwell.

Coates, J. (2004) *Women, men and language* (3rd edition). Harlow: Longman.

Coates, J. and Cameron, D. (eds) (1989) *Women in their speech communities*. London: Longman.

Collins, B. and Mees, I.M. (2003) *Practical phonetics and phonology: a resource book for students*. London: Routledge.

Collins Cobuild (1991) *English guides 1: prepositions*. London: HarperCollins.

Collins Cobuild (1996) *Grammar patterns 1: verbs*. London: HarperCollins.

Colman, A. and Pulford, B. (2006) *A crash course in SPSS for Windows: updated for versions 10, 11, 12 and 13* (3rd edition). Oxford: Blackwell.

Coltheart, M. (2005) Modelling reading: the dual-route approach. In Snowling, M.J. and Hulme, C. (eds) *The science of reading*. Oxford: Blackwell, 6–23.

Como, P. (2006) Elicitation techniques for spoken discourse. In Brown, K. (ed.) (2006) vol. 4, 105–9.

Cook, G. (2001) *The discourse of advertising* (2nd edition). London: Routledge.

Cook, V. (1993) *Linguistics and second language acquisition*. Basingstoke: Macmillan.

Cook, V. (1997) *Inside language*. London: Arnold.

Cook, V. (2001) *Second language learning and teaching* (3rd edition). London: Arnold.

Cook, V.J. and Newson, M. (1996) *Chomsky's universal grammar* (2nd edition). Oxford: Blackwell.

Coolican, H. (1995) *Introduction to research methods and statistics in psychology*. London: Hodder and Stoughton.

Coolican, H. (2004) *Research methods and statistics in psychology* (4th edition). London: Arnold.

Corbett, J., McClure, J.D. and Stuart-Smith, J. (eds) (2003) *The Edinburgh companion to Scots*. Edinburgh: Edinburgh University Press.

Coulmas, F. (2005) *Sociolinguistics: the study of speakers' choices*. Cambridge: Cambridge University Press.

Coulmas, F. (ed.) (1998) *Handbook of sociolinguistics*. Oxford: Blackwell.

Coupland, N., Coupland, J. and Giles, H. (1991) *Language, society and the elderly*. Oxford: Blackwell.

Coupland, N. and Jaworski, A. (eds) (2006) *The new sociolinguistics reader* (2nd edition). London: Palgrave Macmillan.

Cox, B. (ed.) (1994) *The place-names of Rutland*. Nottingham: English Place-name Society.

Cruttenden, A. (1974) An experiment involving comprehension of intonation in children from 7 to 10. *Journal of Child Language* 1, 221–31.

Cruttenden, A. (ed.) (1979) *Language in infancy and childhood*. Manchester: Manchester University Press.

Crystal, D. (1989) *Listen to your child: a parent's guide to children's language*. Harmondsworth: Penguin.

Crystal, D. (1997) *The Cambridge encyclopedia of language* (2nd edition). Cambridge: Cambridge University Press.

Crystal, D. (2001) *Language and the Internet*. Cambridge: Cambridge University Press.

Crystal, D. (2002) *Dictionary of linguistics and phonetics* (5th edition). Oxford: Blackwell.

Crystal, D. (2003a) *English as a global language* (2nd edition). Cambridge: Cambridge University Press.

Crystal, D. (2003b) *The Cambridge encyclopedia of the English language* (2nd edition). Cambridge: Cambridge University Press.

Culpeper, J. (2005) *History of English* (2nd edition). London: Routledge.

Cummings, M. and Simmons, R. (1983) *The language of literature*. Oxford: Pergamon.

Curzan, A. (2003) *Gender Shifts in the history of English*. Cambridge: Cambridge University Press.

Cutler, A. (1982) *Slips of the tongue and language production*. Berlin: Mouton.

Data Protection Act 1998 UK. Available online at <www.opsi.gov.uk/acts/acts1998/80029—l.htm#sch1>

Davenport, M. and Hannahs, S.J. (2005) *Introducing phonetics and phonology*. London: Hodder Arnold.

Davies, A. and Elder, C. (eds) (2003) *The handbook of applied linguistics*. Oxford: Blackwell.

De Villiers, J.G. and de Villiers, P.A. (1973) A cross-sectional study of the acquisition of grammatical morphemes. *Journal of Psycholinguistic Research* 2, 267–78.

De Villiers, J.G. and de Villiers, P.A. (1978) *Language acquisition*. Cambridge, MA: Harvard University Press.

Dictionary of South African English (1996) Oxford: Oxford University Press.

Dixon, R.M.W. (2005) *A semantic approach to English grammar* (2nd edition). Oxford: Oxford University Press.

Dorian, N.C. (1981) *Language death: the life cycle of a Scottish Gaelic dialect.* Philadelphia, PA: University of Pennsylvania Press.

Dornyei, Z. (2001) *Teaching and researching motivation.* Harlow: Longman.

Dornyei, Z. (2002) *Questionnaires in second language research.* Mahwah, NJ: Erlbaum.

Doughty, C. and Long, M.H. (2003) *The handbook of second language acquisition.* Oxford: Blackwell.

Drew, P. and Heritage, J. (eds) (1992) *Talk at work.* Cambridge: Cambridge University Press.

Eckert, P. and McConnell-Ginet, S. (2003) *Language and gender.* Cambridge: Cambridge University Press.

Eckert, P. and Rickford, R. (eds) (2001) *Style and sociolinguistic variation.* Cambridge: Cambridge University Press.

Edelsky, C. (1976) The acquisition of communicative competence: recognition of linguistic correlates of sex roles. *Merrill-Palmer Quarterly* 22, 47–59.

Edwards, J. (2006) Language attitudes. In Brown, K. (ed.) (2006) vol. 6: 324–32.

Edwards, V. (2004) *Multilingualism in the English-speaking world.* Oxford: Blackwell.

Ekwall, E. (1923) *English place-names in -ing.* Lund: C.W.K. Gleerup; Oxford: Oxford University Press.

Ekwall, E. (1925) The Scandinavian element. In Mawer, A. and Stenton, F.M. (eds), *Introduction to the survey of English place-names.* Cambridge: Cambridge University Press, 55–92.

Ekwall, E. (1928) *English river-names.* Oxford: Clarendon Press.

Ellis, G. and Sinclair, B. (1989) *Learning to learn English.* Cambridge: Cambridge University Press.

Ellis, R. (1994) *The study of second language acquisition.* Oxford: Oxford University Press.

Ellis, R. and Barkhuizen, G. (2006) *Analysing learner language.* Oxford: Oxford University Press.

Elmes, S. (2005) *Talking for Britain: a journey through the nation's dialects.* London: Penguin.

European Communities (2003) *Promoting language learning and linguistic diversity: an action plan 2004 – 2006* COM(2003) 449 Final communication from the commission to the council, the European parliament, the economic and social committee, and the committee of the regions. Available online at <http://europa.eu.int/comm/education/doc/official/keydoc/actlang/act_lang_en.pdf> (accessed 31 October 2005).

Eysenck, M.W. and Keane, M.T. (2005) *Cognitive psychology: a student's handbook* (5th edition). Hove: Psychology Press.

Faerch, C. and Kasper, G. (eds) (1987) *Introspection in second language research.* Clevedon, Avon: Multilingual Matters.

Fairclough, N. (2001) *Language and power* (2nd edition). Harlow: Longman.

Farb, P. (1973) *Word play.* Sevenoaks: Hodder and Stoughton.

Farringdon, J., Morton, A., Farringdon, M. and Baker, M.D. (eds) (1996) *Analysing for authorship: a guide to the CUSUM technique.* Cardiff: University of Wales Press.

Fasold, R. (1984) *The sociolinguistics of society*. Oxford: Blackwell.

Field, J. (2003) *Psycholinguistics: a resource book for students*. London: Routledge.

Field, J. (2005) *Language and the mind*. London: Routledge.

Firth, J.R. (1968) *Selected papers of J.R. Firth 1952–59*. Ed. F.R. Palmer. London: Longman.

Fisher, J.H. and Bornstein, D. (1974) *In forme of speche is chaunge: readings in the history of the English language*. Lanham, MD: Rowman and Littlefield.

Fletcher, P. (1985) *A child's learning of English*. Oxford: Basil Blackwell.

Fletcher, P. and Garman, M. (eds) (1986) *Language acquisition* (2nd edition). Cambridge: Cambridge University Press.

Fletcher, P. and MacWhinney, B. (eds) (1995) *The handbook of child language*. Oxford: Blackwell.

Fodor, J.A. (1983) *The modularity of mind*. Cambridge, MA: MIT Press.

Foley, J. and Thompson, L. (2003) *Language learning: a lifelong process*. London: Hodder Arnold.

Foster, S.H. (1990) *The communicative competence of young children*. London: Longman.

Foulkes, P. and Docherty, G. (eds) (1999) *Urban voices: accent studies in the British Isles*. London: Arnold.

Fowler, R. (1991) *Language in the news: discourse and ideology in the press*. London: Routledge.

Fowles, B. and Glanz, M.E. (1977) Competence and talent in verbal riddle comprehension. *Journal of Child Language* 4, 433–52.

Freeborn, D. (1995) *A course book in English grammar: Standard English and the dialects*. Basingstoke: Macmillan.

Freeborn, D. (1996) *Style: text analysis and linguistic criticism*. Basingstoke: Macmillan.

Freeborn, D. (1998) *From Old English to standard English* (2nd edition). Basingstoke: Palgrave Macmillan.

Freeborn, D. with Langford, D. and French, P. (1993) *Varieties of English* (2nd edition). Basingstoke: Macmillan.

Freedom of Information Act 2000 UK. Available online at <www.opsi.gov.uk/acts/acts2000/00036—a.htm#1>

Fromkin, V., Rodman, R. and Hyams, N. (2003) *An introduction to language* (7th edition). Boston, MA: Thomson Heinle.

Fromkin, V.A. (1973) *Speech errors as linguistic evidence*. The Hague: Mouton.

Garman, M. (1990) *Psycholinguistics*. Cambridge: Cambridge University Press.

Garnham, A. (1985) *Psycholinguistics: central topics*. London and New York: Routledge.

Garrett, M.F. (1976) Syntactic processes in sentence production. In Wales, R. and Walder, E. (eds) *New approaches to language mechanisms*. Amsterdam: North Holland, 231–55.

Garton, A. and Pratt, C. (1998) *Learning to be literate* (2nd edition). Oxford: Blackwell.

Gibbs, R. (2006) Metaphor: psychological aspects. In Brown, K. (ed.) (2006) vol. 8: 43–50.

Giglioli, P.P. (ed.) (1972) *Language and social context*. Harmondsworth: Penguin.

Goddard, A. and Patterson, L.M. (2000) *Language and gender*. London: Routledge.

Gordon, E., Campbell, L., Hay, J., Maclagan, M., Sudbury, A. and Trudgill, P. (2004) *New Zealand English*. Cambridge: Cambridge University Press.

Görlach, M. (1991) *Introduction to early modern English.* Cambridge: Cambridge University Press.

Görlach, M. (1995) *More Englishes: new studies in varieties of English 1988–1994.* Amsterdam: John Benjamins.

Graddol, D., Leith, D. and Swann, J. (1996) *English history, diversity and change.* London: Routledge.

Graddol, D. and Swann, J. (1989) *Gender voices.* Oxford: Blackwell.

Grant, T.D. and Baker, K.L. (2001) Identifying reliable, valid markers of authorship: a response to Chaski. *Forensic Linguistics: The International Journal of Speech Language and the Law,* 8 (1), 66–79.

Gray, M. (1984) *A dictionary of literary terms.* London: Longman.

Green, J. (1998) *Cassell's dictionary of slang.* London: Cassells.

Green, J. and D'Oliveira, M. (2005) *Learning to use statistical tests in psychology* (2nd edition). Maidenhead: Open University Press.

Greenbaum, S. (1991) *An introduction to English grammar.* London: Longman.

Greene, J. and Coulson, M. (1995) *Language understanding: current issues* (2nd edition). Buckingham: Open University Press.

Grice, H.P. (1975) Logic and conversation. In Cole, P. and Morgan, J.L. (eds) *Syntax and semantics,* vol. 3. New York: Academic Press. Reprinted in A.P. Martinich (ed.) (1996) *The philosophy of language* (3rd edition). New York: Oxford University Press, 156–67.

Griffiths, P.D. (1986) Constituent structure in text-copying. *York Papers in Linguistics* 12, 75–116.

Groom, B. (1934) *A short history of English words.* London: Macmillan.

Grundy, P. (2000) *Doing pragmatics.* London: Arnold.

Gruneberg, M. (2002a) *Instant recall Spanish vocabulary.* New York: McGraw-Hill Contemporary Books.

Gruneberg, M. (2002b) *Instant recall French vocabulary.* New York: McGraw-Hill Contemporary Books.

Gulli, A. and Signorini, A. (2005) *The indexable web is more than 11.5 billion pages.* Paper presented at WWW 2005, 10–14 May, Chiba, Japan, www.cs.uiowa.edu/ ~asignori/pubs/web-size/size-indexable-web.pdf

Gumperz, J. (ed.) (1982) *Language and social identity.* Cambridge: Cambridge University Press.

Halliday, M.A.K. (1975) *Learning how to mean.* London: Edward Arnold.

Halliday, M.A.K. and Matthiessen, C.M.I.M. (2004) *An introduction to functional grammar* (3rd edition). London: Arnold.

Halsall, E. (1968) *French as a second language: levels of attainment in three countries.* Hull: Institute of Education, University of Hull.

Hanks, P. (2006) Personal names. In Brown, K. (ed.) (2006) vol. 9: 299–311.

Harley, T. (2001) *The psychology of language: from data to theory* (2nd edition). Hove: Psychology Press.

Hart, J. (1569/1969) *An orthographie.* Menston: The Scolar Press.

Hartmann, R. (ed.) (1996) *The English language in Europe.* Exeter: Intellect.

Hatch, E. and Lazaraton, A. (1991) *The research manual: design and statistics for applied linguistics*. Boston, MA: Heinle and Heinle.

Have, P. ten (1999) *Doing conversational analysis*. London: Sage.

Hawkins, E. (1987) *Modern languages in the curriculum* (revised edition). Cambridge: Cambridge University Press.

Hawkins, E. and Perren, G.E. (eds) (1978) *Intensive language teaching in schools*. London: CILT.

Hawkins, R. and Lozano, C. (2006) Second language acquisition of phonology, morphology and syntax. In Brown, K. (ed.) (2006) vol. 11, 67–74.

Heath, S.B. (1983) *Ways with words*. Cambridge: Cambridge University Press.

Hewings, A. and Hewings, M. (2005) *Grammar and context*. London: Routledge.

Hickey, R. (2004) *A sound atlas of Irish English*. Berlin: Mouton.

Hillier, H. (2005) *Analysing real texts: research studies into modern English language*. Basingstoke: Palgrave Macmillan.

Hillis, A.E. (2002) Models of the reading process. In Hillis, A.E. (ed.) *The handbook of adult language disorders*. New York: Psychology Press, 3–14.

Hindmarsh, R. (1980) *Cambridge English lexicon: a graded word list for materials writers and course designers*. Cambridge: Cambridge University Press.

Hinton, P.R. (2004) *Statistics explained: a guide for social science students* (2nd edition). London: Routledge.

Hinton, P.R., Brownlow, C., McMurray, I. and Cozens, B. (2004) *SPSS explained*. London: Routledge.

Hoey, M. (2005) *Lexical priming: a new theory of words and language*. London: Routledge.

Holmes, J. (1995) *Women, men and politeness*. London: Longman.

Holmes, J. (2001) *An Introduction to sociolinguistics* (2nd edition). Harlow: Pearson Education.

Holmes, J. and Meyerhoff, M. (eds) (2003) *The handbook of language and gender*. Oxford: Blackwell.

Hotopf, W.N. (1983) Lexical slips of the pen and tongue: what they tell us about language production. In Butterworth, B. (ed.) *Language production*, vol. 2: *Development, writing and other language processes*. London: Academic Press, 147–99.

Howatt, A.P.R. (1984) *A history of English language teaching*. Oxford: Oxford University Press.

Huang, Y. (2006) *Pragmatics*. Oxford: Oxford University Press.

Hughes, A. and Trudgill, P. (2005) *English accents and dialects: an introduction to social and regional varieties of British English* (4th edition). London: Arnold.

Human Rights Act 1998 UK. Available online at <www.opsi.gov.uk/acts/acts1998/19980042.htm>

Hunston, S. (2006) Corpus Linguistics. In Brown, K. (ed.) (2006) vol. 3: 234–48.

Hutchby, I. (1996) Power in discourse: the case of arguments on a British talk radio show. *Discourse and Society* 7: 481–97. Reprinted in Jaworski, A. and Coupland, N. (eds) (1999) *The discourse reader*. London: Routledge, 576–88.

Hymes, D. (1971) On communicative competence. In Pride, J.B. and Holmes, J. (eds) (1972) *Sociolinguistics*. Harmondsworth: Penguin.

Jefferson, G. (1989) Preliminary notes on a possible metric which provides for a 'standard maximum' silence of approximately one second in conversation. In Roger, D. and Bull, P. (eds) *Conversation*. Clevedon: Multilingual Matters, 166–96.

Jenkins, J. (2003) *World Englishes: a resource book for students*. London: Routledge.

Ji, F. (2004) *Linguistic engineering: language and politics in Mao's China*. Honolulu, HI: University of Hawai'i Press.

Johansson, S. and Hofland, K. (1989) *Frequency analysis of English vocabulary and grammar: based on the LOB corpus*, vol. 1. Oxford: Clarendon Press.

Johnson, S. and Meinhof, U. (eds) (1996) *Language and masculinity*. Oxford: Blackwell.

Joyce, P. (1994) The people's English: language and class in England, *c.* 1840–1920. In Burke, P. and Porter, R. (eds) *Language, self and society*. Cambridge: Polity Press, 154–90.

Kachru, B., Kachru, Y. and Nelson, C.L. (eds) (forthcoming) *The handbook of world Englishes*. Oxford: Blackwell.

Kaplan, R. (ed.) (2002) *The Oxford handbook of applied linguistics*. Oxford: Oxford University Press.

Kaufer, D., Hayes, J.R. and Flower, L.S. (1986) Composing written sentences. *Research in the teaching of English* 20, 121–40.

Kearns, K. (2000) *Semantics*, Basingstoke: Macmillan.

Kenworthy, J. (2000) *The pronunciation of English: a workbook*. London: Hodder Arnold.

Kess, J.E. (1992) *Psycholinguistics*. Amsterdam: John Benjamins.

Knowles, M. and Moon, R. (2005) *Introducing metaphor*. London: Routledge.

Kökeritz, H. (1953) *Shakespeare's pronunciation*. New Haven: Yale University Press.

Kortmann, B. and Schneider, E.W. (eds) (2005) *A handbook of varieties of English*. Berlin: Mouton.

Kramarae, C. (1981) *Women and men speaking*. Rowley, MA: Newbury House.

Kramer, C. (1974) Stereotypes of women's speech: the word from cartoons. *Journal of Popular Culture* 8, 624–30.

Kramer, C. (1977) Perceptions of male and female speech. *Language and Speech* 20 (2), 151–61.

Krashen, S. and Terrell, T. (1983) *The natural approach*. Oxford: Pergamon.

Kreidler, C.W. (2004) *The pronunciation of English: a coursebook* (2nd edition). Oxford: Blackwell.

Kress, G. (1990) Critical discourse analysis. *Annual Review of Applied Linguistics* 11: 84–99.

Kress, G. (1997) *Before writing: rethinking paths to literacy*. London: Routledge.

Kress, G. (2000) *Children's early spellings: creativity and convention*. London: Routledge.

Kroll, J.F. and De Groot, A.M.B. (eds) (2005) *Handbook of bilingualism: psycholinguistic approaches*. New York: Oxford University Press.

Krueger, R.A. and Casey, M.A. (eds) (2000) *Focus groups: a practical guide for applied research*. Thousand Oaks, CA: Sage.

Kucera, H. and Francis, W.N. (1967) *Computational analysis of present-day American English*. Providence: Brown University Press.

Kurath, H. (1949) *A word geography of the eastern United States*. Ann Arbor: University of Michigan.

Labov, W. (1966) *The social stratification of English in New York City*. Washington, DC: Georgetown University Press.

Labov, W. (1969) The logic of nonstandard English. *Georgetown Monographs on Language and Linguistics* 22, 1–31. Reprinted in Gigioli (1972), 179–215.

Labov, W. (1972) *Sociolinguistic patterns*. Philadelphia, PA: University of Pennsylvania Press.

Labov, W., Ash, S. and Boberg, C. (2006) *The atlas of North American English: phonetics, phonology and sound change*. Berlin: Mouton.

Lakoff, G. (1992) Metaphor and war: the metaphor system used to justify war in the gulf. In Pütz, M. (ed.) *Thirty years of linguistic evolution*. Amsterdam: John Benjamins, 463–81.

Lakoff, G. and Johnson, M. (1980) *Metaphors we live by*. Chicago: University of Chicago Press.

Lakoff, R. (1975) *Language and woman's place*. New York: Harper and Row.

Larsen-Freeman, D. and Long, M.H. (1991) *An introduction to second language acquisition research*. Harlow: Longman.

Leap, W.L. and Boellstorff, T. (eds) (2003) *Speaking in queer tongues: globalization and gay language*. Chicago: University of Illinois Press.

Leech, G., Rayson, P. and Wilson, A. (2001) *Word frequencies in written and spoken English*. Harlow: Pearson. Additional tabulations online: www.comp.lancs.ac.uk/ucrel/bncfreq/flists.html (accessed 28 Jan. 2006).

Leech, G.N. (1969) *A linguistic guide to English poetry*. London: Longman.

Leech, G.N., Myers, G. and Thomas, J. (eds) (1995) *Spoken English on computer*. Harlow: Longman.

Leith, D. (1997) *A social history of English* (2nd edition). London: Routledge.

Levinson, S.C. (1983) *Pragmatics*. Cambridge: Cambridge University Press.

Lewis, T. (1991) *Pisspote's progress*. Lichfield: Leomansley Press.

Li Wei, (ed.) (2000) *The bilingualism reader*. London: Routledge.

Li Wei, (2006) Bilingualism. In Brown, K. (ed.) (2006) vol. 2, 1–12.

Lieven, E. (2006a) Language development: overview. In Brown, K. (ed.) (2006) vol. 6: 376–91.

Lieven, E. (2006b) Variation in first language acquisition. In Brown, K. (ed.) (2006) vol. 13: 350–54.

Lightbown, P. and Spada, N. (2006) *How languages are learned* (3rd edition). Oxford: Oxford University Press.

Litosseliti, L. (2003) *Using focus groups in research*. London: Continuum.

Litosseliti, L. (2006) *Gender and language*. London: Hodder Arnold

Livia, A. and Hall, K. (eds) (1997) *Queerly phrased: language, gender and sexuality*. New York: Oxford University Press.

Long, D. and Preston, D.R. (eds) (2002) *Handbook of perceptual dialectology*. Vol. 2. Amsterdam: John Benjamins.

Lovegrove, J. (2001) *The foreigners*. London: Gollancz.

Lowie, W., Verspoor, M. and de Bot, K. (eds) (2005) *Second language acquisition*. London: Routledge.

Luzzatti, C. and Whitaker, H.A. (2006) Acquired impairments of written language. In Brown, K. (ed.) (2006) vol. 1, 18–26.

Lynn, J. and Jay, A. (eds) (1987) *Yes Prime Minister*. London: BBC Books.

MacWhinney, B. (2003) First language acquisition. In Aronoff, M. and Rees-Miller, J. (eds) *The handbook of linguistics*. Oxford: Blackwell, 467–87.

Maltz, D. and Borker, R. (1982/1998) A cultural approach to male-female miscommunication. In Gumperz, J. (ed.) (1982) *Language and social identity*. Cambridge: Cambridge University Press, 196–216. Reprinted in Coates, J. (ed.) (1998a) *Language and gender: a reader*. London: Routledge, 417–34.

Marenbon, J. (1994) The new orthodoxy examined. In Brindley, S. (ed.) *Teaching English*. Milton Keynes: Open University, 16–24.

Marslen-Wilson, W. and Tyler, L. (1980) The temporal structure of spoken language understanding. *Cognition* 8, 1–71.

Mather, J.Y. and Speitel, H.H. (1975) *The linguistic atlas of Scotland*. London: Croom Helm.

McCrum, R., MacNeil, R. and Cran, W. (2003) *The story of English* (3rd revised edition). London: Penguin.

McEnery, T. (2005) *Swearing in English*. London: Routledge.

McEnery, T., Xiao, R. and Tono, Y. (2006) *Corpus based language studies*. London: Routledge.

McTear, M. (1985) *Children's conversation*. Oxford: Blackwell.

Meinhof, U. and Richardson, K. (eds) (1994) *Text, discourse and context*. London: Longman.

Melchers, G. and Shaw, P. (2003) *World Englishes*. London: Arnold.

Mey, J. (2001) *Pragmatics: an introduction* (2nd edition). Malden, MA: Blackwell.

Meyer, C. (2002) *English corpus linguistics*. Cambridge: Cambridge University Press.

Mills, A.D. (ed.) (1987) *The place-names of Dorset*. Nottingham: English Place-name Society.

Milroy, J. and Milroy, L. (1978) Belfast: change and variation in an urban vernacular. In Trudgill, P. (ed.) *Sociolinguistic patterns in British English*. London: Arnold, 19–36.

Milroy, L. (1987) *Language and social networks* (2nd edition). Oxford: Blackwell.

Milroy, L. and Gordon, M. (2003) *Sociolinguistics: method and interpretation*. Oxford: Blackwell.

Milton, J. and Meara, P. (1995) How periods abroad affect vocabulary growth in a foreign language. *ITL Review of Applied Linguistics* 107/108, 17–34.

Mitton, R. (1996) *English spelling and the computer*. London: Longman.

Molfese, V., Molfese, D., Molnar, A. and Beswick, J. (2006) *Developmental dyslexia and dysgraphia*. In Brown, K. (ed.) (2006) vol. 3, 485–91.

Mugglestone, L. (ed.) (2006) *The Oxford history of English*. Oxford: Oxford University Press.

Mulcaster, R. (1582/1970) *The first part of the elementary*. Menston: The Scolar Press.

Munby, J. (1978) *Communicative syllabus design*. Cambridge: Cambridge University Press.

Naiman, N., Fröhlich, M., Stern, H.H. and Todesco, A. (1978/1995) *The good language learner*. Toronto: Ontario Institute for Studies in Education 1978; Clevedon: Multilingual Matters 1995.

Nash, W. (1985) *The language of humour*. London: Longman.

Nation, I.S.P. (1990) *Teaching and learning vocabulary*. Boston, MA: Heinle and Heinle.

Nation, I.S.P. (ed.) (1986) *Vocabulary lists: words, affixes and stems* (revised edition). Victoria, New Zealand: English Language Institute, Victoria University of Wellington.

Nation, P. (2001) *Learning Vocabulary in another language*. Cambridge: Cambridge University Press. Related software available on line: www.vuw.ac.nz/lals/publications/software.aspx (accessed 28 Jan. 2006).

Nattinger, J.R. and De Carrico, J.S. (1992) *Lexical phrases and language teaching*. Oxford: Oxford University Press.

Niedzielski, N.A. and Preston, D.R. (2003) *Folk linguistics*. Berlin: Mouton de Gruyter.

Nippold, M.A. (2006) Language development in school-age children, adolescents and adults. In Brown, K. (ed.) (2006) vol. 6: 368–73.

Nussbaum, J. and Coupland, J. (eds) (2004) *Handbook of communication and aging research*. Mahwah, NJ: Lawrence Erlbaum.

O'Barr, W. and Atkins, B. (1980/1998) 'Women's language' or 'powerless language'? In McConnell-Ginnet, S., Borker, R. and Furman, N. (eds) (1980) *Women and language in literature and society*. New York: Praeger, 93–110. Reprinted in Coates, J. (ed.) (1998a) *Language and gender: a reader*. London: Routledge, 377–87.

O'Donnell, W.R. and Todd, L. (1991) *Variety in contemporary English* (2nd edition). London: Routledge.

O'Grady, W. (2005) *How children learn language*. Cambridge: Cambridge University Press.

Oakhill, J. and Cain, K. (2006) Reading processes in children. In Brown, K. (ed.) (2006) vol. 10: 379–86.

Obelkevich, J. (1987) Proverbs and social history. In Burke and Porter (1987), 43–72.

Olsson, J. (2004) *Forensic linguistics: an introduction to language, crime and the law*. London: Continuum.

Onions, C.T. (ed.) (1966) *The Oxford dictionary of English etymology*. Oxford: Clarendon Press.

Orton, H. *et al.* (1962–1971) *Survey of English dialects: the basic material* (4 volumes). London: Arnold.

Orton, H., Sanderson, S. and Widdowson, J. (1978) *The linguistic atlas of England*. London: Croom Helm.

Partridge, E. (1948) *Words at war, words at peace*. London: Frederick Muller.

Partridge, E. (1977) *Origins: a short etymological dictionary of modern English* (4th edition). London: Routledge and Kegan Paul.

Partridge, E. (2002) *A dictionary of slang and unconventional English* (8th edition). London: Routledge.

Paulston, C.B. and Tucker, G.R. (eds) (2003) *Sociolinguistics: the essential readings*. Oxford: Blackwell.

Pawley, A. and Syder, F.H. (1983) Two puzzles for linguistic theory: nativelike selection and nativelike fluency. In Richards, J.C. and Schmidt, R.W. (eds) *Language and communication*. New York: Longman, 191–225.

Pearson, B. and de Villiers, P. (2006) Discourse, narrative and pragmatic development. In Brown, K. (ed.) (2006) vol. 3: 686–93.

Peccei, J.S. (2005) *Child language: a resource book for students*. London: Routledge.

Peck, J. and Coyle, M. (2005a) *The student's guide to writing* (2nd edition). Basingstoke: Palgrave.

Peck, J. and Coyle, M. (2005b) *Write it right*. Basingstoke: Palgrave.

Perera, K. (1979) Reading and writing. In Cruttenden (1979), 130–60.

Perera, K. (1984) *Children's writing and reading: analysing classroom language*. Oxford: Blackwell.

Perera, K. (1986) Language acquisition and writing. In Fletcher, P. and Garman, M. (eds) (1986), 494–518.

Phillipson, R. (2003) *English-only Europe?: language policy challenges*. London: Routledge.

Pinel, J.P.J. (2003) *Biopsychology* (5th edition). Boston, MA: Pearson Educational.

Pinker, S. (1994) *The language instinct*. London: Penguin.

Pratt, N. and Whitaker, H.A. (2006) Aphasia syndromes. In Brown, K. (ed.) (2006) vol. 1, 321–7.

Preston, D.R. (ed.) (1999) *Handbook of perceptual dialectology*. Vol. 1. Amsterdam: John Benjamins.

Prideaux, G. (1990) *Psycholinguistics: experimental study of language* (2nd edition). London: Routledge.

Psathas, G. (1995) *Conversation analysis: the study of talk-in-interaction*. Thousand Oaks, CA; London: Sage.

Pyles, T. and Algeo, J. (2004) *The origins and development of the English language* (5th edition). Boston, MA: Heinle and Heinle.

Redmonds, G. (2004) *Names and history: people places and things*. London: Hambledon and London

Rees, F. (1989) *Languages for a change: diversifying foreign language provision in schools*. Windsor: NFER-Nelson.

Reid, G. and Wearmouth, J. (eds) (2002) *Dyslexia and literacy*. Chichester: John Wiley.

Reitveld, T. and Van Hout, R. (2005) *Statistics in language research: analysis of variance*. Berlin: De Gruyter.

Richards, J.C. and Lockhart, C. (1994) *Reflective teaching in second language classrooms*. Cambridge: Cambridge University Press.

Richards, J.C. and Schmidt, R. (2002) *Longman dictionary of language teaching and applied linguistics*. Harlow: Longman.

Ritchie, W.C. and Bhatia, T.K. (eds) (1999) *Handbook of child language acquisition*. London: Academic Press.

Roach, P. (2000) *English phonetics and phonology: a practical course* (3rd edition). Cambridge: Cambridge University Press.

Romaine, S. (1984) *The language of children and adolescents*. Oxford: Blackwell.

Romaine, S. (1995) *Bilingualism* (2nd edition). Oxford: Blackwell.

Romaine, S. (2000) *Introduction to language and society* (2nd edition). Oxford: Oxford University Press.

Room, A. (ed.) (1992) *Brewer's dictionary of names*. London: Cassell.

Sachs, J.S. (1967) Recognition memory for syntactic and semantic aspects of connected discourse. *Perception and psychophysics* 2: 437–42.

Sadock, J.M. (1979) Figurative speech and linguistics. In Ortony, A. (ed.) *Metaphor and thought*. Cambridge: Cambridge University Press, 46–64.

Saeed, J. (2002) *Semantics* (2nd edition). Oxford: Blackwell.

Sandred, K.I. (1963) *English placenames in -stead*. Uppsala: Almqvist and Wiksell.

Saville-Troike, M. (2003) *The ethnography of communication* (3rd edition). Oxford: Blackwell.

Schiffrin, D., Tannen, D. and Hamilton, H. (2003) *The handbook of discourse analysis*. Oxford: Blackwell.

Searle, J.R. (1965) What is a Speech Act? In Black, M. (ed.) *Philosophy in America*. London: Allen and Unwin, 221–39. Reprinted in Martinich, A.P. (ed.) (1996) *The philosophy of language* (3rd edition). New York: Oxford University Press, 130–40.

Searle, J.R. (1975) Indirect speech acts. In Cole, P. and Morgan, J.L. (eds) *Syntax and semantics*, vol. 3. New York: Academic Press. Reprinted in Martinich, A.P. (ed.) (1996) *The philosophy of language* (3rd edition). New York: Oxford University Press, 168–82.

Searle, J.R. (1979) A taxonomy of illocutionary acts. In Searle, J.R. *Expression and meaning*. New York: Cambridge University Press. Reprinted in Martinich, A.P. (ed.) (1996) *The philosophy of language* (3rd edition). New York: Oxford University Press, 141–55.

Seliger, H.W. and Shohamy, E. (1990) *Second language research methods*. London: Oxford University Press.

Selinker, L. (1972) Interlanguage. *International Review of Applied Linguistics* 10, 201–31.

Serjeantson, M.S. (1935) *A history of foreign words in English*. London: Routledge and Kegan Paul.

Short, M. and Leech, G.N. (2006) *Style in fiction: a linguistic guide to English fictional prose* (2nd edition). London: Longman.

Shuy, R. (1993) *Language crimes: the use and abuse of language evidence in the courtroom*. Oxford: Blackwell.

Sinclair, J.M. (1991) *Corpus, concordance, collocation*. Oxford: Oxford University Press.

Sinclair, J.M. (2003) *A guide to reading concordances*. London: Longman.

Singh, I. (2005) *The history of English: a student's guide*. London: Hodder Arnold.

Skeat, W.W. (1911) *English dialects from the eighth century to the present*. Cambridge: Cambridge University Press. (Also Kraus Reprint Co., New York, 1973.)

Slobin, D. (1979) *Psycholinguistics* (2nd edition.) Glenview, IL: Scott, Foresman and Co.

Smith, N.V. (1973) *The acquisition of phonology: a case study*. Cambridge: Cambridge University Press.

Smith, P. (1985) *Language, the sexes and society*. Oxford: Blackwell.

Smith, P.T. (1986) The development of reading: acquisition of a cognitive skill. In Fletcher, P. and Garman, M. (eds) (1986), 475–93.

Snow, C. (1986) Conversations with children. In Fletcher, P. and Garman, M. (eds) (1986), 69–89.

Spada, N. and Fröhlich, M. (1995) *Communicative orientation of language teaching observation scheme: coding conventions and applications*. Sydney: National Centre for English Language Teaching and Research.

Spender, D. (1998) *Man made language* (4th edition). Rivers Oram/Pandora.

Sperber, D. and Wilson, D. (1987) Precis of 'Relevance: communication and cognition'. *Brain and Behavioral Sciences* 10, 697–754. Reprinted in Geirsson, H. and Losonsky, M. (eds) (1996) *Readings in language and mind.* Cambridge, MA: Blackwell, 460–86.

Sperber, D. and Wilson, D. (1995) *Relevance: communication and cognition* (2nd edition). Oxford: Blackwell.

Stark, R.E. (1986) Prespeech segmental feature development. In Fletcher, P. and Garman, M. (eds) (1986), 149–73.

Steinberg, D. (2005) *An introduction to psycholinguistics.* Harlow: Longman.

Steinberg, D., Nagata, H. and Aline, D. (2002) *Psycholinguistics: language, mind and world* (2nd edition). Harlow: Longman.

Stevick, E. (1989) *Success with foreign languages.* Hemel Hempstead: Prentice Hall.

Stockwell, P. (2002) *Sociolinguistics: a resource book for students.* London: Routledge.

Stoel-Gammon, C. (2006). Infancy: phonological development. In Brown, K. (ed.) (2006) vol. 5: 642–48.

Stoppard, T. (1979) *Dogg's our pet.* London: Fraser and Dunlop.

Strang, B. (1970) *A history of English.* London and New York: Routledge.

Stubbs, M. (1995) Collocations and cultural connotations of common words. *Linguistics and Education* 7 (4), 379–90.

Stubbs, M. (1997) Whorf's children: critical comments on critical discourse analysis (CDA). In Ryan, A. and Wray, A. (eds) *Evolving models of language: papers from the annual meeting of the British Association for Applied Linguistics 1996.* Clevedon: Multilingual Matters, 100–16.

Stubbs, M. (2001) *Words and phrases.* Oxford: Blackwell.

Sunderland, J. (2005) *Language and gender.* London: Routledge.

Swan, M. and Smith, B. (2001) *Learner English: a teacher's guide to interference and other problems* (2nd edition). Cambridge: Cambridge University Press.

Swann, J. (1992) *Girls, boys and language.* Oxford: Blackwell.

Tajfel, H. and Turner, J.C. (1986) The social identity theory of intergroup behavior. In Worchel, S. and Austin, W. (eds) *Psychology of intergroup relations.* Chicago: Nelson-Hall, 7–24.

Talbot, M.M. (1998) *Language and gender: an introduction.* Cambridge: Polity Press.

Talbot, M.M. (2003) Gender stereotypes: reproduction and challenge. In Holmes, J. and Meyerhoff, M. (eds) *The handbook of language and gender.* Oxford: Blackwell, 468–86.

Tarone, E. (2006) Interlanguage. In Brown, K. (ed.) (2006) vol. 5, 747–52.

Thomas, J. (1995) *Meaning in interaction.* London: Longman.

Thomas, L. (1993) *Beginning syntax.* Oxford: Blackwell.

Thomas, L. and Wareing, S. (1999) *Language, society and power.* London: Routledge.

Thornborrow, J. (2002) *Power talk: language and interaction in institutional discourse.* Harlow: Longman.

Thorne, B. and Henley, N. (eds) (1975) *Language and sex: difference and dominance.* Rowley, MA: Newbury House.

Tirkkonen-Condit, S. (2006) Think-aloud protocols. In Brown, K. (ed.) (2006) vol. 12, 678–86.

Tognini-Bonelli, E. and Sinclair, J.M. (2006) Corpora. In Brown, K. (ed.) (2006) vol. 3: 206–19.

Tomasello, M. and Bates, E. (eds) (2001) *Language development: essential readings*. Malden, MA: Blackwell.

Trask, R.L. (1993) *A dictionary of grammatical terms in linguistics*. London: Routledge.

Trask, R.L. (1994) *Language change*. London: Routledge.

Trask, R.L. (1995) *Dictionary of phonetics and phonology*. London: Routledge.

Trask, R.L. (1999) *Key concepts in language and linguistics*. London: Routledge.

Trott, K. (1996) *'Pink for girls, blue for boys': aspects of lexical development in children aged 4 to 9*. Misterton: The Language Press.

Trott, K., Dobbinson, S. and Griffiths, P. (eds) (2003) *The child language reader*. London: Routledge.

Trudgill, P. (1972) Sex, covert prestige and linguistic change in urban British English of Norwich. *Language in Society* 1, 179–95.

Trudgill, P. (1974) *The social differentiation of English in Norwich*. Cambridge: Cambridge University Press.

Trudgill, P. (1999) *The dialects of England* (2nd edition). Oxford: Blackwell.

Trudgill, P. (2000) *Sociolinguistics* (4th edition). Harmondsworth: Penguin.

Trudgill, P. and Hannah, J. (2002) *International English* (4th edition). London: Arnold.

Truss, L. (2003) *Eats, shoots and leaves*. London: Profile Books.

Tyler, L.K. and Marslen-Wilson, W.D. (1977) The on-line effects of semantic context on syntactic processing. *Journal of Verbal Learning and Verbal Behavior* 16, 683–92.

Upton, C. and Widdowson, J.D.A. (1996) *An atlas of English dialects*. Oxford: Oxford University Press.

Vallins, G.H. (1954) *Spelling*. London: André Deutsch.

Van Orden, G.C. (1987) A ROWS is a ROSE: spelling, sound and reading. *Memory and Cognition* 15, 181–98.

Veith, W.H. (2006) Dialect atlases. In Brown, K. (ed.) (2006) vol. 3: 517–28.

Wallace, M. and Wray, A. (2006) *Critical reading and writing for postgraduates*. London: Sage.

Wardhaugh, R. (1993) *Investigating language* (3rd edition). Oxford: Blackwell.

Wardhaugh, R. (2006) *An introduction to sociolinguistics* (5th edition). Oxford: Blackwell.

Watts, R.J. and Trudgill, P. (eds) (2001) *Alternative histories of English*. London: Routledge.

Wells, G. (ed.) (1981) *Learning through interaction: the study of language development*. Cambridge: Cambridge University Press.

Wells, G. (1985) *Language development in the pre-school years*. Cambridge: Cambridge University Press.

Wells, G. (1986a) *The meaning makers: children learning language and using language to learn*. London: Hodder and Stoughton.

Wells, G. (1986b) Variation in child language. In Fletcher, P. and Garman, M. (eds) (1986), 109–39.

Wells, J.C. (1982a) *Accents of English. Vol. 1: an introduction*. Cambridge: Cambridge University Press.

Wells, J.C. (1982b) *Accents of English. Vol. 2: the British Isles.* Cambridge: Cambridge University Press.

Wells, J.C. (1982c) *Accents of English. Vol. 3: beyond the British Isles.* Cambridge: Cambridge University Press.

Wells, J.C. and Colson, G. (1971) *Practical phonetics.* London: Pitman.

Wesche, M., Paribakht, T. and Reading, D. (1996) A comparative study of four ESL placement instruments. In Milanovic, M. and Saville, N. (eds) *Selected papers from the 16th Language Testing Research Colloquium.* Cambridge: UCLCJ.

West, M. (1953) *A general service list of English words.* Harlow: Longman.

White, J. (1986) The writing on the wall: beginning or end of a girl's career? *Women's Studies International Forum* 9 (5): 561–74.

White, L. (2003) *Second language acquisition and universal grammar.* Cambridge: Cambridge University Press.

Williams, J.M. (1986) *Origins of the English language: a social and linguistic history.* New York: Free Press.

Woods, A., Fletcher, P. and Hughes, A. (1986) *Statistics in language studies.* Cambridge: Cambridge University Press.

World Library 2001. *Complete Works of Shakespeare.* Focus Multimedia. www.focusmm.co.uk/store/productpages/productinfo/ess034.html

Wray, A. (1992a) Authentic pronunciation for early music. In Paynter, J., Howell, T., Orton, R. and Seymour, P. (eds) *Companion to contemporary musical thought.* London: Routledge, 1051–64.

Wray, A. (1992b) Restored pronunciation. In Knighton, T. and Fallows, D. (eds) *Companion to medieval and renaissance music.* London: Dent, 292–9.

Wray, A. (1995) English pronunciation *c.*1500–*c.*1625. In Morehen, J. (ed.) *English choral practice 1400–1650.* Cambridge: Cambridge University Press, 90–108.

Wray, A. (1996) The occurrence of 'occurance' and 'alot' of other things 'aswell': patterns of errors in undergraduate English. In Blue, G. and Mitchell, R. (eds) *Language and education: papers from the annual meeting of the British Association for Applied Linguistics 1995.* Clevedon: Multilingual Matters, 94–106.

Wray, A. (1999) Singers on the trail of 'authentic' Early Modern English: the puzzling case of /æ:/ and /ɛ:/. *Transactions of the Philological Society* 97 (2): 185–211.

Wray, A. (2002) *Formulaic language and the lexicon.* Cambridge: Cambridge University Press.

Yus, F. (2006) Relevance theory. In Brown, K. (ed.) (2006) vol. 10, 512–19.

Zachrisson, R.E. (1909) *A contribution to the study of Anglo-Norman influence on English place-names.* Lund: Håkan Ohlsson.

Zachrisson, R.E. (1913) *Pronunciation of English vowels 1400–1700.* Gothenburg: Zachrisson.

INDEX